Critical acclaim for Peter Rand's *China Hands*

"A splendid job, history vividly evoked . . . A fine book."
—*Arthur Schlesinger Jr.*

"A well-drawn portrait of a generation . . . Rand does a good job of tracing relationships among his colorful characters and brings in personal detail from unpublished letters and interviews."
—*New York Times Book Review*

"Rand writes with an appreciative zest and an understanding sensitivity."
—*Boston Globe*

"China emerges in the pages of this book with its dazzling complexity intact. . . . Worth reading not only for the welcome attention it brings to a largely unexamined chapter in American journalism but for its flashes of insight into the byzantine politics of the Kuomintang."
—*The Nation*

"Rand's work provides an introduction to such fascinating people . . . Insightful observation . . . excellent writing, characterization of the writers, and use of the journalists' letters make this work stand far above most popular histories. . . . Engrossing . . . highly recommended."
—*Library Journal*

"An absorbing account . . . Rand skillfully weaves context into these highly personal narratives and vividly recreates a fascinating, confounding, and ultimately tragic era."
—*Kirkus Reviews*

"Rand vividly recreates the period, lucidly and penetratingly presenting the Chinese experiences of the journalists."
—*Publishers Weekly*

"A sweeping narrative . . . a vivid mural of a generation."
—*Booklist*

CONSPIRACY OF ONE

*Tyler Kent's Secret Plot against FDR,
Churchill, and the Allied War Effort*

PETER RAND

LYONS PRESS
Guilford, Connecticut
An imprint of Globe Pequot Press

Lyons Press is an imprint of Globe Pequot Press.

Photo on page viii courtesy of the Library of Congress.

Author has made all reasonable attempts to establish proper credit for all photographs contained herein. Any failure to credit or mistaken credit is purely incidental and unintentional.

Project editor: Meredith Dias
Layout: Casey Shain
Library of Congress Cataloging-in-Publication Data

Rand, Peter, 1942-
  Conspiracy of one : Tyler Kent's secret plot against FDR, Churchill, and the Allied war effort / Peter Rand.
    pages cm
  Includes bibliographical references and index.
  ISBN 978-0-7627-8696-1
  1. Kent, Tyler. 2. World War, 1939-1945—Secret service—Soviet Union. 3. World War, 1939-1945—Diplomatic history. 4. Spies—United States—Biography. 5. United States—Foreign relations—Great Britain. 6. Great Britain—Foreign relations—United States. I. Title.
  D810.S8K467 2013
  940.54'8647092—dc23
  [B]
                                                          2012051752

Printed in the United States of America

10 9 8 7 6 5 4 3 2 1

For Bliss and James

"What do you think spies are: priests, saints, and martyrs? They're a squalid procession of vain fools, traitors, too, yes; pansies, sadists, and drunkards, people who play Cowboys and Indians to brighten their rotten lives. Do you think they sit like monks in London, balancing rights and wrongs?"

—JOHN LE CARRÉ, *THE SPY WHO CAME IN FROM THE COLD*

Tyler Kent in 1940.

Contents

INTRODUCTION

THE STRANGE CASE OF TYLER KENT, AMERICAN SPY, FIRST CAME TO my attention over lunch one day at Boston University with Dr. Howard Gotlieb.

Renowned as one of the great American collectors, Gotlieb founded and kept what became the Howard Gotlieb Archival Research Center at Boston University. From 1963 until his death in 2005, he assembled an archive of twentieth-century Americana second to none. The center commands a vast array of memorabilia, including literary manuscripts; the papers of painters, sculptors, espionage agents, show business figures like Bette Davis and Douglas Fairbanks Jr.; and the rough drafts of important American journalists, among them Gloria Emerson, Martha Gellhorn, David Halberstam, and Dan Rather. It was Halberstam who declared Gotlieb a boulevardier among collectors, a man you might expect to encounter on the Champs-Elysées, in the lobby of the Adlon or Claridge's, or on the esplanade in Nice in his blue blazer, moving with stately vigor, armed with his cane, a confidant to everyone in the world worth knowing.

Gotlieb enthusiastically supported my work from the day my first novel hit bookstore shelves. He provided a haven at Boston University for my manuscripts and papers. He also invited me to use his valuable resources for my research.

Over lunch, Gotlieb confided to me that some years earlier he had acquired the papers of Tyler Kent, who, he explained, as a young code clerk in the American embassy in London in 1939 and 1940, had created a small archive of his own of top-secret diplomatic documents that he had copied, secretly removed from the embassy in his briefcase over a nine-month period, and squirreled away in his bed-sit apartment at 47 Gloucester Place in the Marylebone area of London. Kent had spent a number of years during his twenties in the US embassy in Moscow, where he had developed his archival habits, and MI5, the British domestic counterintelligence branch, had been keeping an eye on him from the moment, in October 1939, that he first set foot on British soil as an embassy employee. In May 1940, officials arrested Kent on the suspicion that he was working as an espionage agent in London for the Nazis.

I had never heard of Tyler Kent, and it's probable that you never have either—until now. He is one of history's footnotes, a minor player in a vast game, who might have made a difference in the outcome if things had turned out differently.

"He's got a marvelous name," Gotlieb said. "Sounds rather like Clark Kent, who also had a secret side to his character."

It was, as Gotlieb told it, a fascinating story, but a forgotten one that had taken place many years earlier. More than half a century had elapsed. Even at the time, government officials suppressed the story of Kent's arrest, his secret trial, and subsequent imprisonment. Word filtered out eventually, during the course of the war, when members of Parliament discovered that among the documents found in Kent's apartment were secret telegrams that Winston Churchill had sent to President Roosevelt during the early months of the war—telegrams that suggested the two men had been discussing ways in which the United States might help the British war effort at a time of enormous opposition to intervention in the States.

From 1944 on, civil libertarians and former anti-interventionists took considerable interest in Kent's case, wondering what Kent knew that Anglo-American interests felt they had to silence with a secret trial and a long imprisonment. The flurry of publicity around his release and subsequent deportation back to America lasted a short time, but Kent withdrew into silence after issuing a lengthy statement to Congress. History consigned Kent to that limbo where the might-have-beens slumber. It had been closed to researchers by agreement with Kent until his death in the mid-1980s. As it happened, Gotlieb told me, no one had yet seen the Kent archive, including at least one pair of subsequent biographers who had written about Kent after his death.

How had Gotlieb come upon this trove of Kent's papers?

Kent, the eminent archivist told me, had returned to the States in 1945. He was then thirty-four years old. He had spent the war years in an internment camp on the Isle of Wight. When he stepped off a ship in Hoboken, New Jersey, on a cold, blustery November day, a battery of reporters and photographers alerted to his return met him. He appeared, as ever, calm and self-possessed in his Savile Row suit. Still youthful, he projects in the news photos of the time the aura of a modestly famous second-string Hollywood matinee idol fresh from a career-shattering scandal. He has the pallor and the weariness of someone who has had his brush with infamy.

Kent disappeared from public view. Within months he met and married a rich, older divorcée named Clara Hyatt. He settled down on Clara's Maryland farm to the life of a Southern gentleman farmer, an occupation for which his penal servitude as a farm laborer on the Isle of Wight had prepared him admirably. For many years, he lived not far from his ancestral Virginia roots.

A man of leisure, he maintained a luxuriously appointed yacht in Florida, on which he could indulge his favorite pastimes of sailing and fishing. In the 1960s, he and Clara lived in Florida, where, for a time,

Kent operated a local newspaper, from which he propounded the same racist views that had won him friends among British and American antiwar activists. Kent also maintained correspondence with various groups, including military historians, unreconstructed isolationists who believed that the Anglo-American liberal elite had victimized Kent, and even Third Reich apologists.

As the years went by, Kent put on weight and grew an unflattering goatee. We see him, in the 1970s, on the shores of Lake Chapala, in Mexico, where he and Clara have moved. John Toland, the distinguished World War II historian, visited the Kents on Lake Chapala in 1972. In photographs taken on this visit, the portly Kent wears a bolo tie and a wide-brimmed hat. He is, according to Toland, gracious, reserved—and bitter about his wartime ordeal.

Soon after Toland visited them, the Kents' fortunes nosedived. Kent had invested his wife's wealth in the Mexican peso. It was a promising move in those years when oil was transforming the Mexican economy. The oil boom went bust, however; the peso crashed, and so did the principal from which Clara and Kent drew their income. The Kents returned to America and ended up in Kerrville, Texas, not far from San Antonio, in a mobile home.

This is how Kent's papers came to find a home at Boston University. Lurking in the background of Kent's past, furtively prepared to take up his cause, flickered certain loyalists from the doomed past. These occasional courtiers warmed the vanity of the man who had played a role of some importance in the ideological war waged by the anti-interventionists, men like Charles Lindbergh, who thought Hitler invincible. In the twilight of Tyler Kent's life, when he played the genteel country squire in a trailer park and needed money, one of these courtiers stepped forward and brokered the sale of Kent's papers to Boston University.

He kept the Savile Row suits, found neatly pressed and beautifully maintained in the closet of the mobile home he shared with Clara, who survived him and lived into her nineties.

Howard Gotlieb offered me the opportunity to peruse the Kent archive. Among Kent's papers are documents that historians have used from time to time to sketch the tale of Tyler Kent, and some that no others have seen as yet. Among them, I found more than fifty love letters that Kent preserved all those years, penned to him in prison by Irene Danischewsky, his *inamorata*. These letters, written in longhand, open the shutters onto a time long gone and provide a voice of courage and passion to this disquieting tale. The daughter of Russian émigrés who settled in London in 1916, Irene inspired me to write this story. She is the muse of this account just as she was to Kent.

Did he reread these letters in later years, or merely keep them as mute witness to the past? We'll never know. The effort of reliving those years would have caused him too much pain, I suspect. Irene's letters have the freshness of expression that never ages. They would have returned Kent too swiftly to his trial, a time of might-have-beens, when he was young and restless—a time when, on the threshold of life, he glimpsed immortality, and, for a brief moment, possessed the power to change the course of history.

CONSPIRACY OF ONE

ONE

Boy Misfit

Exile immobilizes to some degree the minds of those who suffer it.
It imprisons them forever within the circle of ideas which they had
conceived or which were current when their exile began. For the
exile, the new conditions which have been created in his native
country and the new ways of thinking and behaving which have
been established there do not exist.

—ALEXIS DE TOCQUEVILLE

THE STORY OF TYLER GATEWOOD KENT BEGINS IN CHINA, WHERE he was born in a mission hospital in Newchwang, a Manchurian trading port, on March 24, 1911, eight months before revolution erupted and overthrew the Manchu dynasty, changing the face of China. His father, William Patton Kent, was the American consul in Newchwang.

Imagine first on-screen in the movie of his life, as the opening credits roll, the primitive delivery room, the missionary doctor, the Chinese medical assistants, the cries of our protagonist's mother, young Annie Patrick Kent. Next, a messenger travels the streets of

I

Newchwang, passing barely suppressed scenes of discontent before reaching the somber, graying consul. William Kent sits stiffly behind his desk in a suit with a high, starched collar, learning the news of the birth of his only son in his austere office from his male secretary. From this spare and windswept cold Manchurian outpost, fearful scenes of revolution follow: explosions, fire, screaming, chaos.

We don't linger in China, though. The scenes that swiftly chase one another, each announced by a stark dateline, show the stages of Kent's schooling: first in Leipzig (1915), in the German kindergarten, where, an isolated child, he sits forlorn among the Teutonic offspring of strict German parents; next in Switzerland (1916), among the disdainful children of the privileged international elite; then in Hastings, the British prep school in the English countryside, where we see the boy, at puberty, in a peppermint-striped blazer, his pale, insolent face perhaps smeared with jam as he sits in detention among the snickering British schoolboys. We see him in Bermuda as a young teen, arrogantly discrediting his tutor because the man can't speak French or German. The young man shows off by speaking to his tutor only in foreign languages that the man cannot understand. Finally, we catch a glimpse of him in America, at the Kent School, where he distinguishes himself as a Southerner in a Northern prep school by winning the fifty-yard dash. "Kent left other competitors behind in this race," according to the school yearbook.[1] He makes the honor roll, too. But the haughty, aloof Kent remains a lonely outsider.

These vignettes would show how, as he grows up in a series of alien school settings, the Foreign Service child asserts himself in a manner ever more scornful and combative. His overly attentive mother all but smothers Kent as a boy. In return, he behaves rudely and imperiously to her. A series of schoolmasters of varying nationalities who cannot cope with him ruefully attempt to educate the snotty, unruly lad who keeps to himself—brilliant, yet too obstinate to teach.

As offspring of the Foreign Service, Kent had a facility for learning languages that evolved into a skill. Even as a child, he knew much of world affairs. Born in a land that erupted into revolution soon after his birth, he spent his formative years in the heart of a continent torn open by war, an experience that undoubtedly influenced the boy who grew up to make his name in the history of espionage.

Colonel Hugh Wise, the father of a prep school classmate, once observed: "The trouble with Tyler is that he has such powers of concentration that he can *read over* a textbook and get the point the other boys have to dig for."[2]

"There is always trouble with the boys who come with the remarkable IQ of young Kent," noted the dean of freshmen at Princeton University, where Kent studied for two years. "Princeton has no place for them until the junior year. Before that we must only consider the greatest number and make no exception."[3]

Exile may have enhanced Kent's natural brilliance. It may have given him an edge of sophistication over the American boys with whom he attended prep school and college. It also turned him into a misfit. Kent's father had twice run for governor of Virginia on the Republican ticket. He had campaigned vigorously for Theodore Roosevelt, who, when elected president, obtained for William Kent, as a reward, his job in the Consular Service. Kent put Virginia in his past when in 1906 he married a woman twenty years his junior and immediately set out with her for Guatemala on their Foreign Service adventure.[4]

The native land to which Tyler Kent pledged his allegiance belonged to the nineteenth century. When Kent's parents joined the Foreign Service to live abroad, Virginia, their ancestral homeland, was still—more than forty years later—recovering from the Civil War. To their son, who didn't set foot on American soil until he was nine years old, Virginia represented a romantic heritage of nostalgic dreams.

Kent's parents took enormous pride in their ancestry. Patrician rather than aristocratic Southerners, they had deep roots in the antebellum South. William Kent's family descended from Jacob Kent, born in England in 1730, who settled in America and married Mary Crockett. Through this connection, the Kents traced a relationship to Davy Crockett. When he grew up, Tyler Kent also claimed descent from Pocahontas—as so many Virginians rightfully can. The Kents were farmers, lawyers, teachers, and doctors, not plantation grandees, but that made them citizens of a solid professional character. Anne Patrick Kent descended from John Lewis Ireland, founder of Augusta County, Virginia. One of her grandfathers, Judge Hendron, served as treasurer of the Confederacy. Robert C. Kent, Tyler's grandfather, had held the office of lieutenant governor of Virginia during the Civil War. In the Foreign Service, the Kents became Southern gentry in exile.[5]

In the class system of the Foreign Service, however, the real gentry belonged to the Diplomatic Corps, not the Consular Corps. The distinction was absolute. Consular officials took care of business matters between the home country and the foreign country in which they served, handling practical matters concerning visas and problems encountered by travelers abroad, often in backwaters like Newchwang. Foreign Service officers had a loftier assignment. They represented the policy of their country in national capitals. To these men and their wives, often well born and independently rich, went the glamorous roles and important assignments.

If the Foreign Service had been a passenger steamer, divided by class, the diplomats chatted on the top deck with the eminent travelers and sipped champagne with dukes and duchesses; the Kents, on this ship, would have occupied cabin class, where, among their fellow travelers, they would have commanded a certain prestige without doubt—but within limits. The consular official played a vital though socially inferior role in the Foreign Service.

In this situation and within these limits, without hope of ever crossing the barrier and with no promise in life of grandiose future glory, the Kents made their antebellum Virginia heritage an essential ingredient of family pride, one undoubtedly complicated by the wound of victory inflicted by the Northerners, who ran the country and who, in the diplomatic corps, traveled first-class.

Social demotion complicated the experience of exile for the Kents. A sense of family heritage may have provided some comfort, but it could not, for Tyler Kent, provide all the answers. Virginia supplied the coat of arms with its motto, *Memoria pii aeterna:* "The memory of the pious is eternal." It did not, however, offer Kent the sense of belonging that, as an outsider, he had yet to find.

When Kent's parents returned to America in 1927, they settled in Washington, D.C. His father, born in 1857 and now seventy, retired from government service. Tyler Kent joined his parents in Washington and finished high school at St. Albans, an august Episcopal private school for boys. He may have felt by then that he had already completed his education. This was certainly the impression he gave to those who knew him.

At Princeton, he distinguished himself during his freshman year by cutting classes. As a sophomore, he lived alone, and made few friends. Classmate Otis Wingo tried to offer Kent advice later when he was languishing in a British prison, but in New Jersey, he kept his distance. In his junior year, he suffered a burst appendix, took a medical leave of absence, and departed for Europe. There, to complete his undergraduate education, he studied first at the University of Madrid, and then for a year in Paris at the Sorbonne, where in 1932 he received the equivalent of a bachelor's degree. In Madrid, he seems to have come under the spell of a zealous anti-Semitic cafe philosopher who expounded to his student followers on his theories about the World Jewish Conspiracy. In Paris, Kent learned Russian, later claiming that he achieved fluency in just six months. He once said that Russian grammar was easy, no different from the grammar of any European language.[6] (Russian is a Slavic language written in a medieval semi-Greek script—European on both counts—so his boasting on this count falls a little flat.)

He returned home in 1932, his youthful dreams mixed with the constant dread of not belonging, the conviction tempering his alienation that the world owed him for the insulting way that fate had robbed him of an estate, a setting he could call his own. What he could claim for himself was the Foreign Service, which, though not land surveyable from a stately verandah, offered the perks of an exclusive club, to which he could trace his membership back to the day in March 1911 when he first took breath, the son of the American consul in Newchwang. He had trained all his life for what the Foreign Service exams demanded. He knew the requisite languages: French, German, Italian, Spanish, Russian. He had earned a *diplôme d'études supérieures* degree in Paris. He had no reason not to believe that he had superb qualifications to leap the barrier into first class and enter the Diplomatic Corps.[7]

But when he returned to Washington in 1932, the State Department wasn't hiring applicants to the Foreign Service. He easily might have passed the not-too-exacting State Department examinations then, but the Depression had taken its toll on State Department funds. The department was also suffering the throes of reorganization. Exams were suspended until further notice. Instead of stepping smoothly into an entry-level job in the Foreign Service, as he had intended, Kent signed up for courses at the Georgetown University School of Diplomacy, living at home in an apartment building on Wyoming Avenue owned and operated by his mother and his aging, retired father. They lived in a neighborhood of other retired consuls and colleagues, some of whom still worked in the State Department, in Southern comfort, under the new secretary of state, Cordell Hull, a longtime figure in the Democratic Party, who hailed from Tennessee.

It's hard to say exactly what kind of future Tyler Kent's life in exile had prepared him for; he may have found it hard to imagine turning into someone like his father. He surely didn't plan on living out his life as a consul in foreign cities of secondary importance while updating trade agreements. Perhaps he blithely assumed—as so many young twentysomethings do—that the future would take care of itself, which indeed it did . . . in ways he couldn't have foreseen.

His energetic mother gave Kent a sense that he could accomplish anything he wanted. She adored her son, a precocious prince of a boy in the company of two doting sisters, all of them thrown together into alien surroundings. A misfit he may have been, but no one in the course of his youth ever disabused young Kent of his charm, his masculine appeal enhanced by good looks. Though moderate in stature, his slender frame conveyed the self-satisfied air of someone whose handsome face matched the beau ideal of the Princeton lad whom F. Scott Fitzgerald celebrates. Although he may not have known where exactly he belonged, Kent felt himself a young man held in the hands of destiny. How right he was.

Destiny presented itself soon enough, in 1933, when Kent learned that a clerical job might be available for him on the staff of William C. Bullitt, whom President Franklin D. Roosevelt had appointed as the first American ambassador to the Soviet Union. Bullitt, Kent discovered, was putting together a handpicked staff in Washington to take with him to Moscow, where he was opening an entirely new embassy. Kent couldn't qualify for a Foreign Service job because he hadn't taken the exams. He had no background in office work, either. The only skill he possessed that recommended him for a position in Bullitt's mission

William Bullitt (left), whom FDR (right) appointed as the first ambassador to Soviet Russia, departs for his assignment on November 17, 1933.

was the fact that he spoke Russian. He wanted the job, however, so—
equipped with this helpful language skill and certain well-placed connections in the State Department—he went after it.

This position didn't offer the best path to penetrate the stuffy male
enclave in which his father had served in his subordinate capacity. It
was menial employment. If his father traveled in cabin class in the ship
of state, Tyler Kent would be traveling in steerage among the typists
and file clerks, people he considered his professional and social inferiors. His birth and education suited him far better for first-class travel,
of course. In addition, he was not at all suited to clerical work based
on any formal training, a point well understood by the Division of
Foreign Service Personnel in the Department of State, which oversaw
the assignment of clerical positions according to an established system
of priorities. In the opinion of those who worked there, no clerical
worker had a right to employment who hadn't first passed inspection.

But William Bullitt wasn't a career diplomat, and he didn't play by
the rules. He insisted on running things his way, despite entrenched
State Department traditions of bureaucratic protocol. Immediately
after his appointment, Bullitt invited the outrage of members of the
personnel division by choosing clerical assistants "without reference to
the Division of Foreign Service Personnel," in the words of one veteran diplomat who served under him.[8] The outrage was long-lasting.
It spread over the years and deepened within the department to
embrace in the reach of its hatred the entire Eastern Division, including unqualified clerks who, like Tyler Kent, were considered no better
than stowaways.

His knowledge of Russian won the job for Kent, a language known
only by three or four of Bullitt's chosen career officers, among them
George Kennan, Charles Bohlen, and Loy Henderson. Kent also had
obtained the support of people in the State Department with influence, friends of his father who belonged to an entrenched network
of Southerners. The most important of these was Secretary of State

Cordell Hull, a longtime congressman who was married to a contemporary of Anne Kent's named Frances Witz Whitney of Staunton, Virginia. Another former congressman, Walton Moore, proved more immediately useful to Kent in his quest for the clerical job than Hull, however. A contemporary of the elder Kent in law school, Moore hailed from Virginia, his father having served as a major in the Confederate Army.[9]

Moore also served as assistant secretary of state. While serving in Congress some years earlier, he had received the nickname of "Judge" Moore from a Texas legislator, who called him that because, the Texan said, in Texas it was the honorific you gave to an ugly man. Moore had worked alongside Cordell Hull in Congress, and now acted as Hull's protector in State Department skirmishes. He also received the assignment to open negotiations with Maxim Litvinov when the foreign minister of the Soviet Union arrived in Washington in 1933, after Stalin decided to establish US-Soviet diplomatic relations. This decision was made because the Russian leader thought he might need American protection against the aggression of Japan, which, at the time, was rattling its imperial sabers in Manchuria on the Soviet Union's far eastern border.

In the course of these negotiations, Moore—skeptical of this move on the diplomatic chessboard—quickly grew close to William Bullitt, to whom Roosevelt had assigned the task of crafting an agreement to establish formal relations between the two nations.[10] The negotiations with Litvinov went well. Moore, in his early seventies, became a mentor to Bullitt, and, on Bullitt's account, Moore warmed to the idea of American-Soviet relations. Litvinov agreed to terms with the United States on certain outstanding loans from the time of the Revolution. He also agreed to disengage with the Communist Party in the United States.[11]

At that moment, Stalin was so happy to establish diplomatic relations that he offered the United States a choice piece of land overlooking the Moscow River in the Lenin Hills on which to build an embassy. The site commands a panoramic view of the Russian capital. Here Napoleon, in awe and dismay, first beheld in flames the city that the retreating Muscovites had abandoned to his armies during his doomed invasion of 1812. Stalin made his offer to Bullitt in December 1933, when negotiations ended. The newly appointed ambassador had gone to Moscow with George Kennan, then a promising young Foreign Service officer, to put the final touches on the new accord, and to set plans in motion for the new embassy.

Stalin attended a dinner party in Bullitt's honor given by Kliment Voroshilov, supreme commander of the Soviet army and navy. The entire inner circle of the Soviet leadership attended. Everyone drank an enormous volume of vodka before dinner, and in the course of the meal itself, by Bullitt's calculation, fifty toasts were made. Afterward, Stalin chatted on a sofa for a time with the new American ambassador. The Russian leader, Bullitt wrote the president, wore a soldier's uniform, with boots, black trousers, and a gray-green coat. "His mustache covers his mouth so that it is difficult to see just what it is like, but when he laughs his lips curl in a curiously canine manner."

Stalin told Bullitt, "I want you to understand that if you want to see me at any time, day or night, you have only to let me know and I will see you at once." As Bullitt was leaving, Stalin accompanied him to the door. "Is there anything at all in the Soviet Union that you want? Anything?" he asked.

After some soul-searching, Bullitt told the Russian tyrant that he wanted to build an embassy, modeled on Monticello, on a particular bluff overlooking the Moscow River.

"You shall have it," said Stalin. Bullitt extended his hand, but Stalin took Bullitt's head between his hands and kissed him.

"I swallowed my astonishment," Bullitt wrote, "and, when he turned up his face for a return kiss, I delivered it."[12]

He never saw Stalin again.

In the autumn of 1933, Bullitt set about assembling his embassy staff, which, including officers, military attachés, and clerical workers, came to thirty-four men. Moore urged Bullitt to hire Kent. Support also came from Wilbur Carr, the former director of the Consular Service, now an assistant secretary of state in charge of immigration. An old-timer, Carr had ruled supreme over the Consular Service from 1902 until 1928. It was he who had advanced the career of Kent's father to its bitter end when the consular branch lost its autonomy and folded into the Foreign Service. They were also neighbors on Wyoming Avenue in Washington, D.C. Carr pushed Kent's application on the chief of the Division of Personnel, T. M. Wilson, to whom he wrote, on December 7, 1933, "Will you please have Mr. Kent's application carefully considered in connection with a clerkship?"[13]

Various people of varying importance wrote letters of recommendation for Kent. John Cochran, president of the Franklin National Bank, and Senator Harry F. Byrd both wrote letters on his behalf to the secretary of state. So did the headmaster at St. Albans, the Reverend Albert H. Lucas, who wrote, "Mr. Kent had a very enviable reputation at St. Albans for integrity and scholarship." None who volunteered to recommend Kent, or even those—the postmaster of Princeton, for one—whom the Division of Personnel consulted for information about him, actually knew the young man very well, with the possible exception of Reverend Lucas.

An expat and a nomad, Kent evaded the consistent observation of all eyes but those in his immediate family. As he so eagerly campaigned for the clerical position in Bullitt's embassy, this existence worked to Kent's advantage, for, in the words of an official in the Department of Personnel: "As this young man has spent most of his life abroad, it has not been possible to secure a comprehensive report," one that, in the case of someone who had lived closer to home or lingered in one place, might have disclosed certain flaws of character.[14]

William Bullitt's assignment had historic importance, with long-lasting consequences. His appointment reveals the way that President Roosevelt liked to operate. His choice of Bullitt, a State Department outsider, signaled that he planned to act independently of the department when it pleased him to do so. He led Bullitt to believe they were on close terms. Their personal correspondence is extensive indeed, but it bears out the sad conclusion that George Kennan came to many years later: Although Bullitt poured his thoughts and feelings into his letters to FDR, the president's own replies were never more than cheerful thank-you notes.

Bullitt also may have thought mistakenly that the president and he shared the same attitude toward the Eastern Establishment. Roosevelt's deepest loyalties lay in the small, exclusive province of Groton, Harvard, and Dutchess County, New York. FDR's loyalty to school and home proved steadfast, though it didn't necessarily extend beyond them to include the larger East Coast power structure from which Bullitt, a Philadelphian, had emerged. Bullitt may never have understood the importance to Roosevelt, in particular, of the Groton experience, which formed many of his egalitarian social attitudes. A Spartan school in northeastern Massachusetts, Groton devoted itself to the ideals of Christian service. Its founder, Endicott Peabody, known as the Rector, conceived the school to instill in the sons of robber barons a sense of service. Arthur M. Schlesinger Jr. notes tellingly that no New Dealers ever came out of Exeter, the school that he attended, and when he mentioned this to Averell Harriman, who attended Groton, Harriman replied: "To be a New Dealer you had to be unhappy at Groton."[15]

Bullitt may never have understood this about his leader's school. He may never have told Roosevelt the following story; if not, it doesn't matter, although it may explain some of the animosity they later felt toward each other. A rich boy, Bullitt was ironically—thanks perhaps to his mother—a vehement anti-snob. When the time came, his parents enrolled him in Groton. On the day when young Bullitt, aged twelve, was scheduled to leave, his parents found him sitting at the bottom of the stairs in the front hall, atop his luggage, arms folded. He had decided, he informed them, that under no circumstances would he go to Groton. He knew boys who went there, he said. They were snobs, and he wanted nothing to do with any such place.[16] He attended DeLancey Preparatory School instead.

Even as a child, Bullitt was a force; to contend with him was to lose. Had he gone to Groton, he might have come to know Sumner Welles, class of 1911, who commanded Roosevelt's loyalty and proved Bullitt's undoing—and vice versa. This anti-snob streak remained a Bullitt characteristic throughout much of his privileged, upper-class life. At Yale he founded, along with classmate Cole Porter, an organization for those not chosen by clubs like Skull and Bones and Scroll and Key. They called themselves the Mince Pie Club. His attachment to the Russian Revolution, to the memory of Jack Reed, whose widow he married, and to Roosevelt himself as a "traitor to his class," all reflect his heartfelt mistrust of the class system to which he belonged.[17] He may have been a traitor to his class, but Roosevelt never betrayed his school or its principles, which Bullitt—presuming a greater closeness with the president than he really possessed—discovered to his peril.

Roosevelt wanted his own man in Moscow. He chose Bullitt because Bullitt was a Soviet enthusiast. In 1919, Bullitt was attached to the US delegation to the Paris Peace Conference that brought an end to the Great War. He had traveled to Moscow to meet with Lenin on behalf of Woodrow Wilson and Lloyd George, to bring the revolutionary Russian ruler into the peace process then under way at Versailles. Unfortunately, Bullitt's efforts fell afoul of the Paris negotiators. While he was pursuing his mission, they decided to proceed without the consent of the USSR, disposing of Eastern European boundaries their own way without consulting Lenin. Enraged by the cold shoulder that Wilson gave him after all his efforts, Bullitt denounced Wilson's Peace Plan before Congress,[18] and lived in Europe in the 1920s as a wandering dilettante. He married and subsequently divorced Louise Bryant— widow of John Reed, author of *Ten Days that Shook the World,* and of *Reds* fame. Bullitt remained a fan of the Soviet Union. He also pitched in with great enthusiasm to help Roosevelt's presidential campaign.

FDR gifted the Moscow embassy to Bullitt, with whom he saw eye to eye on the need for coexistence between the two countries. Within the State Department, the president wouldn't have found the enthusiast he sought. The Division of Eastern European Affairs fell under the purview of Robert Kelley, a scholar and diplomat steeped in Russian history. Kelley had built up a staff of brilliant specialists who drew upon a network of sources in Eastern Europe, and an extensive library amassed by Kelley, to formulate a view of current developments in the Soviet Union under Stalin that filled them with misgivings. To Bullitt's credit, however—although he was an outsider, whom many in the State Department mistrusted—he assembled his diplomatic officers from the smartest, best educated of the career Foreign Servicers, even if some already stood at odds with Bullitt and Roosevelt in their assessment of future US-USSR relations.[19]

In addition to the aforementioned Russian-language-trained officers—Kennan, Bohlen, and Henderson—Bullitt also added to his staff Elbridge Durbrow, Bertel Kuniholm, Edward Page, Angus Ward, and John C. Wiley, thoughtful skeptics who were all familiar, if not with the Russian language itself, then with service in areas under Russian influence. Well-educated men, they all had solid experience, even though they were not much older than Tyler Kent.

Willing to work closely with the Division of Far Eastern Affairs, Bullitt called forth from the division an effort to satisfy his unorthodox ways, including his determination to circumvent the personnel office, as in the case of Tyler Kent. He earned the fealty of the division, which in turn earned the Russia experts the bitter enmity of other sections within the State Department. By isolating the Russia hands, Bullitt unknowingly initiated the ruin of the entire Division of Eastern European Affairs, a calamity equaled only by the systematic postwar expulsion from the State Department of the China hands. Yet Bullitt's inspired judgment created the superb corps of experts who cut their teeth in the 1930s in the embassy that he so brilliantly launched. These same men remained in the State Department to guide postwar Soviet policy even without the division that Kelley had nurtured.

With few exceptions, most of the men who signed on were bachelors. Bullitt selected an entirely male and unmarried clerical staff, thus assembling an embassy that in some ways resembled a boarding school. He did so because Russia—Moscow in particular—made for a hardship post, and, more specifically, was suffering a chronic and severe housing shortage. When Bullitt met Stalin in December 1933 in Moscow, where he had gone to complete arrangements for the new embassy, his embassy staff had no living quarters as yet. He left George Kennan in Moscow to make these arrangements while he returned to Washington to gather his people for the return trip. An all-male staff could occupy living quarters more economically as roommates, which others more familiar with conditions in Moscow regarded with misgiving. As Loy Henderson recalled, "Those of us in the Department who were acquainted with conditions in the Soviet Union were concerned at this tendency in the direction of an all-male mission."[20]

Bullitt, himself twice married and divorced, remained for the rest of his life a confirmed bachelor. Perhaps he envisioned his Moscow embassy as a glittering bachelor party in a primitive setting, which, during the spring and summer months of 1934, it often was.

Two

Bad Hat

I recall him as a sort of an odd ball around the embassy, very much a loner, an unpleasant personality, full of himself, and giving the impression of pursuing aims of his own.
—George Kennan to the author, February 26, 2001

Tyler Kent formally received an offer of a position on Bullitt's staff as a clerk. Wilbur Carr, his father's benefactor, informed him of his appointment on February 12, 1934, which Kent accepted by telegram immediately. It set in motion a hurried sequence of exchanges, given what little time it allowed Kent to pack his suitcases, bid farewell to his mother and sisters, say good-bye to his father—whom he never saw again—and to travel to New York, where, on February 15, he dived once again into exile. This time he did so in the company of William Bullitt and his mission of twenty-five-plus people on the SS *Washington*, which steamed out of New York Harbor for Le Havre and Hamburg.[1]

Kent as a young man, about the time that he went to work
for Ambassador Bullitt as a clerk. (PHOTO COURTESY OF THE
STATE DEPARTMENT)

Three days into the transatlantic voyage, Bullitt assembled his staff and made clear to all his intention to eliminate the usual hierarchy based on rank, the very system in which Tyler Kent had spent his child-hood and early youth. "He emphasized that he did not desire his mission to resemble the US embassies that he had visited during his many trips abroad," remembered Loy Henderson many years later.

> In the first place, he was opposed to diplomatic missions being operated on a hierarchical basis. So far as he was concerned, every member of his mission from top to bottom would have equal status. He would not recognize or tolerate any distinctions between officers and clerks. He wished, in particular, to impress upon those who were entering the service of the United States abroad for the first time that they should not feel handicapped because of the lack of Foreign Service experience. In his opinion, previous experience in the State Department and in the Foreign Service might well prove to be a handicap rather than an asset to members of a diplomatic mission operating in the Soviet Union.[2]

This heartfelt speech on the eve of trials unknown might explain some, if not all, of the liberties Tyler Kent subsequently assumed. It established the guidelines according to which Kent operated as an embassy clerk.

Rumor later held that Kent immediately enraged the boss by bedding an older married woman mid-voyage, rather brazenly even if apocryphally. If true, it shows how deftly Kent used Bullitt's anti-snobbism to his advantage by slipping into the first-class stateroom of the lady in question. Bon vivant though he may have been, Bullitt saw in Kent's behavior from the very beginning an insulting insubordination, despite his professed thoughts about hierarchy. Only the young lothario's relationship to Walton Moore, a family friend and backer, stayed Bullitt's reproach.

From that time on, however, Bullitt intensely disliked Kent, trying several times to fire him. The ambassador held this impulse in check, however, for which Kent had Moore to thank, among others. Just twenty-two, Kent was bad, in his own way, in Moscow. In the classless embassy, amid a theoretically classless society, he took Bullitt's words to heart. He disdained the menial tasks that he, as a clerk, had to perform; he did them badly, in his own good time, or not at all—which was easy to do in such chaos.

When the staff arrived in Moscow on March 1, on a cold and windy day, no embassy building awaited them. They had no assigned, permanent living quarters. Staff first moved into the Savoy Hotel, on Kuznetsky Most, a cobbled street, at the top of which looms, to this day, one corner of the immense Lubyanka Prison, site of torture and execution for countless "enemies of the people." The ambassador, when he arrived on March 7, took Spaso House, a magnificent mansion provided by the Soviet government that a rich Moscow merchant had erected before the Great War. A huge, domed entrance hall lit by an immense crystal chandelier gave way to upstairs bedroom suites with balconies. A long, wood-paneled dining room comfortably accommodated up to fifty or sixty guests, and beyond it lay a ballroom made for splendid soirees.[3]

The ambassador lived and worked in Spaso House. Several months passed before the State Department obtained a seven-story structure, the Mokhovaya Building near Red Square, hard by the Kremlin, which combined both office space and living quarters. The entire staff, officers and clerks, devoted themselves classlessly in that time to the task of obtaining supplies, including furniture, some of which lay diverted from America in a Moscow warehouse.

The chaos—the transient nature of the workplace—served Kent's truant purposes. He looked down upon his fellow clerks, disliking the sober, serious, well-educated, and better-paid officers of the diplomatic corps whose needs he was tasked with meeting. The feeling was mutual.

"None of us career officers liked him," George Kennan recalled, "Loy Henderson being, perhaps, the exception."[4]

"We were always a little suspicious of him," recalled Mrs. Kennan.[5]

The greater chaos of Moscow that enclosed the lesser chaos of the embassy enabled those who, like Kent, pursued personal aims. In the spring of 1934, Moscow provided an atmosphere that encouraged Kent's talents as an independent operator to flourish, unsuspected by those who thought they knew him. For many of the new arrivals, especially those single young men in the clerical service who, unlike Kent, could speak no Russian, Moscow proved demoralizing, a crowded, unfriendly, primitive, dour place to live.

"The center of the city was usually so crowded that I found myself being jostled off the narrow sidewalks onto the cobblestoned streets," said Henderson. "The polite words and little acts of courtesy to which a Westerner was accustomed were completely lacking, considered hypo-critical, bourgeois manifestations." He described walking for blocks without hearing a laugh or seeing a smile. "Most of the women and girls who were pushing through the throngs wore drab shawls or scarfs to cover their short-cut hair and to protect themselves from the piercing cold winds." He observed that men intentionally wore stubble because, as he understood it, to appear clean-shaven was to give the impression of being bourgeois.

"It was rare indeed to see anyone with good leather shoes," he also recalled. "Many of them wore boots or shoes of heavy felt with rubber, leather, or what seemed to be thatched soles." People used newspaper to insulate their outerwear. At the theater, Henderson never checked his overcoat with those in the cloakroom because lice and bedbugs proliferated. Also, "In the absence of dry-cleaning establishments in Moscow, the odor of long-worn, uncleaned clothing tended to distract from the enjoyment of the performance."

For the clerical staff, life in Moscow from the very beginning appeared grim, with entertainment options limited to ballet, theater, and opera. Restaurants and nightclubs didn't exist. The streets and shops were squalid and filthy. Good food was hard to find, or buy. Shopping for anything generally proved utterly unrewarding. Members of Bullitt's staff who may have wanted to form friendships with Muscovites discovered the difficulty of doing so. Soviet authorities had created laws that barred them from joining social clubs, and made it dangerous for Soviet citizens to extend hospitality to foreigners.[6]

Only Soviet citizens assigned to do so by OGPU, the Soviet security organization, made contact with foreigners. If others did, they could expect extensive interrogation and possibly punishment. For the entertainment and relief of the all-male staff, the Soviet government provided a selection of call girls in the Nosion Hotel, many of whom understood English, although they pretended they couldn't. On OGPU instructions, these girls met with men on Bullitt's clerical staff—rarely if ever with career Foreign Service officers—eavesdropping on conversations and exchanging sexual favors for whatever payment happened to be available.[7]

In Moscow, Kent behaved the way that certain gifted prisoners do behind bars. His command of the Russian language gave him an advantage. He wasted no time at the Nosion Hotel. He attracted women of a higher quality, and eventually acquired a mistress named Tanya; the daughter of a Soviet professor, Tanya had traveled in Europe and had a grasp, if not command, of English. Good-looking and bright, she undoubtedly had connections to the OGPU.

Bullitt later maintained that within three months of arriving in Moscow, Kent was working as an agent for the Soviets, possibly meaning Tanya. No Russian woman could have associated with an American in the US embassy unless the OGPU had authorized her, and Kent undoubtedly made it worth her while to associate with him. Bullitt never prevented Kent from seeing Russian women, which suggests that at the time, even Bullitt probably saw little harm in whatever exchanges took place. The ambassador himself may have understood that in "prison," standards of conduct decline.

As an illustration, take the matter of the ruble, the Soviet currency. When purchased at the official rate of exchange in Moscow, the "paper ruble," as it was called, had a value of 88 cents. Its value on the black market was 30 to 40 cents. Despite a near parity of official value, a paper ruble had the purchasing power of only 3 or 4 cents—which means that life in Moscow would have been astronomically expensive in 1934. American dollars could buy meals at Intourist hotels or at the Intourist store, called Torgsin, which made available for tourists items unavailable to Soviet citizens in exchange for badly needed dollars, at a rate roughly equal to the black-market ruble. It was illegal, however, to bring paper rubles purchased abroad into the Soviet Union, or to use foreign currency to buy them on the black market.

Members of Bullitt's mission faced a dilemma when they arrived in Moscow: how to survive on legally obtained paper rubles. They could buy certain items with dollars through Intourist. However, the embassy couldn't affordably have solved the problem of transporting furniture from the railway yards to the new office building using legally obtained rubles. Bullitt urged the Soviet government to provide credit through the State Bank to enable the embassy to buy rubles at a reasonable rate. The Soviets agreed to do so—for a limited time. Finally, the foreign minister, Maxim Litvinov, openly told Bullitt to violate the law and import rubles from abroad. The mission reluctantly imported illegal rubles via the diplomatic pouch.[8]

This official license to abuse the diplomatic pouch may have encouraged Kent to extend it to include an operation of his own. With Tanya's help, he and another clerk began to smuggle items cheaply obtained with black-market rubles—furs, jewelry, other portable valuables—out of the Soviet Union for sale at a considerable profit in the United States. Anthony J. Barrett, another embassy clerk, served as his sidekick in the illicit scheme. Barrett returned to America in 1937, and on July 1 of that year wrote Kent from Manhattan to account for, among other business, the appraisal of their booty, much of which Barrett had brought from Russia in suitcases.

The letter curiously begins "Dearest Pucia," an endearment and possibly a cover name for Kent, and reveals the extent of their enterprise:

> The cape has made a tremendous hit here. There is no question about it. It has been appraised at $350.00, and it is Japanese Mink and is supposed to be a very fine fur at that. The fur coat is caracul and has been prized at $400.00, by the New York furriers who know the cost of things. The rings all have been appraised and at figures that will surprise you beyond anything you ever saw. A pair of ear-rings I bought in Leningrad have been appraised at 200% per more than the cost of the things at the rate of five rubles equal $1.00. This would be a tremendous killing. The sapphire ring I obtained from Tanya is considered a very fine one and would be worth anything from $75.00 to $100.00 cash on the barrel. The little ring with the clover leaf is also a very fine one and would cost about $65.00. My cost was $9.00 in Moscow from the old man.

Barrett advised Kent "to concentrate on this sort of thing and bring back as much of it as you possibly can. Your baggage is not inspected in New York at all. What you can do is to send stuff over to Helsingfors in the pouch and have them hold it there for you. Don't forget to concentrate on the jewelry and the furs."

Toward the end of this long letter, Barrett lavishly flattered his accomplice: "My suits have been commented upon by everybody. I go around kissing the women's hands and they get quite a kick out of this also. I have told my girlfriend that I owe my improvement in taste and way of dressing to you. You are to some extent responsible for everything."[9]

Kent found that he could live extremely well in Moscow on what he made, plus whatever else he earned in other ways. Soon after his arrival he obtained an apartment of his own outside embassy precincts. With other embassy colleagues, he also rented a country house, a *dacha,* outside Moscow, in a pastoral setting prized for its birch woodlands, scenic meadows, and mushrooms. Kent, who always managed to lay hands on an automobile, liked to visit the *dacha* for sportive weekends with Tanya and other guests. In this respect, once again, Kent was following William Bullitt's egalitarian spirit, seizing the opportunity to comport himself in the manner of those Foreign Service officers who, superior to Kent in the State Department hierarchy, wouldn't have liked how deftly he had helped himself to perquisites available to all through Bullitt's benefaction.

Those in the mission equipped to enjoy them, despite the vicissitudes of Moscow, looked back upon the first nine months of 1934 as their halcyon days—even though nothing turned out the way that Bullitt, in his ebullient optimistic spirits, had expected. Japan had no immediate designs on Russia after all. This intelligence came to Stalin almost immediately after he had tied the knot with America, with which he was, ideologically speaking, out of sympathy. In any case, he cared very little. At the time, the United States hadn't yet become an international force of any meaningful importance. The kiss was just a kiss.

Bullitt hadn't foreseen the setback. Stalin turned away from this newly accredited diplomatic envoy even before he arrived in Russia to take up his assignment. As Bullitt's train pulled into the Moscow station, a band struck up the "Internationale." Equal to the occasion, Bullitt strode forth full of purpose, head erect . . . only to discover that the serenade was greeting a visiting delegation of women from Kharkov, in Ukraine. No Foreign Ministry official waited on the platform to welcome him. George Ancheychev, an Intourist official whom he had befriended, ushered him to his car for the drive to Spaso House.[10]

So it went.

The Russian foreign minister eventually wormed out of every single agreement that had formed the basis of their original diplomatic negotiations, up to and including the embassy building in the Lenin Hills overlooking the river. Bullitt made contact with Litvinov only with great effort. Every attempt to befriend the Soviet Union and every effort to achieve a meaningful rapport met with hostile, even malicious, resistance on the bureaucratic front. It came as no great surprise to the career officers—a number of whom had served in the Baltic States—and even other Soviets. They understood the nature of the beast. To the idealistic Bullitt, unschooled in Eastern European diplomacy, it was a shock.[11]

He had a wonderfully resilient nature, however. A compact man with a balding head, bright blue eyes, and ruddy cheeks, Bullitt had on his side force of character and a fighting spirit. He carried on at Spaso House in great style, a hunter pitching a resplendent camp in the wilderness. Devoted officers accompanied him. He had a loyal male secretary and batman, Carmel Offie, who later served him in Paris. He also had Charles Thayer, another young Philadelphian and a graduate of West Point. Thayer thought up ways—with Bullitt's acquiescence, encouragement, and even indulgence—to make embassy life at Spaso House and beyond an ongoing festival that had long been absent in Moscow. All sorts of Soviet luminaries with a nose for fun came to his glittering parties. Voroshilov, Lazar Kaganovich, Nikolai Bukharin, all members of the Politburo, made an appearance. So did Karl Radek; Marshal Budenny, the great Russian cavalry officer; and Marshal Tukhachevsky, the chief of staff of the Red Army. "Except for Stalin," Thayer wrote, "practically everyone who mattered in Moscow turned up."[12]

Like some salon in Belle Époque Paris, the embassy attracted a coterie of top Russian ballerinas and those literary lights, chief among them Mikhail Bulgakov, who had not yet fallen from Stalin's favor.

Bulgakov even set a significant scene in his novel, *The Master and Margarita,* in Spaso House. Thayer threw a Christmas party and for the occasion hired from the Moscow circus three performing seals, Lyuba, Misha, and Shura, which entertained the guests by entering the ballroom while balancing on their noses a tray of wineglasses, a bottle of champagne, and a small, candlelit Christmas tree, respectively. They proceeded to other feats, including playing the harmonica and climbing ladders—all to great applause—until the aroma of fish drew one seal down the basement steps. She bellowed and slapped her way into the kitchen, overturning garbage pails, chairs, coal scuttles, and so terrifying the newly arrived Austrian chef that he climbed onto the kitchen table with a frying pan. He hit her on the nose with it—evidently to no effect. Thayer meanwhile was trying to subdue the seal with the help of the assistant seal trainer, the head trainer having consumed too much of the champagne borne by one of his seals to be of any help.[13]

Later that winter, Thayer threw a far more ambitious party at the insistence of Bullitt, who told him, "The sky's the limit, just so long as it's good and different." With the help of Irena, the wife of the embassy counselor, John Wiley, Thayer organized a spring festival, complete with a Czech jazz band, gypsy orchestra, Caucasian *shashlik* restaurant (a restaurant from the Caucasus that serves meat on skewers), one hundred zebra finches loaned from the Moscow Zoo, and a baby bear. General Yegorov held the last of these in his arms, and the little creature vomited on the new army chief of staff. Outraged, Yegorov shouted at Thayer: "What sort of place is this anyway? Do the Americans invite guests just to have them messed up by wild animals? Is this an Embassy or a circus? Tell your ambassador that Soviet Generals are not accustomed to being treated like clowns."[14]

In those warm months that followed the arrival of Bullitt's mission, life in the Moscow swim brightened with the promise of better

Above, in Moscow in 1934, Charles Thayer, Marshal Budenny, and an unknown Russian official watch a polo match, arranged by Thayer and Ambassador Bullitt, between the Soviet cavalry and staff of the American embassy. (PHOTOS COURTESY OF YALE UNIVERSITY)

times, the mood mellow even in the grimy city. In the summertime, Thayer and Bullitt introduced the Soviet Cavalry to the sport of polo—yet another of Bullitt's impractical schemes to eliminate class distinction from the top down. In the Silver Forest—now a parkland of meadows and suburban *dashas*, where birch leaves turn silver in the summer breeze, and the river flows between banks of thick blue-green forest—they found a lovely sheep pasture across the Moscow River for grounds. Somewhere in there, not far from a stretch of the river where Moscow women bathed nude and sunned themselves on the sandy shore, the polo sessions began.

Marshal Budenny, perhaps unaware of its status as the sport of robber barons, assigned twenty of his crack horsemen to the course. From London, the Americans imported the mallets and balls. Budenny assembled a string of sixty-four magnificent ponies from all over Russia. After weeks of schooling, the Red team, under Captain Budenny, lined up for its first match against the Blue team, which Thayer captained. Carmel Offie, Bullitt's private secretary, played for the Blues. Litvinov and Voroshilov, the war commissioner, both came to watch. Fittingly, the Reds won.[15]

Luncheons, receptions, dinners, and dances all livened the spirits of the career Foreign Service staff, but there, it seems, Bullitt's social experiment stopped. Barriers went up, and Tyler Kent had to find his own social scene elsewhere. He did attend summer picnics in the country, though. One, according to legend, provided him with the opportunity to demonstrate for the ambassador, whom a snake in the grass had struck with a vicious bite, a certain presence of mind by taking the affected area in his mouth at once and sucking the venom from the wound. Whatever else Bullitt felt at the time for his clerk, the ambassador expressed a grudging gratitude, very likely, as legend would have it, by canceling once again a request sent to the Department of State to have Kent recalled.[16]

We can picture the cinematic scene: The picnickers, all wearing suits, sit on a large Oriental carpet in the high summer grass, eating off plates served to them by the embassy steward. Kent, in an unseasonable oatmeal-colored tweed suit, sits off by himself while Bullitt and his Foreign Service confidants leisurely sip wine and slurp soup. Kent watches them eat, looking bored and out of sorts. We see the snake sliding out from under an embassy car and slipping over the ground and onto the rug. Kent sees it. He also sees Bullitt put his hand on the rug. The snake strikes. Kent shouts as Bullitt yells, raises his hand, and shakes off the snake, which hisses, slithers, and flops around. While the embassy steward goes after the snake with, say, a bread knife, Kent takes Bullitt's hand in his mouth to suck out the poison.

"Very good work," the ambassador tells him, grudgingly, in front of the others.

The episode didn't temper the ambassador's sentiments the following May, however, when he wrote his annual report on Kent's performance for the State Department:

> *Mr. Kent has shown all the attributes of a spoiled child. He has intelligence and a considerable knowledge of Russian, and if he chooses to work with the sort of spirit that should prevail in the Foreign Service he might become a most useful clerk. His present attitude up to the present time, however, has been that many of the tasks presented to him were unworthy of a Virginia gentleman. We have attempted to do what we could to develop a sense of responsibility and devotion to the public service in Mr. Kent, and in some measure have succeeded. The coming year will show whether or not he may become a really useful member of the Service. At the present time he is doing the summaries of the Soviet press and doing them well; but they could be as well or better done by a local Russian employee at one-third the cost. If the clerical staff here is cut, he should, in justice, be the first to go.*[17]

It was not Bullitt's impression—to judge by his next annual report of Kent's performance—that Kent had yet "become a really useful member of the Service." He wrote, on August 1, 1936:

This clerk, who is now in the Consular Section, was in the former Consulate General during its early days. At that time he was not found suited to the requirements of a consular office and was assigned to the Embassy. It was found extremely difficult to use Mr. Kent in the Embassy because in spite of his native intelligence and knowledge of the Russian language, he was so impressed with the grandeur of his own ego and his relations with high-ranking officials of the administration in Washington that he adopted his patronizing attitude toward all officers in the Embassy. A number of times his dismissal from the Embassy has been discussed by the officers of the mission and myself. This clerk was, however, reassigned to the Consular Section several months ago, and since that time has shown signs of realizing that he must do his full work like any other member of the Embassy with zeal and a proper devotion to the public interest or be dismissed.[18]

This is at best the reluctant endorsement of a headmaster who wants to show good faith to a student on the precipice of expulsion. Bullitt concluded flatly: "He is well-fitted for his present position of reception clerk in the Consular Section because of his knowledge of languages, and he has become interested in the various phases of consular work." By the time he submitted this report, Bullitt had already resigned as ambassador to Moscow and returned to Washington to contribute his talents to the reelection of President Roosevelt, who was running against Governor Alf Landon of Kansas at a time when the country was mired in the Depression. This was a tough time to run as an incumbent.

It was the least of their worries.

—◆—

On December 1, 1934, catastrophe struck.

At 4:30 that afternoon, a disturbed young Communist Party member, Leonid Nikolaiev, loitering in the third-floor corridor of the Smolny Institute, headquarters of the Communist Party in Leningrad, shot Sergei Kirov in the back with a Nagan revolver. The second most powerful man in the Soviet Union, Stalin's right hand, secretary of the Central Committee, member of the Politburo, first secretary of the Leningrad Party Committee, Kirov fell dead to the floor. His assassin, who collapsed beside him in a failed suicide attempt, never gave a coherent reason for his act. He was later executed.[19]

"This killing has every right to be called the crime of the century," wrote Robert Conquest, historian and author of *The Great Terror*.[20] Conquest convincingly believes that Stalin himself hatched Kirov's murder, wanting to eradicate his heir apparent, an immensely influential figure—bold enough to criticize Stalin—who posed a threat to the absolute power that Stalin hadn't yet consolidated for himself over the Soviet Union. Some still refuse to believe that Stalin launched his great purge by plotting Kirov's murder, but Conquest holds that Stalin, a student of Hitler's rise to power, had noted how the *Führer* had used the purge of Ernst Roehm on June 30, 1934, to eliminate a serious rival and at the same time silence his critics, acting on a similar premise. Either way, Stalin immediately seized the opportunity to rid himself of opposition, so paranoid that he liquidated at least twenty million people before he finally died himself.

Life in the Soviet Union never recovered. The halcyon days were over.

In the terror that followed Kirov's murder, no Soviet felt safe from the reach of Stalin's secret service, renamed the NKVD in July 1934, which Stalin—whom the great Russian poet Osip Mandelstam called the "broad-breasted Ossete"—controlled through a sequence of vicious henchmen. Genrikh Yagoda, Nikolai Yezhov, and Lavrenti

Beria acted on Stalin's murderous wishes with ingenious malice, only to end as victims of his system themselves, Beria upon the master's death, the others at his command.

Many Soviet citizens simply vanished, never seen again, to die in one of Moscow's penitentiaries, the Lubyanka prominent among them, celebrated as it was by Arthur Koestler in *Darkness at Noon*. Millions more died in the notorious labor camps in the network of the Gulag, of which Aleksandr Solzhenitsyn so masterfully made the world aware. Frequent Russian revelers who attended Bullitt's embassy soirees and luncheons dropped from sight, sometimes but not always appearing one last time, shaken, pale, uncertain, subdued. One by one, the distinguished political figures, including Bukharin and Radek, fell. Bullitt's staff felt the chill at once. George Kennan, so aghast at what was happening, developed debilitating ulcers and had to be hospitalized in Vienna.[21]

The parties went on for a while. So did the polo. For another year Bullitt struggled with the Russian bureaucracy in order to travel throughout the Soviet Union, but Litvinov's hostility to trade agreements, reparations, and the insulting display with which the *Comintern* openly courted members of the American Communist Party at the seventh All-World Congress of the Communist International in 1935 defeated the ambassador in his larger objectives. By the time he departed, in April 1936, Bullitt's disillusion was complete. He chillingly wrote in a final dispatch that his embassy staff called his swan song: "We should not cherish for a moment the illusion that it is possible to establish really friendly relations with the Soviet Government, or with any communist party or communist individual."[22]

THREE

Anti-Semitism

If the Jew did not exist, the anti-Semite would invent him.
—Jean-Paul Sartre, *Anti-Semite and Jew*

On March 3, 1936, a month before Bullitt's departure, Cordell Hull telegraphed Tyler Kent to inform him of the death of his father at Mt. Alto Hospital in Washington. In one swift passage of time, the two authority figures of his life vanished. His distant father's death may have softened the appraisal that Bullitt later submitted on Kent's performance, and the exodus of the ambassador may have worked to Kent's nefarious advantage. The guiding spirit and leader of the Moscow mission left in his wake a dispirited, leaderless staff in a city gripped by fear.

In this situation, Kent prospered. He purchased the ambassador's Ford, and it was around this time that he strengthened his connection with Tanya and began to prosper from the sale of goods that he was smuggling in the diplomatic pouch. He stayed in Moscow for over three years more, and, although he traveled back to the States in the winter of 1939 for a visit, during his time of exile in Russia he made a comfortable life for himself under two more ambassadors and at least one *chargé d'affaires*, none of whom cast upon Kent the sort of penetrating scrutiny that Bullitt had.

Joseph E. Davies, who succeeded Bullitt as ambassador in January 1937, paid no attention whatsoever to Kent. He left evaluations to his subordinates. In April 1937, in his report, J. K. Huddle of the consular staff observed of Kent that he was "a nice enough young man, without personality," one, however, who "does not give an impression of having much strength of character." He also noted that Kent "has not been taught to work with the expedition which should be realized in this office." In 1938, Alexander Kirk, the embassy *chargé d'affaires*, wrote that Kent was "courteous to superiors and colleagues, but not popular among colleagues who feel that he considers them social inferiors; very pleasant when he so desires, but not always so inclined." Nevertheless, of Kent Kirk wrote: "The attitude of this clerk to his work has improved commendably during the past year. He is becoming more mature and serious."[1]

By then, Kent's work had also progressed to a more serious level. He had risen from junior clerk to junior clerk, class 2, assigned to reviewing the Russian press, drafting dispatches based on press articles, and Russian-English translating. Now twenty-six, he had matured, and in a way so had his political ideas, in the sense that these had ripened and taken their shape in the strange hothouse of his mind.

According to his own account, Kent first began the practice of borrowing certain top-secret documents to which he had access as an embassy file clerk, using a camera to photograph them when he could not obtain carbon copies, so he could read them at his leisure in the privacy of his own apartment and file them for future study. He took up this habit in 1937, when embassy security, practically speaking, didn't exist.

It was the custom, according to J. Edgar Hoover, when the time came to destroy confidential and coded messages, "to pile together all original drafts of confidential messages with the original drafts of the coded telegrams for burning in the basement of the building." No guard or control, he wrote, "was ever exercised to see whether the messages were destroyed. With these documents in his possession, the messenger would be in a position to know the contents of all confidential communications coming from the Embassy and also having the data with which to break the confidential codes." Soviet citizens, some of whom lived in the building, gathered at the close of day, when the bundles of paper were burned in the basement, to watch the fire, and perhaps—though Hoover doesn't explicitly say so—to enjoy its warmth. Hoover did add, however, that "Paper bundles such as the bundles of confidential messages do not burn readily and even after being in the fire for several minutes many messages still may be removed and read. Only the Soviets usually know whether the paper thrown into the fire is completely burned."

Hoover undertook the investigation of the Moscow embassy at the request of the State Department after the British embassy in Washington sent word that confidential information had been "leaking out of the Embassy in Moscow; that as a result of this situation the British were refusing to reveal certain confidential information to the United States Government."[2] Louis Beck, an undercover agent dispatched to Moscow at the State Department's request, performed his task in the summer of 1940 in the guise of an internal messenger.[3] Hoover issued a confidential memorandum to the White House in December of that year, sharing his findings.

"Under the regulations of the Department of State no one is permitted in the code room in the Embassy unless he is an official or has been specifically authorized to use the codes," he wrote. "On the second night of the reporting agent's stay, all safes were open and code books lay on the tables together with messages to be encoded and decoded. . . . The door of the code room was open at all times." On the occasion of the agent's visit, the code clerk, Robert Hall, "left the room for forty-five minutes with the room in complete control of the reporting agent." Messages sent through the Code Room—political, personnel, and visa—went into binders often left on the table outside the Code Room, in the File Room, where, Hoover wrote, "Communications marked strictly confidential are considered choice reading. Throughout entire days a file room clerk would do practically nothing but read confidential matter." By the time of Hoover's memo, Kent had already left, but another clerk was "at this time using liquor to excess and associating with Soviet prostitutes."[4]

By then Germany had invaded Poland, and Britain had declared war on Germany, then allied with the Soviet Union. Embassy morale in 1940, according to Hoover, was ebbing low, and his memorandum contains an entire section devoted to what he called "Sexual Perversion among Staff Members," that is: homosexual acts between a clerk and the ambassador's secretary in the Code Room. In another section, Hoover discussed the ongoing situation at the Nosion Hotel, where men on the embassy staff continued to meet with Soviet prostitutes who reported to the NKVD, which, Hoover noted, assigned individual girls to certain men. "These women, up until a short time ago at least, have had free access to the Embassy building and there was hardly a night when several of them were not there."[5]

The conditions described in Hoover's memo predated the war in Europe, and the Molotov-Ribbentrop Pact of 1939 that triggered it. Henry Antheil, a code clerk in Moscow who shared an apartment with Tyler Kent, had in his possession—it was later discovered—copies of telegrams sent by the Moscow embassy during 1937 and 1938 on the political situation in Russia, many letters from Foreign Service officers and members of the State Department, and various dispatches.

Antheil was relaying their contents to his brother George, in Hollywood, who was writing a book on the situation in Europe. Among the many items later found in the closet of Antheil's apartment in Helsinki, Finland, where he served as a code clerk in the US Legation, was a letter written to Antheil when he was a code clerk in Moscow, dated November 30, 1938, by Alexander Fomin, who wrote to Antheil of his "intended purpose that is, to become a spy, as it is usually put, of a progressive country such as the USA." Fomin's more likely purpose would have been to spy *against* such a country for the USSR. On the shelf in Antheil's clothes closet, a Legation official also discovered two copies of the combination of the Code Room vault before promptly burning them.[6]

The lax security that Hoover describes—a feature of the Moscow embassy for a number of years during the 1930s—of which Antheil's and Kent's behaviors provide examples, derived from circumstances peculiar to US-Soviet relations at the time. The White House required evidence of a rosy relationship, which those who served in Moscow knew to be mere wishful thinking. This falsehood eroded morale among men already depressed by the terror amid which they had to conduct their lives. That rose-tinted view no doubt struck many in the embassy at the time as tangential to the concerns of the United States at best.

That's certainly what Tyler Kent had concluded. He quickly came to despise the Soviet system and the men behind it, including the original Bolshevik revolutionaries, whom he called "Bolos." These men made up Lenin's inner circle, like Lev Kamenev and Grigory Zinoviev, victims of Stalin's first purge trials, and those of his two subsequent show trials, Bukharin and Radek among others, who so recently had enjoyed the hospitality of Bullitt's embassy. The defendants "confessed" their crimes in advance under torture, none remotely guilty as charged.

Kent, of course, sided with the isolationists at home and those in the State Department who hated the Bolos. One clue to Kent's attitude at the time reveals itself in the "Dearest Pucia" letter, in which Anthony J. Barrett wrote, on July 1, 1937, "[Y]ou should put your mother on a right track about the political situation in Europe. She thinks Mussolini and Hitler are just awful bandits, safecrackers and bomb throwers, but on the contrary she thinks that Russia is making wonderful steps toward the improving of people's welfare. I told her a few things and told her you had been my adviser on all these points. She was rather surprised to hear that her views didn't correspond with yours."[7]

On leave, Kent traveled extensively in Europe and visited Germany, but he never identified himself as a Nazi sympathizer, although he did sympathize with Nazi anti-Semitism, and hoped that Germany one day would attack the Soviet Union and destroy it. He surely knew Germans who served in the embassy of the Third Reich in Moscow, some of them the "young apprentices in the Foreign Office" whom Martha Dodd, daughter of Thomas Dodd, the US ambassador in Berlin, mentions in her memoirs: "They danced with the daughters, they sent flowers to the mothers, they escorted the fathers on trips and were in general the young bloods of Berlin social life. During the time I was there, I saw a whole batch or two of them trained and disciplined and sent away to foreign posts. All of them were S.S. men."[8] Kent very likely formed friendships with one or more of these German agents, as his mother asserted in a letter to a State Department official in 1941.[9]

The thoughts that concerned Kent as he read over the classified letters, memos, and telegrams that he had copied in the embassy involved the conversations that he could see taking place—but not hear—between ambassadors and other American officials throughout Europe and officers in the Department of State.

The officials involved—in particular, those in embassies of European nations—all expressed in varying ways their deepening alarm over Hitler's deportment. Wilbur Carr, no longer an assistant secretary of state, served quite admirably, according to George Kennan, as ambassador to Czechoslovakia . . . until the Germans occupied it. Kent also knew William Bullitt, now the American ambassador to France, and Davies, who, after Moscow, went to Brussels as ambassador to Belgium. He may not yet have encountered George Messersmith, who served in Berlin and in Austria, but he knew him by reputation, and Kent had worked in Moscow under career officers now assigned to other European capitals as well. In the dispatches that he read, Kent eavesdropped on the shared opinions of men, moved by the rush of Hitler's aggression to believe that America should flex its muscle to safeguard like-minded political friends—especially France, Holland, Belgium, and Poland—from military onslaught. Bullitt made ardent efforts in the time running up to the German invasion of France to obtain US assistance for the French forces, especially the air force, which was short of fighter aircraft.

In the privacy of his room, Kent's blood boiled as he read how these civil servants were conspiring to draw into the gathering conflict those whom they represented—Americans who, in all innocence, knew nothing of the peril it might portend for them. Perhaps it was then that he conceived the idea to use this purloined information to influence events. Maybe he was sharing some of his hoarded secrets with Tanya, or one of his contacts at the German embassy. At the moment, his possession of these top-secret messages and dispatches gave Kent a sense of importance for which his ego yearned, without yet feeding any grandiose ambitions that he might have begun to entertain.

The career officers for whom Kent had such an aversion had also come to Moscow with strong misgivings. They watched Stalin's show trials unfold with sickening dread. The first show trials—so called because they showed the world that Stalin dealt fairly with "enemies of the people"—took place in August 1936. Kamenev and Zinoviev, two of the early Bolshevik leaders, stood accused of conspiring against Stalin with Leon Trotsky, once believed to be Lenin's preferred heir, and whom Stalin had bested in the power struggle that followed Lenin's death in 1922. The first case was called the "Trotskyite-Zinovievite Terrorist Centre."

A new trial, of the "Anti-Soviet Trotskyite Center," featuring Karl Radek—an important Party theoretician, and a guest of the US embassy along with Yuri Pyatakov, Nikolai Krestinsky, and other important members of the Politburo—took place in January 1937. These two sets of trials and the less-publicized executions of other figures struck fear in the hearts of all who dared espouse the cause of Stalin's nemesis—or so it seemed. The purge trials did shake the morale of the entire Soviet military establishment, and for good reason. The whole nation gasped, aghast, when, on June 12, Stalin carried out a summary execution for treason among the officer corps of the Red Army, including Marshal Tukhachevsky.

"Every field of Soviet official, political, technical and cultural life in the past few weeks has been affected by the swelling wave of arrests and dismissals," Loy Henderson wrote in a confidential report on June 13, 1937, to the State Department. "The Embassy's estimate, based on information obtained from sources usually reliable, of the extent of the dismissals, arrests, or executions, is that no fewer than five People's Commissars, seventeen vice commissars, two former ambassadors; dozens of general officers of the Army, as well as hundreds of officers of lower rank; hundreds of high officials attached to the central apparatus of the Government; thousands of lesser officials throughout the country; scores of the more important Party officials, and thousands of less important Party officials; numerous prominent officials of such government- or party-sponsored organizations as the labor unions, the communist union of youth, the powerful civilian military training society called OSOAVIAKHIM; hundreds of the so-called new intelligentsia, including professors, writers, theatrical people, physicians, musicians, and so forth."[10]

Stalin launched his new summer slaughter when he discovered that his first two trials had failed to discredit Trotsky as he had intended. "Stalin became infuriated," Henderson wrote, "when he learned that his recent trials resulted in increasing the prestige of Trotsky abroad and also within the borders of the Soviet Union, particularly, in connection with the latter statement, with respect to the attitude of the so-called new intelligentsia. In his anger he struck where ever whispers of criticism were heard or where he imagined persons to be whispering. He subsequently learned that his blows tended to increase these whispers rather than to silence them, and then his fears changed to alarm for his present position and safety."[11]

George Kennan attended the Radek-Pyatakov-Krestinksy show trial with Ambassador Davies. Kennan was supposed to be interpreting for the ambassador, but to his dismay, Davies seemed oblivious to the travesty of justice taking place before their eyes. "His own reports make it evident that he placed considerable credence in the fantastic charges leveled at these unfortunate men," Kennan later recalled.[12] Clenching their eyes shut behind those rose-colored glasses, neither Davies nor Roosevelt wanted to hear the misgivings of the career officers in the Moscow embassy. FDR had appointed Davies to represent him in Moscow precisely to preserve a relationship with Stalin and the Soviet Union—not to give him reasons to sever it.

The president believed a smooth relationship with Stalin was key to their coexistence. Davies therefore had to make every effort to maintain a link with the Soviet leader. He all but ignored the qualms of his Foreign Service officers, despite the depth and acuity of their observations.

Those young, perceptive officers didn't despise the Bolsheviks and their cause per se, however. They mistrusted the Soviet political system and the way Stalin had twisted it to his own purposes. Kent, on the other hand, *did* despise the Bolsheviks because so many of them were Jewish—or had been before Stalin executed them. That Stalin was himself anti-Semitic seems not to have influenced Kent's views on the subject one way or another, views that he had brought with him to Russia and nurtured during his long residence in Moscow, where, in that atmosphere of mortal dread, anti-Semitism flourished.

It's harder to imagine now, but Western civilization had suffered openly and not unhappily from the virus of anti-Semitism for many centuries. Practically all the nations of Europe had expelled their Jewish populations at one point or another: France in 1182, England in 1290, Spain in 1492, Portugal in 1497, and so on. The establishment bastions of America, which included the Department of State, harbored this closed-mindedness until the aftermath of World War II. But the career officers in the Moscow embassy—all, without exception—hailed from the modern world. Intellectually astute critics of retrograde ideology, they had graduated from elite universities where, in the dining clubs, social clubs, and fraternities, anti-Semitic attitudes had prevailed. They didn't harbor race hatred in their hearts—but none of them was a Jew.

In the 1920s and '30s, Jews didn't take the Foreign Service exams, nor were they encouraged to do so. The State Department elders, men of old, crusty backgrounds, by and large ran the place like a club. As one writer put it, "Built into the worldview of the majority was adamant opposition to the Communist menace and an unquestioning acceptance of their forebears' antipathy toward Jews, as a sly and untrustworthy race."[13]

To some in Washington, anti-Semitism was even commendable. William Castle, who served as undersecretary of state in the Hoover administration, kept a voluminous diary of Washington life. In one entry, dated December 11, 1936, he mentions the Schoenfeld brothers, both working in the Foreign Service. "The Schoenfeld brothers are specially good Foreign Service men, both of them." One of them, Rudy was "proceeding to Stockholm, and I hope the Swedes will not think that he is just another Jew." Castle continued that Rudy "has been the great Jew hater of the Department who has insisted on resisting the political pressure brought by the New York Jews to make the government interfere every time a Jew is murdered somewhere in the world."[14]

President Roosevelt didn't share that attitude, however. "He didn't have an anti-Semitic bone in his body," Trudy Lash told Arthur M. Schlesinger Jr.[15] The wife of Joseph Lash, Trudy was a Roosevelt biographer, a friend of Eleanor Roosevelt, and Jewish herself.

Roosevelt mistrusted the people at State. Among those he mistrusted, besides those who hadn't attended Groton, were those who worked in the Eastern European Division who themselves mistrusted Stalin, thereby impeding the opportunity the president sought to cultivate the Soviet leader. FDR shuttered the division; dismantled its valuable library; moved its director, Robert Kelley, to serve as ambassador to Turkey; and appointed Bullitt in his place, a man altogether unfamiliar, to quote a State Department insider, with "even the most elementary realities of the Soviet system and of its ideology." These were the words of Bullitt's successor, Joseph E. Davies, the husband of the autocratic Post Toasties heiress, Marjorie Merriweather Post. Davies and his wife, recalled the circumspect Charles Bohlen, "treated the staff as hired help and rarely listened to its views."[16]

Whether FDR trusted "Judge" Moore, Wilbur Carr, or even Cordell Hull makes for a matter more complicated. Although he found these men of the South useful for political reasons, they weren't his people, and he didn't entrust them with any significant power. His man at State was Sumner Welles, the Groton graduate. As Arthur M. Schlesinger Jr. put it, "FDR and Welles spoke the same language." The difference between Welles and Hull, according to the renowned historian, was that Welles could describe a situation to the president in a few vivid words that the president would understand perfectly; Hull, on the other hand, had a tendency to be "wordy."

In 1935, when the number-two job opened up at the State Department, it went to Welles and not Moore. Welles sidelined Moore, who never recovered. The latter's bitterness infected his ability to function, and ultimately created a denouement at the State Department that destroyed both Bullitt and Welles.[17]

Another unhappy conservative at State, after years of personal power, Carr occupied a position important only in name as assistant secretary in charge of immigration, operating with a shrinking budget. Hull, as secretary of state, possessed practically no power whatsoever to make actual policy, and exercised none on behalf of his friends, Carr and Moore. But because he knew how to restrain his instincts on behalf of others, Hull hung on to his job through the third Roosevelt administration. Not a New Deal Democrat, Hull was the son of a Tennessee Confederate, a southern moderate but, in the Senate anyway, a political ally who rallied support for Roosevelt's candidacy among fellow Democrats.

These men in the Department of State had the fealty, if not the express loyalty, of Tyler Kent, the son of their late friend. Among them, only Moore lacked the stain of racism. According to historian Irwin Gellman, Carr opposed the admission of European Jews as immigrants in the 1930s "because of his exclusionary beliefs and his anti-Semitism." He found support in the matter from Hull's first undersecretary, William Phillips, a Bostonian who held similar views about the undesirability of

Jews in general. Never openly anti-Semitic, Hull did, as a presidential aspirant, unsuccessfully suppress the Jewish background of his wife, Frances. According to Gellman, he "feared that this Jewish connection made him vulnerable to attacks from anti-Semites," who "would argue that his wife had forced him to support the Jewish cause, and therefore that he had succumbed to un-American influences."[18] In his role as secretary of state, he consistently evaded the growing Jewish refugee question.[19]

These Kent family friends in the Department of State—older reactionaries increasingly isolated from the anti-fascist, anti-Nazi, pro-Soviet pursuits of the Roosevelt administration and his envoys in Europe—shared some of the views of those in Congress who came to be known as isolationists. They wanted nothing to do with war in Europe.

By 1937, many isolationists—a subset of noninterventionists who included pacifists, communists, and Midwestern and Western conservatives—had formed the impression that, no matter what he said, Roosevelt wanted to go to war against Germany, an ambition supported by the Northeastern establishment, press and business alike. To some isolationists, including Colonel Charles Lindbergh—a Midwesterner of German-Scandinavian heritage, and the most outspoken of their number—Hitler held the winning card in Europe. As the *Führer* went about building up his armed forces, Lindbergh went about America, lecturing audiences on the inevitable rise of the Third Reich, where he maintained a secret, second family, and the folly of trying to oppose it. These views contained a strong, racist component even when not expounded overtly. Lindbergh and others spread the virus that the reactionaries in the State Department harbored, and that, at some stage in his life, had infected Tyler Kent.

One source attributes Kent's anti-Semitic attitudes and their rationale to his mentor in Madrid, the cafe philosopher whose informal "sessions" he had attended as a student in exile. Kent's mother later ascribed these beliefs to the friendship he formed in Moscow with a Nazi in the German embassy. Such a friendship may have played a part in the intellectual argument that Kent advanced against Jews, although in Moscow, even in the darkest days of the Terror, a German official would have met many like-minded souls, eager to speak Russian with an American, if only to report to the NKVD what he had to say.

The toxic ingenuity of the virus, however, is that anti-Semitism usually grows covertly at first among those whom it infects, an argument formulated and refined through discussions in which the premise is already agreed upon in advance. A brief examination of the specific circumstances of Tyler Kent's life may help to explain how it came to flourish independently in Kent's mind.

"I would call anti-Semitism a poor man's snobbery," Jean-Paul Sartre writes in *Anti-Semite and Jew*.[20] In other words, it afflicts those who fear being dispossessed, who seek a sense of belonging that depends on the exclusion of others who may claim greater wealth, knowledge, or intelligence, but who cannot claim ancestral roots in any of those states in which anti-Semitism thrives. In France, it's a condition, Sartre writes, found among those who "belong to the lower middle class of the towns," among "functionaries, office workers, small businessmen, who possess nothing," who "have chosen anti-Semitism as a means of establishing their status as possessors," who, "in representing the Jew as a robber," have "put themselves in the enviable position of people who could be robbed," who have concluded that, because "the Jew wishes to take France from them, it follows that France must belong to them."[21]

Sartre points out that "the anti-Semite is not too anxious to possess individual merit," which "has to be sought just like truth," and responsibly maintained, usually with difficulty. The anti-Semite "flees responsibility as he flees his own consciousness, and choosing for his personality the permanence of rock, he chooses for his morality a scale of petrified values." In this artificially constructed and self-buttressed system of values, "Whatever he does, he knows that he will remain at the top of the ladder; whatever the Jew does, he will never get any higher than the first rung."[22]

The dispossessed aristocrat—postrevolutionary Frenchmen and Russians or antebellum Virginians, like Kent—can succumb to the fallacy just as easily as the impoverished lower-middle-class Frenchman. The key ingredient is perceived disenfranchisement. In Russia, Bolshevik Jews seized ancestral lands, but elsewhere the Jewish enemy moved in and simply bought the land, which the complicit nation had permitted them to do.

"Any anti-Semite," Sartre writes, "is therefore, in varying degree, the enemy of constituted authority. He wishes to be the disciplined member of an undisciplined group; he adores order, but a social order. We might say he wishes to provoke political disorder in order to restore social order, the social order in his eyes being a society that, by virtue of juxtaposition, is egalitarian and primitive, one with a heightened temperature, one from which Jews are excluded."[23]

As the definition of a general condition, Sartre's thoughts quite accurately and precisely describe the attitudes reflected in Kent's behavior, especially as the Moscow era of his life matured. "These principles," Sartre continues, "enable him to enjoy a strange sort of independence, which I shall call an invented liberty. Authentic liberty assumes responsibilities, and the liberty of the anti-Semite comes from the fact that he escapes all of this. Floating between an authoritarian society which has not yet come into existence and an official and tolerant society which he disavows, he can do anything he pleases without appearing to be an anarchist, which would horrify him. The profound seriousness of his aims—which no word, no statement, no act can express—permits him a certain frivolity. He is a hooligan, he beats people up, he purges, he robs; it is all in a good cause."[24]

Tyler Kent, the born exile, twice dispossessed, yearned for a place in the social order, wanting overt recognition as the born aristocrat to whom no merit system need apply. This frame of mind left him susceptible to anti-Semitism and came to influence the course of his conduct.

⌐ ⌐

Kent continued to nurse ambitions for a position in the Foreign Service more important than that of a mere clerk. Now that the State Department once again was offering Foreign Service exams, Kent thought that he had a shot at passing them. He had the goodwill of some of the career officers who served in the Moscow embassy, including Alexander Kirk, soon to be *chargé d' affaires* in Berlin, but presently—in late 1938, early 1939—performing the same function in Moscow, where he wrote a not-uncomplimentary evaluation of Kent's performance. Loy Henderson also sent Kent off with best wishes when our protagonist left Moscow in January 1939 to return to Washington, D.C., to take the exams.[25]

In the years immediately preceding Kent's Russian appointment, the Foreign Service exams consisted of simple, factual questions, put to the applicant in written form, followed by oral questions, also less than exacting. It's hard to imagine that Kent would have had much trouble passing them, thus easily qualifying him for a State Department administered by Wilbur Carr.

In 1939, however, Kent's old supporters had all but disappeared. Moore, at eighty, had yet to resign, but under a State Department directed by Sumner Welles he was performing only minor chores. In 1937, George Messersmith, a career officer, replaced Assistant Secretary of State for Administration Wilbur Carr, also of advanced age. Messersmith belonged to the new breed in the State Department, which the old Eastern elite deeply disliked. William Castle and his friends in the Washington social club circuit liked to entertain the idea that he was Jewish, which he was not. "He had a great reputation as a martinet and disciplinarian," Kennan recalled of Messersmith. "Tough he was, and strong-willed indeed." Henderson described him as a "'hard-line' administrator."[26]

Thanks to a proviso established in 1931 for the benefit of the offspring of Foreign Service veterans, Kent requested and received a waiver to skip the Foreign Service written examinations, by then far more rigorous than they once had been, but he had the misfortune nevertheless to have to undergo the required oral exam when Messersmith happened to be chairman of the Board of Examiners. If Kent's sullied reputation hadn't already done so, this examination arrangement doomed his chances.

On February 2, G. Howland Shaw submitted a report of his meeting with Kent, in which he wrote, "I asked him whether he thought he was lazy, inclined to be snobbish, and generally inclined to have an unduly high opinion of his own worth. He said he did not think he was snobbish, although there were some people apparently with whom he was not particularly keen to associate."[27]

Kent met his oral examiners, Messersmith chief among them, on February 14, 1939. The oral examination, according to one authority, "tests qualities that are not revealed in written answers." James L. McCamy writes, "A candidate is asked specific questions, or is engaged in amiable conversation, and is observed by the examiners for such traits as interest, sincerity, appearance, manners, diction, forcefulness, imagination, initiative, general attitude toward work and career, and the readiness, clarity, and precision with which he talks."[28] Messersmith and others who examined Kent observed in him few of the traits listed by McCamy. The day following his exam, in an *aide-mémoire*, Messersmith wrote: "I told him that we had given him a low mark on the examination of yesterday and that we had been unfavorably impressed by the superficial manner in which he answered most of the questions and by his very evident resentment when he was pressed for greater precision. I told him quite bluntly that until he took himself seriously in hand and got over his superiority complex he was a poor bet from our point of view."[29]

—⁓—

The following month, Kent turned twenty-eight. Any future career he might have imagined for himself as a serious diplomat looked lost. He turned briefly to the possibility of working in Moscow as a correspondent for the International News Service. It came to nothing, Kent later explained, because the USSR knew his views and therefore would never grant him a permit to work there as a journalist.[30] Kent returned to Moscow, to his old embassy job, with what sense of failure and resentment we can only imagine. He also must have returned with fresh impressions of the domestic political scene, gathered from family friends and those he knew in the Department of State who were hostile to the Roosevelt administration and the Eastern establishment.

By 1939, isolationists in Congress and elsewhere had become a vocal minority of unlikely bedfellows: senators and congressmen, labor leaders, hyphenated isolationists of German and Irish heritage, old-time progressives like Senator Burton Wheeler of Montana, and Communists. The year before, the isolationists almost managed to get a bill through Congress calling for a national referendum on the war in Europe. Conservative Southern Democrats and anti–New Deal Republicans who controlled Congress in 1939 blocked Roosevelt's efforts to repeal the 1937 Neutrality Act, which prohibited the sale of arms to his future European allies.[31]

Yet from his vantage point in Moscow, in the File Room and in the seclusion of his apartment, where he could mull over his burgeoning archive, Kent saw an increasingly frantic conversation among American diplomats about ways to persuade the president to help the beleaguered Polish and the French and others in Europe on whom Hitler was preparing to pounce.

On August 23, 1939, Joachim von Ribbentrop, Hitler's foreign minister, signed a nonaggression pact with Vyacheslav Molotov, the Russian premier. Their rapprochement assured the invasion of Poland both by Germany and the Soviet Union—a week later, as it happened, in the case of the Germans. The Russians followed suit, and within weeks struck simultaneously by air, land, and sea at the Baltic States of Lithuania, Latvia, and Estonia.

That same August, as it also happened, Kent, while driving in Moscow, struck a Soviet citizen with his car and broke the man's leg. Kent offered to pay some sort of compensation, but the incident— which came at a moment of enormous international tension—was, in the words of Laurence Steinhardt, the latest ambassador, to Secretary of State Hull, "taken under consideration," by the State Automobile Accident Inspectorate, perhaps not for reasons all that friendly to the American mission.[32]

The matter was settled for Kent, when, the following month, the State Department decided to transfer him to the embassy in London in place of his former Moscow code clerk, Henry Antheil, with whom he had once shared an apartment. Antheil, now in Helsinki, had been reassigned to London to fill a vacancy in the Code Room at the request of Joseph Kennedy, ambassador to Great Britain. Antheil, however, didn't want the assignment to the court of St. James. Madly in love with a Finnish girl, he had done everything he could to arrange a transfer from Moscow to Helsinki, up to falsifying telegrams and withholding others that recommended his assignment elsewhere. In Finland, Antheil continued to falsify and forge telegrams and to alter or cancel messages confirming his reassignment to Stockholm, and subsequently to London, which, for three months, had been promised his services, in short supply there.[33]

Kennedy, for his part, couldn't understand why, when he'd asked for a code clerk, he instead got Tyler Kent, a file clerk with no previous training in code work. Kennedy dispatched an angry message to the State Department. "For a clearing house as busy as the London Embassy, first class code clerks are essential, not merely clerks in other lines," he wrote Hull on September 17.[34] Evidently no one in Washington, D.C., or Moscow bothered to explain to Kennedy the circumstances that had led to Kent's departure from Moscow and arrival in England.

Kent left Moscow so quickly that he had no time to pack the possessions he'd acquired during his five and a half years there. He left behind a library of over one hundred Russian-language volumes among his other effects. Some items he put in a briefcase, which he locked and gave to Charles Thayer to store in the embassy safe until Thayer could forward it to Kent in the embassy pouch, which he never did.[35] The documents in his secret archive he committed to flames, probably in the embassy basement, just before his hurried departure.[36]

In September 1940, Ambassador Steinhardt wrote Secretary of State Hull to inform him that two Foreign Service inspectors had discovered the briefcase. They opened it without breaking the lock in the ambassador's presence. The briefcase contained:

- one Colt "police" .38 caliber revolver
- one box of .38 caliber smokeless lead cartridges
- one dirk (a short straight knife)
- two boxes of calling cards
- two framed photographs of Tatiana Alexandrovna Iliovskaya, otherwise known as Tanya
- two nude photos of Tanya
- one photograph of a Moscow church
- one photograph of "a nude woman identified by the staff as an actress in one of the smaller Moscow theatres"

- one small photograph of a nude man and woman
- two volumes of Langenscheidt's pocket German-English dictionary
- a pocket edition of Lyall's *Guide to 25 Languages of Europe*
- a letter, dated May 9, 1939, from the INS
- a bill from H. Frederking of Riga, dated June 23, 1939
- the first page of a memorandum dealing with the August automobile accident in Moscow
- a package of typewriter paper
- and "One volume entitled *Le Portier des Chartreux* (pornographic), published in London, 1788"[37]

On his journey to London, Kent gave a wide berth to Germany, which in the last week of September was mopping up the remains of its slaughter in western Poland, while the Soviet Union took unto its cruel embrace those Poles who had fled eastward into the arms of its advancing warriors. He left the Soviet Union on September 23, traveled by train and boat across Finland and Sweden to Norway, whence he made the North Sea voyage to Newcastle, where he disembarked in the company of a passenger named Ludwig Matthias, a naturalized Norwegian of German-Jewish origin.

This is why MI5, the British counterintelligence agency, had a record on Kent. They had reason to believe that the Gestapo had sent Matthias on an undercover mission to Great Britain, now officially at war with the Third Reich after Hitler's forces invaded Poland. On a tip from Norway, MI5 dispatched agents to Newcastle to track Matthias on his arrival in England. They reported that Matthias ("5'4", stout, dark rather Turkish appearance; well dressed") had met Kent in the Cumberland Hotel lounge in London, at 4:00 p.m. on October 4. The two men entered the hotel restaurant. Then at 6:45 they paid a brief visit to Kent's room. They left together, Matthias carrying a bulky envelope, ten inches by six. The two men dined together in Jermyn Street, walked to the Park Lane Hotel, and had drinks in the lounge. Matthias, when last seen in London, was driving off in a taxi in the company of a prostitute, destination unknown.[38]

British counterintelligence agent Maxwell Knight filed his report without informing the US embassy that their newly arrived embassy official had been spotted with a suspected agent of the German secret police.[39]

FOUR

Code Clerk

Even so we should abandon all sentimentality in our views of the traitor, and recognize him as a thief and a liar. He may be other things; a criminal is very rarely simply a criminal. But to a marked degree the traitor is also a thief and a liar.

—REBECCA WEST, *THE NEW MEANING OF TREASON*

TYLER KENT'S JOB IN THE CODE ROOM OF THE LONDON EMBASSY, where he reported for work on October 5, 1939, presented him with an opportunity vaster in scope than he had enjoyed in Moscow for eavesdropping on diplomatic correspondence. Before long he returned to the practice of copying discarded telegrams, which he removed from the embassy precincts via his briefcase to the privacy of his quarters, where, as in Moscow, he assembled a private diplomatic archive of his own—file folders stored in suitcases.

"In view of the importance of the American Embassy in London as one of the focal points in the European political scene," Kent later wrote in a memorandum labeled "Strictly Confidential" that he prepared for Congress, "it will readily be understood that the quantity of such relayed messages was very large, and that these messages covered the most important political developments in Europe as a whole." He added, "Bear in mind the fact that the dates of the communications at my disposal go back as far as 1937, thus covering the most important period prior to the outbreak of the recent war and the early months thereof."[1]

Conditions in the London embassy differed significantly from those in Moscow, where security, as J. Edgar Hoover's secret agent soon discovered, was scandalously slipshod. In London, the Code Room remained locked at all times. So did the File Room, next door. Under the stewardship of Ambassador Kennedy, here morale, even in early-wartime London, was by comparison effervescent and purposeful, central as it was to international events and American interests. Everything hummed right along.

But the change in climate didn't inhibit Kent's archival inclinations. He swiftly adapted himself to the new circumstances. No one in the London embassy for a moment supposed that a code clerk or anybody else in the embassy would even consider keeping copies of diplomatic telegrams for private use. In the absence of any signal from Maxwell Knight about Kent's questionable association with a Gestapo agent, or even someone suspected of being one, the possibility that Kent might himself be a Nazi agent didn't occur to anyone—this despite the force of his pro-German views.

His new responsibilities and opportunities inspired him to don Savile Row suits, tweed jackets, silk neckwear, and good leather shoes. Like a young British banker, he wore his thick, smooth, brown hair precisely parted, evenly trimmed. His pale, plump, good-looking face went along perfectly with his entire look.

Kent worked alone in the Code Room and could easily make duplicates of official incoming and outgoing dispatches that passed through his hands. He could remove other documents already on file from the File Room at times when he had the place to himself.

A changed man—chastened, perhaps—he performed his job well and attracted none of the animus directed his way by colleagues in Moscow. Although not surprisingly one fellow clerk, Page Huydekuper, recalls finding him "smug" and thinking him Midwestern. Twice Kent invited her out on a date. Once he asked her to go sailing, a pastime he had enjoyed in his boyhood and had now resumed. He also asked her out for dinner with another couple. Both times she declined.

Huydekuper worked in the File Room, she explains, because it was the most exciting place to be in the embassy. She saw Kent every day. Kent, because he worked the night shift, usually arrived in the late afternoon, and Huydekuper caught glimpses of him when he passed through the File Room en route to the Code Room. He had the gait, she says, of someone who thought he was important. He was always impeccably dressed, but, according to her definition, not dapper. "That implies someone more handsome," Huydekuper says. "He was good-looking, but his cheeks were too filled out, not carved enough."

He had no male friends in his life, she also recalls. "He kept clear of them."[2]

The night shift permitted Kent more ease with which to indulge his habit of perusing files and copying documents when, in the early hours of the morning, especially, he had the place to himself.

Kent didn't like living in London at first, and never very much. It's hard to say quite why, except that of course he entirely lacked sympathy with the British war effort. He may have felt more at home on the Continent, where he'd often lived and traveled. In Europe, he could practice his gift for languages and the camouflage they provided. He always fared better when less known to others.

"Once I asked him whether he liked being in London," a Russian émigré named Sabline recalled of Kent. "He answered that he found life here very dull, and that he would not mind returning to Russia, or going to Germany, for he considered life in the totalitarian world more

The entrance to the building in the Marylebone area
of London, where Tyler Kent lived. (PHOTO BY AUTHOR)

interesting than in a democracy. He did not seem to have friendly feelings towards this country." Sabline found Kent's knowledge of Russian "amazing," however. "He not only spoke perfect Russian, but he even knew intricate idiomatic phraseology now used in modern-day Russia of which I myself am ignorant."[3]

When he first came to London, Kent liked to eat out in Spanish restaurants—the Southern European nation then under the totalitarian control of General Francisco Franco—but for company Kent sought out members of the Russian émigré community, like Sabline, in order to maintain his Russian skills. He also thought, rightly, that they would want to hear about recent conditions in the Soviet Union. In time, Russian émigrés like Catherine Ridley, granddaughter of Count Benckendorff, the last imperial Russian ambassador to London, sought him out. By the end of 1939, he had entered the rather rarified social stratum of the dispossessed members of Russia's landed gentry, most of them impoverished exiles who now lived in London.

This is how he came to meet May Straker, of Greenville, Virginia, active in the Russian Red Cross, who contacted Kent through the embassy. Years earlier she had met Kent's mother in London, and Count Benckendorff had mentioned Kent's name once in passing. Straker introduced Kent into the Russian émigré social scene. He met Irene Danischewsky at a White Russian New Year's Eve ball on January 20, 1940. The old Russians observed the Old Style Gregorian calendar, and the New Year fell later. Her father, Peter Mirinoff, had moved to London with his family in 1916, when Irene was four. She grew up in England, attended good Catholic schools for young ladies, and had been married for some time to Alexander Danischewsky, newly enlisted in the British Army. Her father-in-law, a prosperous and eccentric Russian businessman, had made his fortune in Archangel in shipping and insurance, but left it behind when he fled the

Russian Revolution, first to Norway, thence to Sydenham, a southern London suburb, where he once again prospered, this time in the bath oil business, among other enterprises.[4]

The comely Irene and the handsome young Kent became lovers at once. In mid-January, Kent moved into a brick row house, 47 Gloucester Place, where, on the second floor, Irene made a regular practice of coming to see him around nine o'clock in the morning when Kent was working nights. Although they spent those mornings together in the seclusion of Kent's rooms, they often spent afternoons walking the city, sometimes making excursions to the countryside by car in the early spring.

Kent compartmentalized his life. Irene later wrote him that she never knew where he went when he left her to meet someone for lunch. She also intimated that she knew she wasn't his only sexual interest—a matter that didn't bother her at all, she insisted. Honest as she appears to have been in every other way, this isn't hard to believe. She regretted only that in those morning assignations she had not expressed herself as a lover in a more imaginative way.[5]

Irene later claimed to know almost nothing of Kent's political views or his subsequent activities, and he for his part appears to have kept his vehement anti-Semitic opinions to himself, along with his burgeoning archive. Kent surely left unsaid opinions certain to hurt someone married to the son of a Hasidic patriarch, to whom Irene was deeply attached, her passion for Kent notwithstanding. Kent, if Sartre may continue to guide us through the anti-Semite's condition, might have found an added sexual charge in this proximity to Irene's Jewish husband. If we follow the philosopher further, one element of the anti-Semite's hatred "is a profound sexual attraction toward Jews."[6]

But through the Russian émigré social scene, Kent found an outlet for the anti-Semitic feelings and his enraged, if simmering, political resentment. At a Russian Red Cross ball in February 1940, he made the acquaintance of the parents of Anna Wolkoff, a baroness. Older than Kent by a decade, she held no sexual appeal whatsoever for the otherwise erotically busy young American code clerk. A stocky, short, unlovely exile, she had prematurely white hair and a voice that Kent's landlady's cook later recalled as "gruff." But Kent, who preferred the company of women, as we have seen, had the socially useful talent for flattering women of all ages. He doubtless enjoyed the nonstop, coruscating anti-Jewish badinage that flowed from the baroness's overheated mind.

She had a certain social wit, Baroness Wolkoff. Kent fell under her spell. He took to visiting the Russian Tea Rooms in South Kensington, run by Wolkoff's father, an admiral in the czar's navy and the naval attaché in the czar's London embassy. There, émigrés could obtain reputedly the best imported caviar in all of London. Kent dismissed the small, dark, crowded establishment as "an oilcloth kind of place," however. He came here to meet the baroness, who helped her father run the place when not in her shop, where she made dresses for ladies of fashion. One such client was the charismatic Wallis Simpson, herself newly enduring a more richly appointed if no less bitter exile.

Bitterness gave the baroness a force of character that enchanted Kent. By the time he began to visit her at the Russian Tea Rooms, her pro-Nazi feelings had fueled her already-smoldering hatred of Jews, whom she blamed for overthrowing the czar and robbing her family of its land and titles. The previous summer she had visited Germany and traveled to the Sudetenland, where she had made a tour of inspection. She committed herself to the belief that Hitler would restore the old order once he'd driven the Bolsheviks from power in the Soviet Union, but her animating animosity aimed itself squarely at Jews and those who befriended them.

Kent cut a debonair figure in this twilight world of dispossessed Russians, when not engaged in his other sexual and archival pursuits.

He stood ready to leave at a moment's notice if the opportunity presented itself, as he thought it might. On February 24, not long after he had met Baroness Wolkoff, he wrote the *chargé d'affaires* in Berlin, Alexander Kirk, under whom he had served in Moscow, asking whether Kirk would consider him for a code clerk post in the Berlin embassy. Recommending himself for that job if it became available, Kent made the request without informing Ambassador Kennedy.[7]

Meanwhile, in the Code Room, Kent saw much that was happening behind the scenes within the State Department and the foreign policy establishment, and in the interactions between Washington and the capital cities of Europe. It was clear to almost everyone that Hitler was preparing to invade France and Northern Europe, including the Scandinavian countries, with or without the active assistance of Mussolini, his nominal Italian sidekick.

Ambassador Bullitt in France urgently lobbied on behalf of the French government for the air support needed to fight the Germans, who had noted the danger that Bullitt's friendship with Roosevelt could pose to their plans. Aware of the suspicions that the American isolationists entertained—that Roosevelt was secretly designing with his allies ways to draw the United States into the war—the Germans produced a volume of letters and telegrams between Bullitt and Tony Biddle, US ambassador to Poland, that they claimed to have captured in Warsaw. These documents, which Kent had also seen and copied, promoted the idea of an American invasion. In the words of the German home office minister, who later read them, the documents "displayed an anti-German attitude on the part of the American representative and shed light upon Jewish activities in Poland."[8]

The Molotov-Ribbentrop Pact of August 1939 may have delivered a body blow to the isolationists' cause, as one historian suggests, but if so, they seemed not to know it. They had the power, in 1940, to influence the foreign policy of the president, who, at heart an interventionist, as yet remained unwilling to come to the military assistance of those whom Hitler threatened. It was after all a presidential election year.

"There have been a number of fierce national quarrels in my lifetime—over communism in the later Forties, over McCarthyism in the Fifties, over Vietnam in the Sixties—but none so tore apart families and friendships as the great debate of 1940–41," writes Arthur M. Schlesinger Jr. in his memoir, *A Life in the 20th Century.*[9] Ambassador Kennedy, Kent's boss, held views diametrically opposed to those of William Bullitt, and had friends in the British government who shared them, all taking the vocal position that Great Britain could never expect to resist a German invasion successfully.[10] Kennedy believed that Bullitt's role in Warsaw appeared correctly in the German White Paper of letters and telegrams. He hated Bullitt and resented Roosevelt, who undercut Kennedy by establishing a back-channel correspondence with Winston Churchill,[11] whom Neville Chamberlain had appointed to the position of First Lord of the Admiralty after Britain declared war on Germany in September 1939.

On October 4, the day that Kent arrived in England, a letter came in the diplomatic pouch. Roosevelt invited Churchill to drop him a line anytime, and send it via the pouch. On October 5, Churchill invited Kennedy to the Admiralty to read him the letter. "Another instance of Roosevelt's conniving mind which never indicates he knows how to handle any organization," Kennedy confided to his diary later that day. "It's a rotten way to treat his Ambassador and I think it shows him up to the other people. I am disgusted."[12]

The invitation rested on a friendship formed when Churchill was First Lord of the Admiralty during the Great War and Roosevelt was Assistant Secretary of the Navy. It provided Churchill with an opportunity to solicit help for the British war effort in an unofficial manner that suited Roosevelt, who couldn't risk open communication regarding ways to circumvent the Neutrality Act. He wanted to help British naval efforts against Nazi aggression and in favor of American shipping in waters patrolled by the British.

Prime Minister Chamberlain had given his consent to this private, ex officio exchange between Churchill and Roosevelt, but he was not privy to the contents of the correspondence, with the exception of certain messages that Churchill sent to the Foreign Office to be vetted. Signing them "Johnson," Churchill altogether sent seven messages to Roosevelt through the US embassy Code Room as First Lord of the Admiralty. After he ascended to the position of prime minister, on May 10, 1940—while Kent was still code clerk—he sent two more messages that he signed "Former Naval Person."[13]

The Neutrality Act prevented Roosevelt from taking a stand against Nazi hostilities in the western and south Atlantic; he conceived the idea of a "Neutrality Zone" around the Western Hemisphere, which formed the subject of the first Roosevelt-Churchill communiqués. This proposal would exclude all belligerents from a zone of up to six hundred miles deep in the Western Hemisphere. The zone concept was designed to frustrate Nazi U-boat activity in western waters and, consequently, to help the British naval effort—at least indirectly. It was an Anglo-American act of cooperation cleverly concealed in the rhetoric of neutrality. The two leaders exchanged these early dispatches via the help of Tyler Kent.

In subsequent messages, Churchill kept Roosevelt informed of the successes and failures of Britain's naval war, including the loss of the British battleship *Royal Oak* at Scapa Flow to a Nazi submarine attack, as well as British violations of the "Neutrality Zone," which Roosevelt quite understood and forgave, though the State Department did not. His private, sub-rosa correspondence circumvented the growing, official acrimony between the UK and America over not only the ways

reat Britain violated the Neutrality Zone, but also British
policy. By that latter policy, Britain justified the interception
of ships, American included, passing through British patrolled waters,
which British ships then escorted to Kirkwall, a Scottish port, where
the British inspected them for contraband, a form of harassment many
Americans resented.[14]

As he informed President Roosevelt on January 29—in a telegram
Kent copied and kept at 47 Gloucester Place—Churchill went over
the heads of his prime minister and Cabinet colleagues and absolved
US shipping of this inconvenience. US shipping lines, which now
easily moved into and out of Scandinavia through British controlled
waters, happily made this known to the nations that were still subject to the strictly enforced policy, as Churchill informed Roosevelt.
Churchill hoped the president would yield to his urgent request for
destroyers, and in their correspondence he planted the seeds of what
emerged, months later, as the Lend-Lease program—seeds of American intervention that the isolationists so bitterly feared Roosevelt was
plotting. Here was proof.[15]

❧

From the time, prior to the Great War, when he served as Home Secretary and Great Britain was experiencing a wave of anti-German spy
fever, Churchill had nurtured an obsession about the presence in Great
Britain of underground organizations composed of foreign residents
or British citizens dedicated to helping the overthrow of the British
government by nations or groups dedicated to that end. He developed
in the years that followed a keen interest in the craft of espionage and,
in the various positions he held, came to rely on certain loyal individuals for information. Often these people occupied positions within the
intelligence community that he had helped them procure.[16]

Very little went on in the government and within the intelligence establishment of which Churchill was unaware by the time he was once again First Lord of the Admiralty. Foremost among the concerns that preoccupied him was the likely existence of a Fifth Column. Coined during the recent Spanish Civil War, the term referred to the presence in Madrid of Loyalist followers secretly charged by Generalissimo Franco to subvert from within the Republican government then in power. Churchill was certain that Hitler had planted a similar secret organization of Nazis in London to undermine the British war effort. Not surprisingly this became a preoccupation of the people in counterintelligence, notably Maxwell Knight, whose agents had spotted Tyler Kent on the gangway in Newcastle on the day that he disembarked on British soil.[17]

Knight had scored significant success in tracking down Communist infiltrators, a particularly dangerous breed of enemy agent in the view of Winston Churchill, and scored some moderate success with agents, Guy Burgess among them, infiltrating into Anglo-German friendship societies not unfriendly to the Nazis. The most famous of these was the Link, founded by Sir Barry Domvile, once the head of British Naval Intelligence.[18]

Himself a naval person, Knight had a gaunt face and would have looked the model rear admiral in uniform had he not chosen another career, in which he managed nevertheless to convey an appropriate impression, according to one old friend, who wrote, "My wife often says how sinister he looked with his tall figure and aquiline features (he always said he had a nose like a Jewish bookmaker), wearing a mackintosh and a brown trilby with a turned-down brim."[19] It has been said with some authority that Ian Fleming modeled the character of "M," James Bond's shadowy overseer, on Maxwell Knight. A great devotee of the adventure novels of John Buchan and dedicated to the thrill of intrigue, Knight himself authored detective novels.

According to those who worked for him, Knight made a thrilling and shrewd employer and enjoyed the stagecraft of spying, operating with a kind of imaginative derring-do. His talent for mystery, however, may have come as a by-product of his ambiguous sexual identity. He liked to hire, and even marry, attractive women drawn to his charming personality, but ultimately he turned as sexually cold-blooded to them as the snakes and other reptiles that he carried in his pockets with which to amuse himself and others, concealing much of the time a sexual attraction to other men, his double life aligning with the talent he showed for spy-craft.

This is the conclusion to which Joan Miller eventually came. Knight had hired Miller as an agent, one of the women he cultivated, only to disappoint sexually. She was sharing a house in the country with him when she discovered that he had placed a want ad in a local newspaper: "Gentleman requires help from motorcycle experts afternoons at weekends." A mechanic eventually showed up. "He worked wonders," Knight told Miller. "A marvelous mechanic. The bikes have been thoroughly overhauled."

Soon after, Miller happened to look out the window, on an occasion when a mechanic was visiting, and noted with surprise that Knight was walking in a very effeminate way, which she had never seen him do before. She began to speculate on his sexual preferences and quickly began to fear that he knew of her speculations. "I couldn't help dwelling on the things I knew about M that underlined the ruthless side of his character," Miller writes in her memoir. "I thought of his first wife's death, an obscure and sinister event as far as my knowledge of it went, tied up with M's disquieting interest in the occult. There was an unedifying Canadian, I remember, an ex-drug addict and jailbird known to me as Frank, who'd performed some unofficial jobs for M, such as getting rid of an unreliable double agent in the middle of the North Sea. It didn't cheer me to envisage this sort of end for myself,"

Miller admitted, adding, "The threat of blackmail must be a constant worry for someone in his position; once he realized he'd given himself away, he would have to take steps to destroy in advance the value of any information I might lay against him. God knows what that particular exercise would entail."[20] Miller didn't wait around to find out.

By March 1940, Knight was operating under great pressure. After the outbreak of war—the Phoney War (1939–40)—MI5 took the position that suspicious aliens from countries with Axis or pro-Axis governments should be interned. MI5 possessed no authority to make this happen, however. As an organization, it fell under the jurisdiction and political consideration of various ministries, including the Home Office, which were reluctant to impose a policy potentially unpopular with the British public—especially in the absence of any evidence that a Fifth Column existed. MI5 hadn't been able to produce this evidence because the Germans, until 1937, had discouraged espionage in Britain in the hopes of winning the British as allies.[21]

By the spring of 1940, MI5 stretched to the breaking point as its agents tried to keep track of aliens suspected of enemy activity reported by the police and the public. MI5 needed a better case for the internment of enemy aliens just to survive. To B Branch, the section of MI5 responsible for investigating all threats to security—and to its director, O. A. Harker; his deputy and successor, Captain Guy Liddell; and, not least, to Maxwell Knight—fell the task of finding, if not actually creating, a Fifth Column to justify the internment of enemy aliens. Churchill increasingly favored the move as a political necessity.[22]

Even if not acquainted personally with Knight, Churchill knew his professional activities. Vernon Kell created MI5 shortly before Churchill went from being Chancellor of the Exchequer to becoming Home Secretary. The two men had worked closely together thereafter. In 1925, Kell hired Knight and trained him in the craft of counterintelligence. Knight, a master of surveillance and an agent-runner extraordinaire, found and trained spies willing to risk their lives to penetrate Communist and fascist strongholds. Kell had such a high regard for Knight that he allowed him to operate independently of MI5 supervision from an apartment on Dolphin Square in Pimlico, just south of Westminster. There he had greater secrecy, and, because the building lay on the Thames Embankment, not far from the Anglo-German Information Service on Parliament Street, Knight and his agents could keep a close eye on the activities of the Nazis.

Churchill received his most intimate intelligence information not from Vernon Kell, however, but from Desmond Morton, his protégé and confidant, and director in the 1930s of the Industrial Intelligence Centre, a position that provided Morton with access to information available through the Secret Intelligence Service and MI5. Three prime ministers reportedly authorized Morton throughout the 1930s to convey to Churchill, "in the wilderness," highly confidential information. "Out of office he may have been," one historian writes, "but he was frequently better informed about both British and Nazi rearmament than many cabinet ministers."[23]

Morton worked closely with Knight and, as such, provided a conduit between the two men, so Churchill would have known about and even encouraged the like-minded Knight's efforts to uncover the Fifth Column even before he ascended to Admiralty House in 1939. Knight would have understood well the complex, subtle calculations that Churchill devoted to counterintelligence matters. Ambitious as he was, he also would have understood, as David Stafford puts it, that the intelligence that Churchill "sought and exploited was as much a tool of his political crusade as one of objective and dispassionate analysis."[24]

That crusade entailed the unconditional destruction of Hitler. It by no means enthralled all, or even most, British subjects—even after Hitler had invaded Poland and Great Britain had declared war on Germany.

—◆—

As First Lord of the Admiralty, and even as prime minister, Churchill had opponents in the War Cabinet, in Parliament, and on the streets who favored appeasement. He counted among his bitter foes those landed aristocrats in and out of the House of Lords who espoused indifference to the European turmoil and declared themselves quite willing to live with a Nazi continent ruled by Hitler—provided that he left them in peace on their estates. They shared his antipathy toward Jews, whom they loathed and feared as a race ever scheming to strip them of their inherited wealth and position. To these Britons, among others, Churchill—son of Lord Randolph Spencer-Churchill, third son of the seventh duke of Marlborough—seemed a traitor to his class, a reactionary warrior among conservatives.

Those who opposed Churchill's crusade because they favored rapprochement with Hitler didn't ally themselves with those who favored Anglo-German friendship. This second group had a counterpart of sorts in the isolationist movement in America. They comprised the membership of clubs that opposed war with Germany altogether: the Anglo-German Fellowship; the Nordic League; the British Union of Fascists, founded by Oswald Mosley; the Link, Sir Barry Domvile's organization; and the Right Club, an organization formed for the purpose of promoting anti-Semitism and anti-Communism in government and throughout London by Captain Archibald H. Maule Ramsay, a member of Parliament from Peebles in Scotland. A stated enemy of Winston Churchill, Ramsay had sustained wounds in the trenches of the Great War. He was Christian, a slightly mad patriot, and earnest, if not awfully bright.

Ramsay entered the names of his Right Club members, its officers, and outstanding dues in weirdly scrupulous, actuarial penmanship on the gilt-edged pages of a fat, red leather-bound volume marked PRIVATE LEDGER, secured by brass fasteners and fitted with an automatic lock. Certain august names appear in its pages: Princesse de Chimay (a name familiar to readers of Marcel Proust), Princess Blucher, Prince Turka Galitzine, Lord Carnegie, the duke of Wellington, the duke of Westminster. Lord Redesdale's name also appears in it, his daughter Unity a favorite of Hitler's. Another Redesdale daughter, Diana, married Sir Oswald Mosley, the founder, in 1932, of the British Union of Fascists.[25] At least five or six members of Parliament paid dues to belong to the club.

Ramsay wanted to have twenty Foreign Office administrators in the Right Club and twenty members from the War Office. The most notorious member, William Joyce, an American of Irish descent, lived in Berlin, where, as a Nazi propagandist during the war, he earned the title of "Lord Haw-Haw" for broadcasting shortwave radio messages designed to undermine the morale of British subjects. Baroness Wolkoff and her father, the former admiral, also belonged to the Right Club, which boasted a membership some three hundred strong in June 1939.

At that point, Captain Ramsay closed it down to forestall anticipated accusations that his organization was unpatriotic, although, as Captain Knight's agents discovered, the Right Club was still kicking, if secretly, at the Russian Tea Rooms in South Kensington. Marjorie Mackie, one of Maxwell Knight's agents, had ascertained this little fact. A "cosy middle-aged lady" who used the name Marjorie Amor, Mackie had taken to frequenting the Russian Tea Rooms. There she had earned the confidence of Anna Wolkoff, aide de camp to Captain Ramsay.[26]

━━◆━━

"M/Y"—the abbreviated code name of Miss "Amor," as it appears in MI5 reports—first came to report to Captain Knight on Right Club activities on September 23, 1939. Mrs. Ramsay, the wife of the Right Club founder, had known M/Y since 1931, when she and the Ramsays belonged to the Christian Protest Movement, formed to protest the persecution of Christianity in Soviet Russia. On behalf of her husband, Mrs. Ramsay called M/Y to ask her to "get a job in some Government department in order to carry on some sort of penetrative work on behalf of Captain Ramsay and his associates," according to a summary of reports submitted by M/Y over the nine months that followed. M/Y had contacted Mrs. Ramsay and met her for tea that summer, at Knight's suggestion. "He seemed particularly anxious to get someone into the Postal Censorship" who was "Jew-wise," M/Y reported. Doing so would help the Right Club circumvent censorship.

M/Y met with Captain Ramsay on the 29th. At this meeting, he "stressed the fact that members of the Right Club should confine their work to the distribution of various leaflets and contacting 'useful people,' and spreading propaganda." Once M/Y had obtained a job with the Postal Censorship office, assisted in this endeavor by Captain Knight, Mrs. Ramsay invited her to meetings, held every Wednesday evening at her flat in Onslow Square in South Kensington, of "the inner circle of the Right Club." The coven met at Mrs. Ramsay's, although Ramsay himself was rarely if ever present. Solicitous of his health, Mrs. Ramsay didn't want him to come home, as he usually did at 9:30 p.m., to confront a gathering of women.[27]

In early October, M/Y stood poised to provide the information that Knight needed to form an idea of the scope of Right Club activities and how they might be construed. At first, and for several months, nothing that M/Y reported about the Right Club could have been interpreted in any way as traitorous. In one report, for example, M/Y relates that Mrs. Ramsay told her: "Captain Ramsay thinks you will be most useful when the time comes. We think that it will be a Communist rising and then we shall have to take over. Mosley has tried often and hard to get Jock [Captain Ramsay] to join in with him and, this is for your private ear, he promised him Scotland; but I asked Jock about this and he is firmly resolved on two things, no pogrom of Jews that is unnecessary, and no joining with Mosley."[28]

The M/Y reports begin to show more promise after her introduction to Baroness Wolkoff, on December 6 in Mrs. Ramsay's apartment, where, it appeared to M/Y, the latter was "vetting" her. Unlike anyone else M/Y had met thus far, the baroness seemed actually to know people in Nazi Germany. "Anna bragged a great deal about her trip to Germany and Sudetenland during the summer of 1939," M/Y reported, after a subsequent meeting. "She claimed that she had met many leading Nazis, including Rudolph Hess. She also referred familiarly to Conrad Heinlein, the Sudetenland Nazi." But mostly, the reports that M/Y submitted concerned members of the Right Club, others who sympathized with it, or those in the police or military, General Ironside among them, who might in some way support Right Club objectives. Rather vague, those objectives involved inciting anti-Semitic feelings in Londoners through activities that Captain Ramsay had outlined for M/Y at their first interview. Ramsay seems never to have countenanced any activity contrary to the war effort, although, on February 21, according to the summary of her reports, M/Y "had been given to understand that Captain Ramsay was compiling a special black list of Jews who were to be dealt with 'when the time comes.'"[29]

Of all the Right Club members, it seems that only Mrs. Ramsay's friend, Mary Sanford, who had been in contact with Miss Margaret Bothanley, "a British subject at present at liberty in Germany," made any effort to contact anyone in Germany. Through Anna Wolkoff, M/Y learned that the club had a contact in the Belgian embassy named Jean Nieuwenhuys, a second secretary, who provided the club with newspapers "from neutral countries." She learned as much in the last week of February, soon after Wolkoff met Tyler Kent for the first time. Although she claimed that Nieuwenhuys had agreed to dispatch letters through the Belgian diplomatic pouch on her behalf to his friend

Antoine, in Brussels, who would send them by regular mail to Lord Haw-Haw in Germany, he evidently never did any such thing. The example Anna Wolkoff showed M/Y was, in fact, a letter written by Mary Sanford to a certain Monsieur Price in Belgium, which she had given to M/Y to mail for her through the Postal Censorship office, intercepted by MI5.[30]

This reference to Nieuwenhuys makes for a small, significant item of note, however. It indicates that the baroness was considering ways to communicate with Lord Haw-Haw, and that she knew of the diplomatic pouch as an intelligence device. Perhaps of even greater significance, MI5 was willing to offer a Right Club member assistance in her effort to evade censorship when mailing a communication abroad.

By April, Knight had concluded that the Right Club and Anna Wolkoff in particular presented perhaps the only promising evidence of the kind he needed. Most MI5 agents in 1939–40 were women, and Knight had acquired and trained an upper-class young woman of striking good looks named Joanna Phipps, twenty-two at the time, who called herself Joan Miller, yet another of those lovely moths whom the mercurial agent-runner fatally drew to his cold flame. He decided to use Miller to infiltrate the Right Club with the help of Marjorie "Amor," who, at the Russian Tea Rooms, on April 9, introduced the former agent to Wolkoff. Knight wanted a list, even if only partial, of the club's members in order to establish with reasonable certainty that a Nazi Fifth Column existed, composed of certain well-born British subjects.[31]

Certainly the Right Club continued to function. Mrs. Ramsay had continued to sign on new members and hold meetings at night in her apartment in Onslow Square, located within blocks of the Tea Rooms. Right Club headquarters now occupied an apartment above the Russian Tea Rooms. Those who attended meetings, usually ten or twelve people, mostly women, endorsed the anti-Semitic views promoted by

Captain Ramsay, who authored pamphlets and anti-Semitic verses, including one entitled "Land of Pope and Jewry."[32]

As Joan Miller discovered when finally invited to attend a meeting, the membership ladies protested the war at night during blackouts by pasting anti-Semitic stickers on lampposts and public surfaces. "Anna instructed her helpers to keep to the dark side of the road, paying particular attention to shadowy doorways where an alert policeman or air-warden might lurk, and to carry out the sticking while continuing to walk," writes Joan Miller in *One Girl's War.* "Passersby who observed the Right Club's papers adhering to lamp posts, telephone kiosks, belisha beacons [amber globes on posts used in London for additional street lighting], church boards and so forth, were informed that the war was a Jew's war. This was the Right Club's famous 'stickyback' campaign. What these labels said: 'A bayonet is a weapon with a worker at each end. War destroys workers, not Hitlers.' They also used greasepaint to deface ARP and casualty station posters. Jeering at Winston Churchill when he appeared on cinema newsreels was another of their practices."[33]

"She was quite mad" on the subject of Jews, Kent later testified of Wolkoff, who was on epistolary terms with Celine, the French novelist who made no bones about his hatred of Jews.[34] "And this Jewish question!" Celine wrote Wolkoff in a letter. "In Paris it no longer arises, since it is forbidden to write about it. It is finished—the Jew is absolutely king, and a supercilious Asiatic king."[35]

Anna Wolkoff was, if not unstable, surely destabilized, and those who knew her regarded the baroness as dangerously indiscreet in her chatter and emotionally excitable—hardly someone capable of operating successfully as a foreign agent. That conclusion, however, is precisely what Captain Knight began to reach in view of Joan Miller's reports, even if the mad baroness wasn't yet an agent.

Should the opportunity arise, as it was soon to do, certainly she was all for it. Captain Knight then may have decided to shift the emphasis of his infiltration from the acquisition of the club's membership list to the task he now assigned to his agents—although it's more likely that Knight needed both a comprehensive list *and* proof that Wolkoff was acting as an agent. He decided to do so around the time his agents reported the appearance in Anna Wolkoff's life of Tyler Kent—of whom Knight hadn't lost sight. We can assume that the conjunction of these two separate subjects of inquiry quickened the pulse of the counterintelligence officer, for whom so much effort had so far yielded so little of any importance, the Fifth Column having failed to materialize as desired.

Knight's agents were superbly prepared for the job. In addition to Marjorie "Amor" and the glamorous Joan Miller, the captain had also released into the precincts of the Russian Tea Rooms—as he might have released one of his friendly garden snakes—an MI5 agent recently recruited named Hélène de Munck, a Belgian who had known Wolkoff and her sister since 1936. De Munck shared Wolkoff's anti-Semitic views, which gave her a plausible cover with the mad baroness. Miss "Amor" and Joan Miller, by this time—February 1940—both possessed the silver Right Club badge on which appeared an eagle dismembering a viper. The latter creature, according to Miller, signified the "Communist and Jewish element in society." They all were placed excellently to assist Wolkoff in her efforts to expand the club's activities on the Continent, de Munck perhaps more so than the other two, who were hatching schemes with the Special Branch—the civilian counterintelligence section of Scotland Yard that worked closely with MI5—to tap the telephones in Mrs. Ramsay's apartment.[36]

Secret Sharer

THE UNEXPECTED means misfortune from without.
—Wu Wang / Innocence (The Unexpected),
The I Ching

Tyler Kent proved to be a significant addition to the life and times of Anna Wolkoff. He later admitted that he made no more than three or four visits to see her at the Russian Tea Rooms, yet, even if true, he came to know her well enough to share her car, which he ultimately purchased from her, and he became acquainted with a number of her Right Club friends.

He incited her political ardor with his appealing, youthful conviction, which in turn greatly enhanced her sense of self-importance—that a person who held a position of such consequence in the US embassy, with views that echoed her own, had fallen under the spell of her brilliant wit. Although ten years older than Kent, she may also have entertained the idea of taking him as a lover—even though nothing

79

could have strayed further from Kent's desire. She introduced him to "Jock" Ramsay during the week of April 10. Kent, at Ramsay's invitation, eventually joined the Right Club in early May 1940, awarded the rank of steward.[1] This was an honorific.

Kent opened up to Ramsay and Wolkoff, and the latter, indiscreet, hotheaded creature that she was, let everyone, including Joan Miller and Miss "Amor," know that she had this wonderful new friend in the Code Room at the American embassy who hated the prospect of war with Germany. The baroness liked having well-placed friends, and it added to her sense of grandeur that she also knew the Duca del Monte, a military attaché at the Italian embassy whom she referred to as "Macaroni."

It's hard to say who, if anyone, incited Wolkoff to get in touch with Right Club members or agents in Europe. Surely not Jock Ramsay, who considered himself among the patriots of the Empire, who never wanted to join the Fascists, never pro-German, and had reinstated his club because he wanted to influence the government against going to war however he could. No doubt he didn't want to see his sons subjected to the wartime horrors that he and the rest of his decimated generation had experienced. Wolkoff, however, wanted to spread the word about the Right Club's anti-Semitic activities.

The urgency of the coming *blitzkrieg* (literally "lightning war," for its speed and intensity) in Europe, two months hence and ticking, influenced the way everyone behaved in March 1940, Captain Knight included. Kent knew this better than anyone because he read the cable traffic. All hell was preparing to break loose in Europe.

Without informing Secretary of State Cordell Hull, President Roosevelt dispatched Sumner Welles to travel to the capitals of Italy, Germany, France, and England to determine once and for all what chance, if any, there was for a peaceful solution to the tensions that threatened to break out into war.[2] If Welles could bring him news of no such chance, FDR could then formulate a policy based on what he could justifiably describe as German aggression to people like Endicott Peabody, the founder of Groton School. As did so many others, Peabody intensely disliked the idea of taking sides against Germany in cahoots with Great Britain, especially under Churchill. The rector considered the First Lord of the Admiralty unstable, unlike Chamberlain, whom he knew and liked, and who, by the bravest whisper of hope, was still serving as prime minister to the king.[3]

Welles had sundered the hopes of Walton Moore, Kent's champion in the Department of State who, though almost eighty, still remained, if only to destroy Welles. Roosevelt enraged not only Hull, by sending Welles to Europe without first informing him, but also Bullitt, who thought he had the president's ear. Bullitt hated Welles, as FDR must have known, because Bullitt championed Walton Moore and resented the privileged position that FDR's Groton protégé now occupied; he protested the Welles peace trip by decamping to Florida. When Welles arrived in Paris, he'd find the ambassador absent. It was an impulsive, even childish move that FDR quietly noted.[4]

Meanwhile, in Berlin, there was no ambassador. Roosevelt had recalled Hugh Wilson after the outrage of *Kristallnacht*. Welles's peace trip wasn't exactly going to go according to plan.

Welles sailed for Naples in February on the Italian liner *Rex*,[5] accompanied by his wife, Mathilde; his English valet, James Reeks; Jay Pierrepont Moffat, another Groton graduate, and chief of the European Division of the Department of State; and a secretary named Hartwell Johnson, a young Foreign Service officer.[6] The undersecretary of state married women of great wealth and presided in Washington and elsewhere over large establishments. Arthur M. Schlesinger Jr., who knew him slightly, describes Welles as "a frosty patrician who drank too much and made passes at everyone, fish, flesh or fowl."[7] Welles—like others, actively bisexual—kept his powerful homosexual urges under wraps until they burst forth, ultimately to his undoing, when he had been drinking.

Welles refused to communicate in advance with officials of the US embassies in the countries upon which he descended. Once there, accompanied by the ranking official in the embassy, he would hold interviews with various heads of state and other dignitaries, but he would not issue public statements about those meetings. Reporters who covered the European beat dubbed him "Sumner the Silent." He met with Mussolini, von Ribbentrop, Goering, and Hitler, and traveled to Paris, where he met with various French officials, before flying to London for talks with Prime Minister Chamberlain.[8]

Ambassador Kennedy met him in London and recorded in his diary that the Belgian ambassador in Berlin had confided to Welles that he considered that the two "most dangerous men in Europe to the cause of world peace" were von Ribbentrop and Bullitt. "Welles then told me again about Bullitt," Kennedy wrote. "How the Germans had taken the file from the Polish Foreign Office showing that Bullitt had told the Poles not to negotiate with the Germans, that the U.S. would back them up." He also wrote, "He said he was amazed at what Bullitt had told the French. That they were practically sure of our support by our coming in." Welles reported to Kennedy that Roosevelt had told him Bullitt had written him that he was all tired out because he was practically running the French government. "Welles said, 'My God, look through all your mail and make sure there is no such record available.' The President said he would."[9]

Tyler Kent needed no such record for his archive. He may not have been privy to Kennedy's diary, but he well knew how matters stood between Kennedy and Bullitt, the latter of whom Welles called a "double crosser"[10] to Kennedy later that month. It was a prescient criticism: Bullitt soon informed FDR, who already knew, that Welles—in his cups on the train that bore him back to Washington from the funeral of House Speaker William Bankhead—had sexually solicited at least two black railway porters. It ultimately proved to be Welles's undoing.

But by forcing the matter on Roosevelt in a private conversation at the White House, Bullitt invited his own undoing. When Sumner Welles dies, the president later informed Bullitt, he'll go to heaven; when your time comes, you'll go to hell.[11]

Kent may also have known that both Welles and Chamberlain were holding out hope that Mussolini—in the words of Welles, "a man of genius," but "at heart and in instinct an Italian peasant"—by remaining neutral in Europe would somehow deter the Nazis from further conquest. When he returned to Washington, Welles so informed the president, and also advised him that ultimately only an American peace plan, boldly advanced, could possibly stop the German juggernaut.[12]

At his trial the following October, Kent would testify that although he had been copying classified embassy documents for his own purposes for months, those purposes remained unclear to him until, under the pressure of international events, he began to believe that he should consider ways to get his documents into the hands of members of anti-interventionists in Congress. He was, it seems, very attuned to the matter of timing. Also, he had in his possession copies of telegrams that Churchill had sent through the Code Room to Roosevelt, irrefutable evidence that the president was already aiding the British behind the backs of American voters.

"Jock" Ramsay found it both hard to believe and of very great interest that Kent also had evidence that Churchill was engaging in secret negotiations that could imperil a British peace process. It came up in the course of a discussion in which the Right Club founder told Kent that he remained sure Roosevelt and Churchill were conspiring toward intervention, but had no evidence to support the idea. We can imagine how Kent might have responded that he had in his apartment in Marylebone just that very thing. It was the key moment in his life to change the course of history and retrieve the Kent escutcheon from cabin class, to which through no fault of his own it had fallen.

Soon after their first meeting, Ramsay drove his red racing car over to Gloucester Place, accompanied by Baroness Wolkoff, to see what the young man had to show him. Kent had arrayed his wares on every surface of his front room, files he'd organized neatly in folders marked Chamberlain, Churchill, Halifax, Hore-Belisha, films, Jews, and, also alphabetically, the names of countries, from Belgium to Turkey. The MP from Peebles browsed over these documents with some interest and took note of the Churchill telegrams, although he left without asking for copies of these, which may have disappointed Kent.

Kent had concluded, he testified later, that, although he now had decided to get his archive before Congress, doing so would pose a problem because, though the diplomatic pouch suggested the best available means of transporting it, State Department employees at the other end could easily uncover it during an inspection. He had begun to think, if not to hope, that Ramsay could help him, perhaps if he submitted them to Parliament.

The baroness also took a keen interest in what Kent put on display for Ramsay. She came back several days later on April 13 and asked him to "loan" her two Churchill telegrams so that, Kent assumed, she could copy them for the captain. He let her have them.

Wolkoff took the documents to a man she knew named Smirnoff, an émigré like herself, who had served in the czar's London embassy in 1906 with her father, and who now made his living as a photographer. While she waited in the kitchen with Smirnoff's wife, the photographer made negatives of the documents on glass plates. The baroness returned the telegrams to Kent the next day.[13]

Ten days later she returned to his apartment with the glass-plate negatives. She handed them to him in a brown paper package, along with some stickers that she asked him to keep for her. When Kent asked her why she had copied the documents, she replied rather loftily that he would be informed later. The chain of command—so hidden in shadows that Wolkoff herself never knew where it began—could have been traced, first of all, to Captain Knight, and upward from him to Winston Churchill.

Six

The Onslaught

Roosevelt would bring the whole country into the war now if he possibly could.
          —DIARY OF CAPTAIN GUY LIDDELL, MAY 17, 1940

ABOUT ADOLF HITLER, PRIME MINISTER NEVILLE CHAMBERLAIN declared on April 4, 1940: "One thing is certain: he missed the bus."[1] Churchill later said that this observation "proved an ill-judged utterance."[2] As Mussolini had made clear to Sumner Welles at their last meeting, Hitler had never even entertained the inclination to negotiate anything. All winter long he had been preparing his assault on France by positioning divisions on the German border. Meanwhile, the Low Countries were trying to steel themselves against the coming onslaught.

In Great Britain, the First Lord of the Admiralty stood with the minority of those in the War Cabinet who felt the urgency of Hitler's menace. Churchill proposed to mine the waters around Norway to strike a blow at the German armament industry, which received its iron ore almost exclusively by ship from Scandinavia. The British

Navy received permission to do so—belatedly—but not before the German Naval Staff, fully aware of British plans, launched an invasion of Norway by sea, which also co-opted Churchill's follow-up plan to land British troops in Norwegian ports. The British fleet, en route to Norway to intercept the German invasion, abandoned this effort and steamed north. Although the British, under Churchill's command, engaged the Germans and inflicted heavy losses on German ships in the northern fjords, they lost Scandinavia to Hitler. It failed, but it was a daring and imaginative attempt to inflict an early defeat on Hitler and seize the initiative before he launched his forces on France and the Lowlands.[3]

Thus April brought disaster to the British and paved the way for the month of May in ways unforeseen, especially by those like Captain Ramsay and Ambassador Kennedy, who thought this so-called "second Gallipoli" would bring an end to Churchill's career.[4]

Captain Ramsay wanted to block Churchill's plans, and he may have thought that the Norwegian debacle had done just that, because he didn't raise in Parliament the matter of the secret Churchill-Roosevelt correspondence. What, then, did Anna Wolkoff intend to do with the three plate-glass copies that Smirnoff had made of the documents she had borrowed from Kent? She may have intended to mail them to Berlin via the Italian diplomatic pouch with the help of her acquaintance, the Duca del Monte, an assistant military attaché in the Italian embassy. It was he whom she hoped would act as an intermediary and send messages to Lord Haw-Haw in Berlin for his English-language propaganda broadcasts from Hamburg over the New British Broadcasting Station there.

This use of the diplomatic pouch for devious purposes sounds awfully like something that Kent might have discussed with the baroness during one of their not-infrequent meals together that March. However she may have learned of this instrument, Wolkoff never could keep anything to herself, and made quite sure that her associates knew of her operational skills. "So," Joan Miller recalled, "while Anna boasted to me about her contact at the Italian Embassy, and dropped hints about certain materials she intended to forward to the notorious traitor William Joyce [Lord Haw-Haw], I tried to work out exactly how the information I was gathering could be used against her."[5]

Pleading illness, Francesco Marigliano, the Duca del Monte, withdrew from the meeting at which Wolkoff planned to propose her scheme to use the Italian diplomatic pouch. This move, according to Miller, who was working under instructions from Knight, provided the opportunity that MI5 needed to convert Wolkoff into a Nazi agent. Wolkoff mentioned to her that del Monte had reneged. "I told her," Miller recalls, "(quite untruthfully) that I believed Helen [de Munck, Knight's anti-Semitic Belgian-born agent] was in a position to use the Romanian diplomatic bag." Miller wrote: "Anna lost no time in cornering Helen: 'Why didn't you tell me you had a friend at the Romanian Legation?' She went on to confess that she was in something of a quandary. She had in her possession a coded letter, addressed to William Joyce at the Rundfunkhaus, Berlin, and full of tips about the line he should take in his German propaganda broadcasts. Helen, briefed by M, offered to use her own contact to get this important missive on its way."[6]

At the Kent trial, the judge read aloud to the jury excerpts of the coded message that Wolkoff gave to de Munck. "Talks effects splendid news bulletins less so," she wanted Lord Haw-Haw to know. "Palestine good but I.R.A. etc. defeats object. Stick to plutocracy avoid king." She also wanted him to have information that would help him get better broadcast reception: "Why not try Bremen at 500. Bremen 2 on longs very weak needs powerful set to get. On shorts Podie Grad difficult. DXQ easier but always distorted even on big set." When it came to communications, the baroness clearly knew her stuff. "Here

Kriegshetze only among blimps," she wrote. "Workers fed up, wives more so. Troops not keen. Anti-Semitism spreading like flame everywhere all classes."

But of course there was more; there was always more. "Note refujews in so-called Pioneer Corps guaranteed in writing to be sent into firing line. Churchill not popular. Keep on at him as Baruch tool and war-theatre-extender, sacrificer Gallipoli, etc. Stress his conceit and repeated failures with exproselites and prestige."[7]

She unquestionably was helping the Nazi propaganda broadcaster to do a better job undermining the morale of British civilians with information of a technical nature. It was enough to indicate that Wolkoff, regardless of whether she authored the sentiments, had ambitions to act as an enemy contact on British soil. She had not, as yet, become an agent. Indeed, so much was she not one that she couldn't even figure out how to get a message from London to Berlin.

In April 1940, any agent trained in rudimentary spy-craft could have transmitted a message like this across the North Sea. As it was, MI5 did this on her behalf to help her establish her credentials. She gave her message to de Munck, who gave it to Captain Knight. The next day, Wolkoff asked for it back, though, because she wanted to add to it.

"You're in luck," de Munck told her. By the time the baroness arrived, de Munck had retrieved the message, to which, on de Munck's typewriter, Wolkoff added a postscript.[8]

"She rounded off the letter with a drawing of an eagle and a snake—the Right Club emblem—and the letters P.J.—'Perish Judah,'" Miller recalled. She and Captain Knight then drove down to Bletchley together to give it to the wartime code-breakers. Wolkoff's code was so simpleminded that ironically it stymied Bletchley's "Top Boffins," as Miller calls them, who had prepared to deal with something truly challenging.[9]

Back in London, Knight and Miller, still along for the ride, took the message to the son of "Miss Amor," yet another naval person, who actually did have access to the Romanian pouch. That way the message made its way to Lord Haw-Haw, who acknowledged that he'd received it in one of his broadcasts with a prearranged signal: the use of the name "Carlyle." Wolkoff had found a thrilling new activity, an outlet for her anti-Semitic obsession—thanks to MI5.

For the baroness, April 1940 hummed with feverish activity. In the course of this month, with the assistance of MI5, she dispatched a radio message to Lord Haw-Haw; sold a car to Tyler Kent; "borrowed" two Churchill telegrams from him, which she put in the hands of Nicholas Smirnoff to copy; returned the original documents; formally opened new Right Club premises at an apartment at 24 Manson Mews; and, on April 16 or thereabouts, called once again on de Munck for assistance, this time in Belgium, while de Munck was there on a four-day visit. There, at Wolkoff's request, de Munck agreed to pick up a document from one Guy Miermans, the Right Club "representative" in Belgium, who, de Munck later testified, "told me that this game was very dangerous and that he advised her and asked her to stop it."[10]

Throughout April, Wolkoff and Kent met frequently and spoke often by phone in Russian, a language unknown to Knight's agents, who, by now, with the help of Joan Miller and "Miss Amor," had tapped the telephones not only of Mrs. Ramsay but also of Anna Wolkoff's Right Club quarters over the Russian Tea Rooms on Harrington Road in South Kensington. Thus they learned that Tyler Kent had been taking documents home with him from the embassy to 47 Gloucester Place. Although she spoke Russian with Kent, in telephone chats with Right Club friends like Enid Riddell and Christabel Nicholson, the baroness used English. Wolkoff, ever the compulsive talker, spoke of secret documents and her friend in the Code Room, and alluded to the contents of messages that she'd seen.

"She is a very silly woman, mind you," Maule Ramsay said in the course of a long police interrogation. "[S]he talks as if she is going to do this, that, and the other; in fact, I have had to warn people at the Right Club about her, because she is such an ass with her tongue."[11]

～～

In the reports of M/Y, Tyler Kent began to appear by name as of March 29. He must have seemed to Maxwell Knight a kind of godsend.

M/Y first reported that the Right Club had a new contact at the American embassy on February 24, the date of Kent's letter to Kirk in Berlin, and noted that this person, name incorrectly given, had served in Moscow and had been in Great Britain for about six months.[12] A month passed before M/Y reported that Wolkoff was "spending a great deal of time with this man from the American Embassy and was concentrating upon him," according to a summary prepared by Knight. He wrote, "Anna had said that he was definitely pro-German and it was clear that he was engaging in disseminating defeatist and anti-Allied propaganda."[13]

Only on March 29 did M/Y report Kent's name, thereby revealing to Knight that Kent was the man his agents had spotted in the company of Ludwig Mathias, the suspected Gestapo agent, the previous October. Knight might have contacted the US embassy—but he didn't. Instead, he continued to let M/Y and Joan Miller report on Kent's activities and keep watch on his friendship with Wolkoff as it developed. On April 16, "another Mi5 agent," probably Miller, "reported that Anna Wolkoff was obtaining a great deal of information through Tyler Kent. She had dined with this man at the Russian Tea Rooms on April 12th, and she claimed that Kent had given her confidential information regarding the North Sea battles, stating that they had been grossly exaggerated and were only British propaganda designed to cover heavy naval losses sustained by the air attack on Scapa Flow."[14] In addition, the baroness claimed that the information Kent had given her had come from an interview between Joseph Kennedy and Lord Halifax, although Knight's notes state this somewhat unclearly.

Actually, on May 5, the date of the summary Knight prepared, he had only an inkling, based on hearsay obtained from his agents, of what Kent had been up to. Knight knew at that time only that, on a regular basis, Kent was relaying various chunks of information gleaned from sources at the American embassy to Wolkoff. Knight primarily suspected Wolkoff of using Kent as a conduit to the embassy pouch. The spymaster also had come to understand through M/Y that Wolkoff had been trying to send, perhaps through Kent, photographed copies of reports regarding the Norwegian Expeditionary Force. Whatever he may have learned about Kent and his documents through the telephone taps clearly wasn't worth mentioning, and may have been conjecture. However talkative she may have been, Wolkoff doesn't seem to have boasted in any great detail to her coven about Kent's archive and what it contained, even though she had seen it in all its glory and made use of it, probably on behalf of Captain Ramsay.

Knight had no idea that Kent possessed such a wealth of documents. He thought that Anna Wolkoff had given Kent some Right Club documents to store in an embassy safe. Of her visits and Ramsay's to Kent's apartment, he knew nothing.

These visits, according to Ramsay, occurred more numerously than Kent acknowledged. Ramsay's testimony before a Home Office Advisory Committee also explains why this upstanding if deranged Member of Parliament never considered that Kent's behavior might have surpassed misconduct such that he ought to have reported Kent to Scotland Yard or MI5.[15]

Originally, his purpose in visiting Kent's place was to examine the Churchill telegrams, as he did. He found little of interest, although in his later testimony he did recall mentioning that it "would be a good thing" to have some photographs to show to Prime Minister Chamberlain to document his claims about the Churchill-Roosevelt correspondence, unaware that Chamberlain already knew about this. What he did find of interest in Kent's rooms was the documentary history, going back to 1928, of the role that US diplomats had played in European events. He made no copies of the absorbing correspondence Kent had assembled, but he did return to study it. "I used to go when I could get away from the House of Commons, you know we work at the House at odd hours, and I went at odd times when I could," Ramsay told the Advisory Committee. "Between Committees I would take a taxi up to his house. I would look at these papers for whatever time I had, put them back in the folder, back in the locker, and come away again, and that was all there was to it."[16]

Of course, a number of the documents Kent had copied included telegrams sent by Ambassador Kennedy to Washington, and also matters relating to the confidential meeting between Kennedy and Lord Halifax—one of the few clues Knight possessed that Kent was feeding confidential information to Wolkoff. Ramsay made a study of Kent's archive, though, to build a case to present to Parliament that "plans for establishing Marxist socialism under Jewish control in the country were far advanced."[17]

In a statement composed during his internment, Ramsay wrote: "As a Member of Parliament, still loyal to Mr. Chamberlain, I considered it my duty to investigate." The combined perceived threats of international Bolshevism and world Jewry had evolved over more than a decade into an obsession that had finally unhinged a man "made of the finest stuff of Empire. He was educated at Eton and Sandhurst and obtained his Commission in the Cold Stream Guards," the undersecretary of state for the Home Office wrote in a long report on July 18, 1940, urging the continuing detention of Captain Ramsay. "He served in the Great War and was wounded in France in the year 1916. The wound was of a serious nature, cutting his heart muscle and one of his kidneys and, as a result, he was invalided out of the army in 1920, and has been in receipt of a wound pension ever since."[18]

Captain Ramsay, the undersecretary also wrote, "had been twice married and has four sons," two of whom were "serving in the present war, one of whom was wounded in the recent fighting in Norway," adding that "one of his step-sons is also serving in his Majesty's forces." His anti-Semitism, the undersecretary explained, grew from his campaign, as a Member of Parliament, against Russian Bolshevism. "Having studied the matter and read extensively," the former Cold Stream Guardsman "became finally convinced that an international group of Jews had immense power over an international revolutionary organization through the power of finance." The effort to explain this menace "to the peace and happiness of the world," as Ramsay put it, proved enormously difficult—for obvious reasons—and Ramsay "gave an account of the immense difficulties he had had to confront in making his views known both in Parliament and outside it, and said that all his activities, whatever they might have been, were actuated only by the desire to confront and defeat the harmful influence of International Jewry wherever it was to be found."[19]

The pressures of his mission—not to mention the pressure of events, and the war itself, on the verge of explosion—had begun to reveal themselves in Ramsay's behavior. One contact of the Home Secretary, a Scotsman named Atholl, who had seen the MP not long before, wrote him on May 24. "Maule Ramsay has been very queer for some time past," Atholl reported. "About four months ago, when I was in the Front Hall of the New Club, Edinburgh, he suddenly went down on his knees in front of me, pulled out papers from every pocket, and begged me to do what I could about the Jew menace. He handed me a whole lot of papers and raved generally in a very mad way, telling me that many prominent people, including Vansittart, were Jews trying to ruin the country." Atholl concluded: "I really think he is probably only 'Jew' daft."[20]

But what Ramsay found in the Kent archive provided him with much material to ponder. It was perhaps in gratitude for providing such a trove of evidence for the connivance of American diplomacy and international Jewish financial conspirators in America that Ramsay conferred upon the young code clerk membership in the Right Club, with the rank of steward. Ramsay had another use for Kent, however, unknown to M/Y, Captain Knight, or even Wolkoff.

By early May, Scotland Yard officers working with MI5 had begun to question members of the Right Club. Aware of this development, and that the police had entered and searched the premises of politically suspect people he knew, Ramsay took the Red Book, his Right Club ledger, to 47 Gloucester Place for safekeeping. It remains unclear how long he intended to leave the locked ledger, to which he retained the key, in that location. He did so before leaving for a ten-day vacation in Scotland on May 9 or 10, because he knew what value it would have if it fell into the hands of the police. Ramsay believed that in his absence it would lie beyond their reach in the custody of Kent, whose premises, as he misunderstood it, were protected by the rules governing diplomatic immunity from police search.

Neither Knight nor any of his agents knew this. The most telltale piece of evidence in Knight's possession was the hearsay version of Anna's report to M/Y about the meeting between Lord Halifax and Kennedy that M/Y had passed on to Knight. By May 4, however, in a report for Vernon Kell, director of MI5, Knight noted what he had learned about Wolkoff's meetings with Kent: "[I]t seems urgently necessary for something to be done about this man, and it is suggested that the matter should be discussed with Dy. B [the directory of B section of MI5], with a view to approaching our contact in the American Embassy."[21]

"Fifth Column Panic" somewhat tamely describes the sudden fear of subversive aliens that ravaged Great Britain after the defeat of British naval forces in Norway. Had someone leaked information to the Germans about British naval plans in the North Sea? This was the turning point for those in MI5 and elsewhere in the government, who all along had been arguing that a Fifth Column had been at work.

Knight and Churchill needed to prove that such a faction existed, but, even so, in the dark fog that made everything so uncertain during the so-called Twilight War, it wasn't hard to believe. Knight probably believed it by the time he wrote his note, which conveys the feeling he must have had—that not much time remained before MI5 had to act decisively. Given this sense of urgency, it does seem odd that they did nothing of the kind for two more weeks.

Hitler invaded the Lowlands on May 10, 1940. Fifth Column Panic struck full force that day. Also on that day, Chamberlain resigned, forced to do so by Parliament over the Norway debacle. The man who took his place engineered the coup—none other than Winston Churchill, for whom it was a day of triumph. The very menace he had foreseen appeared to have materialized, along with his new powers. "The iron of Gallipoli had entered into the soul of my Right Honorable Friend," one staunch Churchill champion said at the time.[22]

"Churchill was *belliciste,* and that was why Parliament, which had formerly been pacifist, turned to him," Joseph Lash wrote.[23]

In his triumph, Churchill behaved magnanimously. On May 11, he sent a message to Chamberlain: "No one changes houses for a month."[24] Churchill remained at Admiralty House, and Chamberlain at No. 10 Downing Street, official London home of the prime minister. Chamberlain also remained in Churchill's War Cabinet, a valued presence who might help Churchill negotiate his aims with those who favored some kind of compromising peace with Hitler.

But Churchill opposed compromise of any kind with Hitler. To wage all-out war on the *Führer*, he needed absolute authority as minister of war, more power than he possessed as yet even as prime minister. The coming weeks, he understood, required of him the genius of a visionary orchestra conductor—to put it mildly. Still, he felt this moment of destiny as an occasion of profound joy. The overture, the Black Fortnight, though brief, proved momentous, a time of furious, muffled debate within the War Cabinet over this issue of whether to make peace with Hitler, as Lord Halifax and the conservative element in Parliament wanted.

Meanwhile, the German army roared across France from the Meuse and forced its will, from the north, on the Dutch and the Belgians. The British Expeditionary Force, sent months earlier to reinforce the French, tried to hold the line in Western France, which soon proved an impossible task.

For the time being, Churchill continued to correspond with Roosevelt via the US embassy Code Room, though he still signed his messages "Former Naval Person."

"Although I have changed my office," began the message that Tyler Kent transmitted at 6:00 p.m. on May 15, "I am sure you would not want me to discontinue our intimate, private correspondence." Churchill knew this preamble to be inaccurate and untrue. The rhetoric of his message was formal because it was subject to the inspection of a man whom he knew to detest him, and another who leaked privileged information. The former was Ambassador Kennedy; the latter, Tyler Kent.

Churchill may have had reason by then to believe that any message he sent to the president via the US embassy was insecure. Nonetheless, he wrote to ask the president for help. "I trust you realize, Mr. President, that the voice and force of the United States may count for nothing if they are withheld too long," he warned. "You may have a completely subjugated, Nazified Europe established with astonishing swiftness, and the weight may be more than we can bear." He needed, he explained, "the loan of forty or fifty of your older destroyers" to cover British needs while warships of their own were being constructed, "several hundred of the latest types of aircraft" to be repaid with those currently under construction for the British in the United States, "anti-aircraft equipment and ammunition," and other materials.

He also asked the president to send a squadron on a prolonged visit to Irish ports, where, he wrote, reports had reached him of "possible German parachute or airborne descents." Finally, he wrote, "I am looking to you to keep that Japanese dog quiet in the Pacific, using Singapore"—still a British colony—"in any way convenient." Churchill may have tried to do so himself two days later when he lunched with his wife and secretary at the Japanese embassy. By then, he had received a reply from the president, even less intimate and also in the form of a telegram. It refused Churchill's request for destroyers and otherwise ducked his bluntly stated plea, which included the sentence: "As you know, the American fleet is now concentrated at Hawaii where it will remain at least for the time being."[25]

This was the telegram that Christabel Nicholson had copied by pencil from a copy of the original, which Wolkoff had brought to her house to show her and the admiral, her husband. Nicholson subsequently photocopied the copy, although it was the penciled version that she sealed in an envelope and gave for safekeeping to her charlady, Mrs. Welberry. To Mrs. Welberry, she gave instructions that if anyone found it, she must tell them that it contained the admiral's will. The following day Nicholson said to Welberry, "I thought you had been seized by the police or someone, with the papers," and added, "For goodness sake, either stick them in your corsets or bury them in the garden."[26] Mrs. Welberry later opened the envelope and gave the contents to Arnold Sleight of MI5, who gave them to Inspector Pearson of Special Branch, who gave them to Maxwell Knight on May 26.

Wolkoff more than likely stole the first copy of this document from Kent's apartment. She had made copies of the keys to the doors at 47 Gloucester Place, and, Kent later testified, on at least one occasion she was waiting for him when he returned from work. It's also possible that Kent, once again, had loaned her this telegram. By this time, he and Anna Wolkoff were thick as thieves, for thieves they were. Perhaps by now Wolkoff had involved Kent in some of her more subversive schemes. He later confessed to Maxwell Knight that he had indeed known the identity of Wolkoff's friend, Francesco Marigliano, the Duca del Monte, assistant naval attaché at the Italian embassy, whom she had tried to use as a mail drop for her messages to Lord Haw-Haw.[27] Wolkoff and Kent had dined with the duke at L'Escargot in Soho—perhaps on the night of May 9—in the company of Enid Riddell, Wolkoff's friend and a Right Club member.

At first, and for some years thereafter, Kent denied that he knew the duke's identity. Wolkoff in her snide and cutting way had called him "Mr. Macaroni." Kent described "Mr. Macaroni" as a man of "45, short-ish, thick-set, dark hair and complexion," with whom they'd later gone on to the embassy club, after which, on the way home, sometime around midnight, while driving the Italian home to 67 Cadogan Square, Kent's Austin Eight sustained a flat tire, which they changed in "Mr. Macaroni's" garage.[28] In his first sworn statement to Maxwell Knight, Kent asserted: "It occurred to me at the time that this was a pseudonym." In his final meeting with the MI5 agent-runner, Kent admitted that this pseudonym, "Mr. Macaroni," was in fact a code name.[29]

Not that it seems to have mattered. The first time Wolkoff sent something via Mr. Macaroni—an envelope of photocopies of documents related to the invasion of Norway—it vanished. On May 16, after listening to a broadcast of her message to Lord Haw-Haw, Wolkoff went to Cadogan Square with M/Y and left in his letter drop a story that she'd written. They took the number 30 bus from Knightsbridge to Beauchamp Place. The baroness did this because she knew that if the story she'd left with Mr. Macaroni made the rounds the next day at the Italian embassy, she'd be sure her conduit was working, little knowing (or perhaps never suspecting) that her cohorts in all this nonsense were working for MI5.[30]

For his part, Tyler Kent was no less oblivious of the attention that MI5 was training on his activities. During his social rounds, the young code clerk was, in his own blithe way, as outspoken about his views as secret agents seldom, if ever, are.

June Huntley described Kent as a "loud talker." By this, according to a Scotland Yard agent who interviewed Huntley, she meant that "he was very boastful and wanting to impress" people "with his knowledge of various subjects." Huntley, an American, was the wife of British actor Raymond Huntley. She met Kent through Hyman Goldstein, a fellow clerk at the embassy and one of the rare Jews employed for this work by the Department of State. Goldstein makes a strange, brief appearance, by name only, in the transcript of Kent's trial. Through the introduction of Kent to June Huntley, Goldstein somewhat enriched the social life of the code clerk, who, the agent reported, "was always saying he knew so few people and that he had wanted to go to Berlin and was disappointed about being sent to London."[31]

Although Kent was conducting an intense affair with Irene Danischewsky, and by March had begun to meet often with Wolkoff and others in the Right Club, Mrs. Huntley reported that she "never once heard him talk of anybody he knew in England." She introduced him to a number of her friends, and he joined her for Easter on the weekend of March 22 in Bexhill, a sailing village near Hastings on the southern coast of England. They stayed at Digby House, a boardinghouse, and entertained various of Huntley's friends. "He struck me as a very charming, interesting and intelligent young man," one of them recalled, "with a good deal of money and a rather cultivated air of laziness; this air of laziness is belied by the fact that his eyes are very wide awake and miss nothing. I don't know exactly how much is known about him, but he admits to speaking seven languages. His main passion seems to be sailing, and he did quite a bit of this at Bexhill, taking me with him on one occasion."[32]

An air of braggadocio clung to Kent throughout his life like a chronic, malodorous condition. Because he derived such gratification from it, it became a source of his appeal, sexual and emotional. But not everyone warmed to it. Another guest at Digby House, Sergeant W. G. G. D. Smith, had a less-favorable impression when he met Kent, from whom he purchased the Austin Eight, damaged in a crash en route to Bexhill, which Kent replaced with the one he purchased in April from Wolkoff. According to another report, Smith formed the opinion that "Kint [sic]" was "rather anti-British in his views." Smith, the report's author noted, "was surprised that a member of the American Embassy should air his views in public," although he also added that "the whole party had a fair amount of drinks during the evening."[33]

None of these newfound social acquaintances suspected at any point that Kent was acting as a spy, although, in her meeting with a Scotland Yard inspector, Mrs. Huntley said that Kent on one occasion infuriated her when he told her that "[t]he Americans would soon take on the German views when the Germans got into America." Her husband, the actor, attended this interview with the police in June. Looking back, he did recall, he said, that "one evening when they were listening to the radio, Tyler Kent said, '[T]he British radio isn't anything—you should hear the broadcasts from the anti-British station.'"[34]

Kent's views and his way of expressing them, odious though they were to June Huntley et al., had found a response in the White Russian community and continued to advance his social appeal elsewhere. Jane Aitken, a pro-fascist friend of June Huntley, met Kent at a party where, Huntley told Scotland Yard's agent, "she had agreed with everything Kent said and since that [time] she had often been out with him." Always the ladies' man, Kent had so struck Patricia Dalgliesh at a dinner party with his "Anti-British and pro-German conversation, that she had rung him up recently and asked him to lunch with a view to trying to put forward the British point of view," according to yet another report.[35]

Kent's social successes emboldened his table talk. While some, as in the case of Sam Allen, husband of Wolkoff's American pro-Nazi friend Barbara, found him "precocious and conceited and inclined to be anti-British,"[36] others weren't so put off by Kent's manner. At this particular lunch, he discoursed on all sorts of topics he'd studied in the Code Room: "That all available British aeroplanes were now in France; [t]hat Turkey would not stir a hand beyond her frontier to aid the allies, and that if the Germans invaded Romania it would be a two day job;" that "further resistance by the British was useless and they had better make peace as soon as they could; that there were five German divisions in Genoa; that the British were afraid of the Italian Navy."[37]

The last observation ruffled the feathers of a guest or two. Nearly every sailor, he gathered, had expressed a "keen desire" to fight the Italian Navy, according to Mrs. Dalgliesh, and a certain Mrs. Bull, both women at the lunch with Kent that day, held at the flat of Mrs. Mitchell Innes. The report adds: "[W]hen he was further asked whether he could name a single British naval officer who was apprehensive on this score, he replied with great emphasis and apparent certainty: 'The British Admiralty.'"[38]

That was on Saturday, May 11.

The following Saturday, the 18th, as he testified in a statement for Knight, Kent and Anna Wolkoff took an afternoon drive in the Austin Eight that Kent had bought from her. "We visited Enid Riddell," he stated, "who was staying with her grandmother at a sort of hotel-sanitorium on the Reigate road."[39] It was the last time that he would see the baroness outside the precincts of justice.

SEVEN

The Raid

I forced the lock and I produce the book.
—MAJOR MAXWELL KNIGHT TESTIMONY

AS OF MAY 18, 1940, NEITHER WINSTON CHURCHILL, MAXWELL Knight, nor anyone else planned to arrest Tyler Kent.

As Knight informed embassy counselor Herschel Johnson when he paid him a visit that afternoon, as Kent and the baroness went for tea on the Reigate road, what they wanted was the right to search 47 Gloucester Place for evidence that might strengthen the government's case that Wolkoff was conducting Fifth Column activity. Knight had no hard evidence to offer Johnson—already "profoundly" shocked to learn of Kent's association with Wolkoff—that Kent had done anything other than provide her with information. Still, that information about incidents that Johnson recognized suggested "a serious leakage of information through the Embassy."[1]

Churchill knew no more than Knight, but, as of that Saturday afternoon, he realized that he had in hand an incident with which to embarrass the American ambassador, a nasty adversary with known pro-German sympathies, now harboring an associate of a Nazi agent. It gave Churchill an instrument, moreover, with which to stick it to Roosevelt.

Kennedy was in Windsor, where he'd acquired a retreat to which he could repair if the Germans bombed London. Herschel Johnson called him right away, went down to see him Sunday morning, gave him the full story, filled him in on the Right Club, Ramsay, his Fifth Column activities, those of Wolkoff, and Kent's encounter back in October 1939 with Ludwig Matthias. Kennedy learned that Scotland Yard was preparing to arrest Wolkoff on Monday, the 20th.[2]

Kennedy shot off a telegram to the State Department for instructions about waiving diplomatic immunity that indicated he had already done so.[3]

Maxwell Knight, in the meantime, had obtained an 18B order, signed on the morning of Sunday, the 19th, by Home Secretary Sir John Anderson, to arrest Wolkoff the following day. With this order, the Home Office officially capitulated to Fifth Column Panic, which at last allowed the men and women of MI5 and Churchill to intern not only foreigners but also British subjects deemed enemies of the state.[4]

That night Churchill composed a telegram to Roosevelt that he knew would put him on the spot once the activities of Tyler Kent came to his attention in short order. It was his withering response to Roosevelt's cold telegram of May 16: "I understand your difficulties," he wrote, "but I am very sorry about the destroyers. The battle in France is full of danger to both sides. Though we have taken heavy toll of the enemy in the air clawing down two or three to one of their planes, they have still a formidable numerical superiority." The British needed as many Curtiss P-40 fighters as soon as Roosevelt could divert them from being delivered to the US Army.

Churchill continued: "[O]ur intention is to fight on to the end in this island and, provided we can get the help for which we ask, we hope to run them very close in the air battles in view of individual superiority," but he warned the president that, "Members of the present administration would likely go down during this process should it result adversely," and explained that while under "no conceivable circumstances" would his Cabinet consent to surrender, those who succeeded "amid the ruins" of his own administration might, "if this country was left by the United States to its fate," have to be forgiven if they bargained the British fleet for peace with Germany. "Excuse me, Mr. President," he wrote, "putting this nightmare bluntly. Evidently I could not answer for my successors, who in utter despair and helplessness might well have to accommodate themselves to the German will. However there is happily no need at present to dwell upon such ideas. Once more thanking you for your good will."

"Here's a telegram for those bloody Yankees," Churchill said that night to John Colville, his private secretary. "Send it off tonight."[5]

Colville was "somewhat taken aback," he confided to his diary, considering "the soothing words he always uses to America, and in particular to the President,"[6] but the secretary sealed it in an envelope, along with a letter, which he addressed to Herschel Johnson.

The envelope arrived by courier at the Chancery of the US embassy at about 1:30 that morning. Croft, the doorman, took it upstairs to the Code Room, where he gave it to Tyler Kent, who, although not authorized to do so, opened the envelope and showed its contents to the officer on night duty, Vice Consul Palmer—but not before he had, in the words of Rudolph Schoenfeld, "scribbled a pencil copy of the entire text for his archives."[7]

Colville reported in his diary that at 2:30 a.m., to his annoyance, the prime minister woke him to have the telegram message retrieved from the embassy so that he could review it. According to Schoenfeld, a Captain Elliot of Admiralty then called the embassy and said "it was now desired not to have Churchill's message sent. The Prime Minister wishes to have it back by six AM—may I come and fetch it?" Schoen-feld described Elliot as a "tall dark officer wearing an RAF uniform for some reason." This Elliot may have been Churchill's scientific adviser, Professor Frederick Lindemann, Lord Cherwell, sent undercover to retrieve the telegram. "Later that day," Schoenfeld testified, "May 20, the Churchill message was returned to the Embassy for transmission, quite unaltered,"[8] which contributed to the annoyance of Colville, who felt that the prime minister had deprived him of sleep to get the tele-gram back for no reason.

Why Churchill did so remains a mystery to this day. He never mentions the matter in his war memoirs. He never, for that matter, mentions anything about Tyler Kent. He may have retrieved his tele-gram because on second thought he wanted to reassure himself that he had expressed himself clearly to the president. He may also have arranged to get it back in order to send it after the search of Tyler Kent's premises, to give his message extra urgency, indicating to Roo-sevelt that the latter's reluctance to come to British aid in wartime, in light of Kent's behavior, insulted the Anglo-American friendship. Or perhaps the prime minister was playing a little game in which he satisfied his need to test the code clerk when the message came back, removed without authorization from a sealed envelope intended for the eyes of Herschel Johnson and no one else. Churchill may have known that Johnson wouldn't have reported for work at the US embassy that late at night on a Sunday, especially because, as no doubt he knew, the counselor had spent the day traveling back and forth to Windsor.

It wouldn't have been at all unlike Churchill to pull such a move. No one could ever guess with absolute certainty what the prime min-ister might do, or for what reason. He found great joy in the sport of outfoxing the fox wherever the fox lay. At 1:30 in the morning on May 20, the fox seemed to be lying low in the Code Room of the US embassy on Grosvenor Square.

—◦—

Kennedy suspended Kent's diplomatic immunity so that Knight could search Kent's living quarters untroubled by international legal sanctions and, if necessary, bring the code clerk under police guard for questioning at the embassy. He had authorization to do so under an executive order[9] signed by President Roosevelt in September 1939 that permitted the executive branch of the US government to revoke the diplomatic immunity of Foreign Service employees, who had previously inhabited a special realm immune to legal consequences. Kent had occupied that realm for all but several years of his entire life.

The ambassador decided to suspend Kent's privilege of immunity sometime on Sunday, May 19, before Churchill sent his message to Johnson, who, by prearrangement, had called Knight that evening to inform him that the ambassador had obtained, or was going to obtain, the necessary suspension.[10]

On Monday morning, Knight, accompanied by Scotland Yard detectives, arrested Anna Wolkoff at her apartment at 10 Roland Gardens. Here he obtained evidence of her friendship with Kent, including a letter, later produced as evidence in court, dated March 21, 1940, in which Kent wrote from the embassy that he was enclosing some Chesterfields. "I am driving down to the South Coast early tomorrow morning for the Easter holidays," he had written, "and expect to be back in London on Tuesday next at which time I hope to see you and make the acquaintance of more of your interesting friends."[11] He closed with a question addressed to the baroness in Russian. How much more Knight ascertained about this friendship remains unclear, but it's not unreasonable to suppose that he may have learned from Wolkoff something of the size of Kent's archive. The constabulary took her away to be booked as a suspicious alien.

Flanked by the ubiquitous Inspector Pearson of Special Branch and two Scotland Yard detectives, Scott and Buswell, Knight proceeded to the US embassy where, at 11:15, on instructions from Ambassador Kennedy, second secretary Franklin Gowen was waiting on five minutes' notice to join them in their car for the five-minute ride to 47 Gloucester Place. Gowen's official report provides a detailed account of what followed.[12]

Pearson rang the bell at No. 47. A maid opened the door and Pearson "asked" for Tyler Kent. The maid cannot have found the sight of five men on the narrow steps altogether reassuring. She told Pearson that she would have to go downstairs to the basement to call the landlady, Mrs. Welby. As she started down the stairs, the men pushed in after her.

One man went downstairs behind the maid. The others, including Gowen, ran up to the second floor, came to an open door on the landing, went through it, and there found Mrs. Welby, to whom the police, Maxwell Knight among them, displayed a warrant issued to search her house, in addition to their police credentials. They inquired whether Tyler Kent was in.

"Mrs. Welby pointed to a door on the same landing and said that it was Kent's room," reports Gowen.

Kent indeed was in. He had come home to his rooms that morning from the embassy at eight. Jut then he was lying in bed in his front room with Irene Danischewsky, who had arrived that morning sometime around nine for one of their regular assignations.

Inspector Pearson turned the handle of Kent's door. The door had a Yale lock, the key to which Mrs. Welby retained, which Kent therefore never used. On this particular morning, however, Kent had bolted the door for the first time, to Mrs. Welby's knowledge—although this very well may have been his practice when Irene came to visit. Unable to open the door, Pearson knocked, heard no response, and knocked again.

This time, a "man's voice answered in a loud tone: 'Don't come in.'"

Pearson knocked again.

The voice inside again called out, "Don't come in."

Then Pearson "crashed through the door and we all followed him into the room."

Kent was standing beside his bed, wearing the bottom half of a pair of striped pajamas. "Captain Knight immediately told him that the house was being raided by the police, and that all his effects would have to be searched."

Disheveled, Kent still managed to convey the discomfited air of someone intruded upon by a visitor intent on reading the gas meter. But as a police officer made for the door to Kent's other room, he "shrieked," according to Gowen, "You can't go in there; there is a lady." His cry had no effect on the officer, who "entered the other room," where he found Irene wearing the upper half of Tyler Kent's pajamas—and nothing else.

Knight informed Kent that anything he said might be used against him, and asked him "[w]hether he had in his possession in the house or elsewhere any documents pertaining to the American Government, and more particularly to the American Embassy in London."

"I have nothing belonging to the American Government," Kent replied. "I don't know what you mean."

Knight then "asked Kent whether he knew certain people, and mentioned several names, including that of Ernst Ludwig Matthias, the German Jew and naturalized Norwegian in whose company MI5 had observed Kent following his arrival in the UK. In most cases Kent said that he did know these people, and when Captain Knight asked him whether Kent thought these people were loyal to Great Britain or their particular countries, Kent said that he could not answer; but after a moment's hesitation he turned to me and said: 'Do you think I should answer these questions?'"

"By all means; answer everything," Gowen told him.

Knight gave Kent and Danischewsky permission to dress "under police supervision" while he made a thorough investigation of the premises in Gowen's presence. His efforts disclosed a great trove. In one light brown leather portmanteau, he found, neatly packed:

- confirmation copies received from the Department of State of telegrams dated July 1939
- copies of telegrams marked "For the Ambassador's file," November 1939
- a folder marked "Telegrams January 1–31, 1938"
- an unmarked folder containing telegrams to and from the Department of State, February 1938
- "flimsies" of "miscellaneous" telegrams
- an unmarked manila envelope containing miscellaneous telegrams sent over the period of April 22 through October 31, 1939
- four folders, each marked by month sent, containing telegrams from the Department in June and July 1939, and miscellaneous telegrams from July and August
- six packs of incoming telegrams, numbered 1–540, dated January–July 1939

In addition to these facsimile communiqués the portmanteau also disclosed an envelope containing keys, a "small box of photographic plates," and an envelope containing Kent's personal correspondence.

The keys became a matter of importance in Kent's trial because they were duplicates that he had commissioned Wolkoff to obtain at Woolworths. They belonged to doors to the File and Code Rooms at the embassy, and Kent had no authority to copy them. He asked the baroness to do so because he knew that if the ambassador or one of his officers transferred him from the Code Room to some other duty he would have to relinquish them and his access to those rooms, which he intended to retain. The skullduggery surrounding Kent's archival habits was damning.[13]

The photographic plates were the same that Smirnoff, the émigré photographer, had used, and that Wolkoff had given to Kent for safekeeping. These, like the keys, further contributed to the unpleasant truth that Kent was dishonest. When Knight asked the code clerk on the spot how he came to have the glass negatives, Kent—to spare Miss Wolkoff, of whose arrest he was as yet unaware—lied.[14] He told the MI5 agent that he himself had photographed the documents that appeared on the negatives because he had wanted to try out a Leica that Hyman Goldstein, another embassy clerk, had offered to sell him. Later that day when he learned of Wolkoff's internment, he admitted to Knight in a subsequent interrogation that he had lied about the negatives, and that on the spur of the moment he had introduced Goldstein in this fictitious exchange because he was en route to a new assignment in Madrid,[15] and at that moment was unavailable to verify or disprove what Kent had said. No doubt he also wanted to implicate a known Jew in this illegal activity.

A second piece of evidence, a cardboard box that Knight had found in Kent's rooms, contained itemized files entitled Chamberlain, Churchill, Halifax, Hore-Belisha, American and European Affairs, Films, Jews, and so forth, along with files identified by country or region, of which there were sixteen. Of the material in Kent's archive, 1,463 pieces originated in the London embassy between January 1939 and May 1940, a period that included correspondence concerning the German occupation of Czechoslovakia in March 1939, the end of the Spanish Civil War in April 1939, the Soviet wars with Finland, the expulsion of the USSR from the League of Nations in December 1939, the German-Soviet nonaggression pact, the Soviet occupation of Lithuania, and the German invasion of France, not to mention the German invasion of Poland that started World War II.[16] Of the discoveries that Knight made among the effects in Kent's rooms, none better suited the purposes of his search than the locked, leather-bound Right Club ledger, the infamous Red Book, which Captain Ramsay had given to Tyler Kent for safekeeping.

Knight told Irene that she was free to leave. "Captain Knight told me that the police had nothing to fear about her," writes Gowen, "because it was a case of real infatuation for Kent, and the police already knew that she was frightened lest her liaison with Kent became known to her husband." He added, "Captain Knight added that anyhow the telephone at her house is tapped and she is under constant observation." The police packed up the rest of Kent's archive in suitcases found on the premises and they all went down to the street.

Captain Knight summoned a taxi, into which went the suitcases, and in which Gowen then rode with the MI5 agent-runner to the embassy, in a kind of convoy with the police car, in which rode the other officers and Tyler Kent.

"On arrival at the Embassy," Gowen reports, the suitcases and their contents "were immediately brought to the Ambassador and opened in his presence." Kent, in police custody, was locked up in room 119 at the embassy until later that day, when he was summoned to an interrogation conducted in the ambassador's office by Ambassador Kennedy and Maxwell Knight, in the presence of Herschel Johnson and John Erhardt, first secretary, who, as a Foreign Service veteran, had known Kent in the days when he had served in Northern Ireland with Kent's father, William Kent.

Whatever his plans before he entered Kent's rooms, it's likely Knight never expected to arrest the errant code clerk. The hoard of documents he had found once Pearson had forced entry—and, in particular, the discovery he made of the Right Club ledger—undoubtedly inspired in him new possibilities. He now possessed convincing evidence that

Kent had been conspiring with Wolkoff to aid the enemy. Here was the material he needed—which otherwise he lacked—to prove that Wolkoff was acting as an enemy agent. Thus he had a plausible reason to argue that Wolkoff, as Captain Ramsay's Right Club aide-de-camp, formed part of a Fifth Column composed of Right Club members, an argument he could strongly reinforce now that he had the Red Book in hand.

As Knight inspected Kent's archive, as he held in his hands the Right Club ledger, as he supervised the processing of evidence, all the while he was calculating the heft of his revelations and what he had to do now to achieve his aims. He would have more time to do this once Kent fell under embassy lock and key, while he and the ambassador sorted through the haul of documents packed away in the suitcases. It was approximately at this time—one o'clock in the afternoon—when Churchill's message, unchanged and redelivered to the embassy, went out over the wires from the Code Room to Washington, where, still early in the day, it would appear before the president as he learned of the Kent debacle. In light of Knight's revelations, the incident must have appeared very damaging indeed, certainly to Joseph Kennedy.

For the ambassador, the situation he now beheld was appalling for several reasons. But he seems not to have confided his innermost thoughts about the matter to his diary, wherein no evidence survives that any such mess had come to pass, although he composed an extensive if unrevealing *aide-mémoire* on the subject.[17]

Uppermost in Kennedy's mind must have been his panic that Kent had compromised all of the secret State Department codes. The Department of State ordered an immediate blackout worldwide of coded communication. Fury also raged in him that Kent had read and copied memoranda of his own top-secret, pro-German—arguably anti-British—musings and discussions. Now it looked like this ambassador, who held such outspoken defeatist views, had harbored a Nazi agent in his Code Room for nine months. At the very least Kennedy appeared under these circumstances not to have been vigilant. He understood at once how his apparent inattentiveness must have compromised the president's relationship with Churchill, and how this fiasco had changed the equation of his own interaction with the prime minister, whom Kennedy had disparaged as an irritating souse—always offering him a whiskey and soda no matter what time of day[18]—who had outlived his usefulness.

The great fear that encompassed this variety of anxieties was that Kent's activities would quickly come to the attention of the press in both the UK and the United States. Knight and Kennedy each worked in the employ of men, Churchill and Roosevelt, respectively, whom above all they were obliged to protect. The fate of the world in part depended on them. The information that Kent possessed about their secret correspondence could easily have undermined Churchill's popular authority just then and ruined his efforts to control deliberations in the War Cabinet over how to deal with Hitler. Imagine if his political enemies had used it to show that as the First Lord of the Admiralty, he had secretly plotted to bring America into the war by offering Roosevelt shipping privileges, among other inducements, not available to other neutral powers. Churchill no doubt had already imagined such a possibility. In the ambassador's office, Knight would have understood that as well even as the men were examining the documents.

Kennedy had achieved transatlantic notoriety for views that he had expressed on the subject of German military strength and British vulnerability. Foremost a fan of Neville Chamberlain, the architect of appeasement, Kennedy may even have had designs on his employer's job, which on May 20 appeared up for grabs at the forthcoming Democratic National Convention in Chicago—although his aspirations may have reached further than that. He disagreed with the president's inclination to stop Nazi aggression; nor did Roosevelt any longer have much use for the ambassador's thoughts on the topic. Even so, Kennedy owed his diplomatic post to FDR. He remained, on record, a Massachusetts Democrat. While Tyler Kent cooled his heels under police watch in room 119, and, with Maxwell Knight beside him, Kennedy examined the code clerk's trove, he understood how this documentary matter would look to isolationists in Congress—how it could so quickly disrupt the president's carefully managed election-year inscrutability, expose him as secretly plotting to get America into the war, and thus destroy his presidential options.[19]

Together, Knight and Kennedy decided Kent's fate in those few hours.

They couldn't allow Kent to leave the UK to argue his case at home—within the confines of the Department of State or in a court of law—because that would enable him to take his evidence straight to Congress and arouse the isolationists. This publicity, both men recognized, would endanger both the president and the prime minister. Kennedy hadn't yet received a final okay from Cordell Hull to relieve Kent once and for all of his diplomatic immunity. This had never yet been permitted in any instance. Kent became the first and thus far only State Department employee stripped of diplomatic immunity in US history. Kennedy couldn't have done it without a hearing if Kent had been a Foreign Service officer. As it happened, Kent was an employee, who, although he had spent his entire life within the ambit of Foreign Service privilege, served at the discretion of Ambassador Kennedy. Kent might have expected his boss to sympathize with his own goals, given the outlook they seemed to share. But quite to the contrary, Kennedy fumed at what Kent had done and decided to fire him.

That's how simple it was. Diplomatic immunity didn't cover someone who no longer worked for the Department of State. Knight and Kennedy discussed the matter by telephone with Norman Kendal, the head of Special Branch, the section of Scotland Yard assigned to police the activities of political extremists. In a letter he wrote immediately afterward to a high official at the Home Office, Kendal reported that Kent had apparently "been stealing confidential information from the Embassy." As he informed F. A. Newsam, Esq., of the Home Office, "the Ambassador feels very strongly that he ought not to be allowed at liberty for one moment. He told me himself," Kendal added, "that if it should turn out that we cannot prosecute him here, they will prosecute him in America." He was writing to inform Newsam that the ambassador "refuses to claim any diplomatic privilege for Kent," and that he, Kendal, had "arranged for Kent to be kept at Cannon Row for the time being." He concluded his letter: "I suggest that either a Deportation Order should be made to cover his detention or an Order under 18G, the latter really on the grounds of his close association with Wolkoff and the probability that the American secrets 'stolen' were passed on to Germany."

To protect the president and himself, Kennedy decided more or less on the spot to hand his code clerk over to the British, now free to arrest the clerk for larceny and put him in a holding cell while MI5 "put everything," as Norman Kendal wrote in his letter to Newsam, "in shape for the Director's consideration" concerning whether the evidence recommended legal action against Kent for violating the Official Secrets Act of the United Kingdom.[20]

In exchange for handing over this priceless quarry, Kennedy received from the British the promise of absolute secrecy "regarding publicity," as he put it in a message to Hull on May 24, after a telephone conversation with Sir Alexander Maxwell, undersecretary of the Home Office, who had discussed the matter with the chief censor.

"I have been assured by them that nothing either here or abroad will be permitted to be printed," Kennedy wrote Hull. "Since this case smells to heaven may I suggest utter caution that nothing is given out in the United States from Washington."[21]

Franklin Gowen concludes his report of Kent's arrest, under the heading "Comments," in which he observes, "The sudden appearance of the police officers who crashed into Kent's room with me on May 20th did not seem to upset Kent very much. He gave me the impression that he was not overly concerned as to what his fate might be; perhaps he was only showing off or has powerful and prominent friends who are involved in his activities."[22]

Kent maintained this appearance of unconcern—equanimity, even—when later that day he answered questions during his "First General Interrogation," as the transcript is titled, "held in Ambassador Kennedy's office," by Kennedy and Knight. He didn't yet know that Kennedy already had decided to fire him and, by so doing, to strip him of his diplomatic immunity. Even so, under interrogation, Kent conducted himself with the presence of mind rarely displayed in such circumstances by anyone not possessed with the serenity of his convictions. He didn't endear himself to either of his inquisitors.

"From the kind of family you come from—people who have fought for the United States—one would not expect you to let us all down," Kennedy told Kent at the outset.

"In what way?" Kent immediately wanted to know.

The ambassador replied, "You don't think you have? What did you think you were doing with our codes and telegrams?"

"It was only for my own information," Kent responded.

"Why did you have to have them?"

"Because I thought them very interesting."

Then Knight took over. "I think it is just as well you should know you can be proved to have been associating with this woman, Anna Wolkoff."

Kent hadn't yet learned that Wolkoff had been arrested, but answered, "I don't deny that."

Knight then informed him that he could prove that Wolkoff had "a channel of communication with Germany" that she had used at the very least to communicate "pro-German propaganda," and pointed out, as the ambassador already had, that Kent had been "found with documents" that he was not entitled to have. "You would be a very silly man," said Knight, "if you did not realize that certain conclusions might be drawn from that situation, and it is for you to offer the explanation, not us."

Then Knight moved immediately to the subject of the locked, red, leather-bound book. "What is this?" he asked.

"I don't know what it is," Kent replied.

"Who gave it to you?"

"I think probably if you opened it you would find out."

Knight tried a different approach. "Who has the key?"

"I haven't any idea," replied Kent.

"By whom was it given to you?" the MI5 officer asked him.

This time Kent told him. "It was given to me by Captain Ramsay," adding, "what it contains I don't know."

When Knight asked him why Ramsay had given it to him, Kent answered: "He asked me to keep it," and when Knight wanted to be sure that Kent knew none of its contents, the code clerk said, "Positively none."

"Don't you think it strange," Knight pressed, "that a Member of Parliament should come to you, a minor official in an Embassy, and give you a locked book to take care of for him? Now seriously, doesn't it strike you as odd that a Member of Parliament should bring you a locked ledger and ask you to take care of it for him?"

"I don't know," Kent replied.

"You are adopting a sort of naive attitude that doesn't deceive me for a moment," the exasperated MI5 officer said. "You are either hiding something or—"

Kent cut him off. "Well, the fact remains that I don't know what is in that thing and I haven't seen it open. He simply requested that I keep it for him."

"That is not answering my question," Knight insisted, although Kent had, in fact, answered his question—if not in the way Knight had wanted him to. "I have asked you whether you did not think it curious that a man in Captain Ramsay's position should bring to you—a young and obscure man—a book to which he apparently attaches some importance, and ask you to keep it for him."

Knight may have thought that a dart aimed at Kent's vanity would sting him into discussing his role in Right Club activities, and he turned to the subject of Captain Ramsay's relations with Wolkoff. Then he produced the letter Kent wrote to Wolkoff when he sent her the Chesterfields and quoted the passage, "I hope to see you and make the acquaintance of more of your interesting friends."

"Now," said Knight, "who are the 'interesting friends'?"

Captain Ramsay was the person he'd had in mind when he wrote that, Kent replied. "Then I did meet him and found him rather interesting."

"In what way?" Knight asked.

"In conversation. We had sort of common views, to a certain extent."

Knight then revealed quite skillfully to Kent how his associations with Wolkoff and others, from a strictly British viewpoint, had compromised Kent in a way that until then he had not comprehended. "The first time you came to my attention was in February 1940 when your friend, Anna Wolkoff, was telling people that she had made an extremely useful contact with a young man at the American Embassy. I am going to speak now extremely bluntly. I am afraid that I must take the view that you are either a fool or a rogue, because you cannot possibly be in any position except that of a man who has either been made use of or who knows all these people. I propose to show you how."

He then did exactly that. On April 16, 1940, he told Kent, he learned that Wolkoff had been telling her Right Club associates a story "purported," he said, turning to Kennedy, "to be based on an interview you, Mr. Ambassador, had with Lord Halifax, and it concerned the landing of the Germans in Norway and the difficulties that had been encountered by the British Navy in connection with that."

"I don't remember what I said in conversation in April 1940," said Kent.

"You have a very good memory for what you have not said, but not a very good memory for what you have said," Knight snapped.

This was a riposte worthy of the author of a courtroom thriller, if something of a gamble, unless Knight had already concluded that Kent had lied about Goldstein's camera. This was the only false statement Kent is known to have made in the case.

Maxwell Knight now turned to the visit that Ludwig Matthias had paid to Kent's room at the Cumberland on October 8, 1939, after which he was seen leaving Kent's room with an envelope.

"I certainly don't remember that incident at all," Kent replied. "I am guilty of one thing, and that is smuggling a box of cigars through the British Customs which I subsequently lost, and that was the object of his visit to my room." How Kent had lost his alleged box of cigars, how Matthias fit into this incident, and whether the envelope contained the cigars was never explained, and Knight showed no desire to explore the connection. Instead, he gave Kent other examples of confidential information that Wolkoff had claimed came from Kent, and asked him if he'd ever sent messages in the "diplomatic bag to anyone other than those in his family to whom he'd sent personal letters."

"No," Kent answered.

When the MI5 interrogator raised the subject of Lord Haw-Haw, Kent's knowledge appeared to be rather vague, so the former returned to the subject of the ledger. "You definitely state that to the best of your knowledge and belief, you had no knowledge of what the contents of this book are?"

"No. It was given to me, and I made no attempt to open it."

"And you still cannot offer any explanation as to why he should give to you a book for safekeeping?" the MI5 officer insisted.

"I haven't thought about it much, to tell the truth," Kent replied.

"You really mean," said Knight, "it didn't strike you as odd."

Kent conceded, "Well, I suppose it does seem a bit odd," as if to say that perhaps to someone unfamiliar with the circumstances it might, indeed, look stranger than it really was.

Kent deftly exhausted Knight's line of questioning. "It is not for me to discuss your position with regard to these documents belonging to your government," Knight said, "because that is not my affair at all. But your explanation about this appears to me to be extremely unconvincing,"

"Well, give them to me again and I will try to be a little bit more clear. You mean the fact that I had the documents at all?"

"That is my interest," Ambassador Kennedy said. "You don't expect me to believe you for a minute that you had them for your own entertainment?"

"I didn't say entertainment, I said interest," Kent told him, revealing a sound memory for what he had said already.

Knight came to Kennedy's aid, saying to Kent, "Do you consider yourself entitled to have them to refresh your memory about their confidential documents?"

"I think in the future it would have been very interesting."

"You know you are in an extremely bad position," Knight said. "If you were English you would be in a very difficult position. You don't impress me by your cocky manner."

Kent told him that he had not been trying to be cocky or to impress him. Knight wanted to know why he thought the documents would be of any use to him, to which Kent replied, "I hadn't any definite plan as to what use I'd make of them. But they are doubtless of importance as historical documents and throw an interesting light on what we are going through."

"You know, of course, that it is against the law for you to have these documents?" Kennedy said.

Kent said that he was not aware of this fact.

"Well, let me assure you that it is," Kennedy replied, trying to get at Kent. "You were not by any chance going to take them with you to Germany when you asked for a transfer there, without our knowledge?"

Kent seemed not at all taken aback that Kennedy had come upon the letter he had written on February 24 to Chargé d'Affaires Alexander Kirk in Berlin to sound him out about a job. "No," Kent said, "I couldn't have gotten them out. I'm not entitled to exemption."

"But I think you will find that in regard to many countries you'd get it," Knight hastened to say.

"No," Kent insisted, "that was very far from my thoughts."

Knight asked him once again about Wolkoff. He wanted to know what Kent thought of her loyalty, as a British subject, a matter about which Kent had not expressed himself with a straightforward answer that morning.

"Well," said Kent, "if you mean that she holds some views that are apparently at variance with some of the ideas possibly of the British Government, that is quite true; but it doesn't mean that she is not a loyal British subject."

"Does a loyal British subject communicate—" the MI5 officer began to ask, but Kent cut him off again.

"No, but I have absolutely no knowledge of that. That is the first I have heard of it. If you say that she is in communication with the enemy, why, of course she is not a loyal British subject; but when you put the question to me this morning I didn't know that."

"But this morning you wouldn't say yes or no," said Knight. "A person is either loyal or disloyal."

"If you think that everybody that doesn't approve of what is being done by the country is disloyal, that would—"

It was Knight's turn to cut off Kent. "Now you are merely trying to talk like a parlor politician, but we are dealing with fundamentals."

"As far as fundamentals are concerned, I have no knowledge of Anna Wolkoff," Kent replied.

Then the ambassador delivered his coup de grace. He phrased it as a question to the British intelligence officer. "If you prove that she is in contact with them, she is more or less a spy," he said. "If the United States Government decides to waive any rights they may have, do I understand that that might very well make Kent part and parcel of that?"

"Subject to the production of evidence under the law," Knight replied, "yes."

"I think honestly," Kennedy said, "that at this stage, nothing very useful is to be got by carrying on this conversation."[23]

In an undated *aide-mémoire* composed weeks if not months after Kent's arrest—a testimonial piece intended for the appraisal future historians might make of his role in the affair—Ambassador Kennedy explained that he "agreed to waive any future immunity for Kent" because he realized that "the whole matter deserved a very thorough investigation that could only be effectively carried out by the British police, and that the evidence pointed to an offense under British law."[24] Historians may detect behind this glib explanation a self-serving spirit.

Maxwell Knight's sting operation held Kennedy captive as much as Kent, both victims of Knight's blackmail. Veiled and presented as a genuine crisis to the security of wartime Britain, Knight's message to Kennedy was unambiguous: If you know what's good for you, you'll hand Kent over. Kennedy, in this instance, proved the right man for the job to which President Roosevelt had appointed him. He saw at once that MI5 and Scotland Yard had compromised US security by withholding from the ambassador the information that his code clerk might be a spy for the Nazis. He also understood at once that they now had it in their power to sabotage the appearance Roosevelt wanted to convey to the world of scrupulous neutrality.

"I was naturally distressed by the incident," Kennedy wrote in his memoir, "and by the failure (that I had no hesitancy in commenting on) of the Scotland Yard officials to bring their suspicions about Kent to our attention months before. Their failure had led us to continue Kent in our employ in the most confidential of all positions, and had led to the dissemination of much confidential information as well as spreading broadside data in the form of the readings that would make insecure our most secret codes."[25]

The British police had the means to determine whether Kent was a spy, and the evidence—which included a copy of Kent's letter to Alexander Kirk in Berlin, requesting a job there, and Kirk's reply, which Kent had filed in a metal dispatch box in the Code Room—on the surface suggested that he probably was. Furthermore, Kennedy knew that the British had the power to suppress information that Kent had obtained and revealed to Captain Ramsay in the form of telegrams that Churchill had sent through the Code Room. Those telegrams could endanger any consideration that Roosevelt might have been entertaining about running for a third term, and any career that the ambassador might have been designing for himself.

That Tyler Kent had intentionally or inadvertently compromised the code system employed by the Department of State globally created for Kennedy a frightening possibility for which he had to assume responsibility, along with the likelihood that Kent was a spy. Kennedy wrote a secret telegram to the secretary of state, marked RUSH, fired off on the evening of May 20: "Copies of the readings of the strip cipher were found among the papers in Kent's possession at his home, and it is therefore impossible to say now that the strip cipher system has not been compromised." On May 23, Kennedy assured the secretary of state that "All codes have been at all times accounted for and none is missing," and that "the Embassy discounts likelihood that he made photographs of codes." He could not, however, assure the secretary that the codes were secure. Indeed, he asserted in his memoir that they were "no longer safe, and their violability imperiled the secrecy of our own diplomatic communications throughout all of Europe."[26] On May 25, this was a possibility—even if incorrect. Either way, the codes were already due for an overhaul.

No document has ever surfaced which indicates that, when Kennedy waived Kent's diplomatic immunity so that Scotland Yard could search his apartment, the ambassador had yet received State Department permission to do so, or that he had the okay to hand Kent over to the police—both of which he did once he and Knight had concluded their interrogation. Kennedy had distinguished himself as having a mind so fast that no principle could flag it down when roaring forward at full speed.

EIGHT

Usual Suspects

No Fifth Column existed in Britain.

—WINSTON CHURCHILL

AT 10:30 A.M. ON MAY 22, 1940, HOME SECRETARY SIR JOHN Anderson met with members of the War Cabinet. Those present included Chamberlain, Attlee, Halifax, and Greenwood, all authorized to act on matters that required immediate decision in the absence of the prime minister, himself en route to Paris to meet with Reynaud, the French prime minister, and Weygand, the new, if aged, commanding French general. Churchill hoped to impress them with the urgent need to launch an all-out attack against the German forces Hitler had unleashed.[1]

This visit formed part of Churchill's campaign to dominate the Allied war strategy in the War Cabinet and on the European Front, a strategy still in contention. Churchill insisted on all-out war against Hitler, but on both sides of the Channel, some still wanted to make peace with the Third Reich and thus continued to look for ways to compromise. Churchill believed that Hitler must be defeated in France, and under no circumstances, even if he successfully invaded Great Britain, should the British government negotiate with him. Such was the premise of his argument in the War Cabinet, with Lord Halifax, and, in Parliament, with those of his Conservative opponents who wanted to bargain for peace.[2]

On that Wednesday, Paris hadn't yet fallen to the Germans. This was the day, also, on which Hitler halted the Panzer advance to the British Channel, an action that historians now believe lost him the war. It gave the British the time that they needed to move their Expeditionary Force to the coast of Flanders, where a fleet of warships and small civilian craft, marshaled at short notice, assembled at Dunkirk to evacuate them from Friday, May 26, until June 4. That rescue operation saved the lives of 337,000 Allied soldiers, 110,000 of them French.

These were desperate days. The news blackout in Britain had somewhat anesthetized the British public to their dire plight. Yet already a fever of panic influenced how everyone thought. The two categories of people who provided an immediate and palpable source for that panic were enemy aliens at liberty in the country, and those whom MI5 deemed members of the so-called "Fifth Column."[3]

MI5 had failed to provide any solid evidence to convince Sir John Anderson that the latter indeed existed, or that Sir Oswald Mosley and his organization, the British Union of Fascists—politically anti-Semitic, violent, pro-appeasement, and noisy though they were— had any covertly traitorous ambitions that identified them as a Fifth Column.[4] Until May 22, Anderson refused to endorse any effort to intern British subjects who happened to hold views inimical to those of the wartime British government. No argument that the director of Military Intelligence advanced to curtail civil liberties could alter the constraints of British democracy without the assent of the Home Secretary at this time.

The secretary's power was of a peculiar nature. He couldn't issue the order to round up suspicious British subjects or enemy aliens on British soil and detain them en masse. The Home Secretary wasn't yet even technically a Cabinet member. But his position empowered Sir John Anderson to present the evidence that he thought recommended consideration by the War Cabinet for internment of people in Britain who posed a threat in wartime. On the basis of what he now knew, this is what he did on the morning of Wednesday, May 22, forced as he was by the circumstances of his job to report to the Cabinet about the Monday arrests of Wolkoff and Kent.[5]

Once the Cabinet made the general decision to intern enemy aliens and subversive British subjects and drafted a law to this effect, which Parliament expediently voted to pass that night, Sir John then had the power to implement it. Kent supplied the ingredient that made the formula effective. Churchill, MI5, and the military chiefs of staff so keenly wanted to intern civilians for one reason or another that, had Kent not come along, soon enough someone else would have no doubt served the purpose. But it was Kent who came along, and that remains his historical significance to the actions of World War II.[6]

In the eyes of those who knew of his activities and associations, Kent was in all likelihood guilty of espionage. As a suspected foreign agent, he associated with Captain Ramsay and Anna Wolkoff, themselves in communication with someone who worked in Germany for the Hitler regime.

Anderson presented the situation at the Cabinet meeting: Ramsay, the MP, had engaged in subversive activities; Wolkoff had been involved with Kent; Ramsay in another context had been in contact with Mosley. Anderson also drew to the attention of those present that MI5 had produced no evidence to show that Mosley and the British Union of Fascists had participated in any Fifth Column activity. In the minds of some, including Churchill, Mosley was positioning himself, in the event of a successful Nazi invasion, to be foremost among those whom Hitler would enlist to govern Great Britain on his behalf. Anderson never said so explicitly, but that outcome was obvious. In his opinion, both Ramsay and Wolkoff could have been prosecuted for violating the Official Secrets Act. (Then again, a subsequent examination of Ramsay's activities by the law officers of Special Branch didn't disclose an offense under the Official Secrets Act.)

As Right Club leader, Ramsay had met with Mosley, but not in connection with anything that involved the alleged espionage of Tyler Kent and Anna Wolkoff. Mosley, therefore, couldn't have been detained for subversive activities under the current law. Nor did the facts, in themselves, justify an amendment in the law to permit internment. Nevertheless, the association between Mosley and Ramsay supplied the rationale that finally prompted Anderson to suggest that, if it decided to authorize the internment of Mosley, the Cabinet should create a new law to do so, because the old, deactivated law that had served this exact purpose in the Great War had proved so unpopular because of the stifling of Britons' liberties.[7]

Churchill had slipped away to Paris and left the matter in the hands of Chamberlain, to whom he'd said, "I will agree to whatever the Cabinet thinks best."[8]

At the meeting, Chamberlain characterized the Right Club as "carrying on pro-German activities, and secret subversive work with the object of disorganizing the Home Front and hindering the prosecution of the war." At the meeting, the Cabinet instructed Anderson and the law officers to decide whether to intern Ramsay or to arrest him.[9] The War Cabinet swiftly decided to amend the old law, DR18B, and, under a new amendment, DR18B (1A), ordered the immediate detention of Ramsay, Mosley, and those of their followers, members of the Right Club and the British Union of Fascists, whom they believed to pose a danger to the state—despite a lack of hard evidence.[10]

By May 25, the British police had interned most if not all Fifth Column suspects in the Right Club and the British Union of Fascists. Knight or someone else at MI5 had broken the lock on the Right Club ledger, which subsequently supplied the police with names of people for whom he may have wanted an excuse to arrest. Inspector Pearson, accompanied by Officer Buswell, arrested Ramsay at 8:30 a.m. on Thursday, May 23.

"Captain Ramsay said it was ridiculous to accuse him of acts prejudicial to the public safety or the defence of the Realm," Pearson wrote in a report following the arrest, which he made at Ramsay's flat, at 24 Onslow Square. "He said he was the founder of the Right Club, which was an organization to combat Jewish and Communist influence in this country, and he went into a tirade against the British government, alleging that it was Jew-ridden and controlled, that the press was in the hands of the Jews, and that the war had been engineered by Jews. On 73 occasions, he said, he had risen in his place in the House of Commons to speak on the subject of Jews and Communism, and failed to catch the speaker's attention. Capt. Ramsay said he was the only member who dared attack the government on their policy and he was being removed to prison as a menace to that policy."[11]

Scotland Yard plainclothes police were waiting for Mosley when he returned to London from their farm with his wife, Diana, the daughter of Lord Redesdale, a Right Club member. In London, the Mosleys occupied an apartment on Dolphin Square, adjacent to the quarters from which Maxwell Knight's outfit operated. "As we turned into the road leading to the entrance of our Dolphin Square block of flats I immediately saw that four or five men were standing about on the pavement near the doorway," Diana Mosley recalls in her memoir, *A Life of Contrasts*. "They were not talking, as a group of friends might, but were aimlessly staring into space. 'Look coppers,' I said to M. We got out of the car and one of them stepped forward and said he had a warrant for M.'s arrest. We went up on the lift with the policemen; on the landing of the seventh floor there were a couple more. All of them were in plain clothes. We went up in M's flat and he asked to see the warrant. They said that he was to go to Brixton prison and that I could visit him the following day. M. and I said goodbye. We went down in the lift and they drove him away. A cold fury possessed me, I can feel it now as I write."[12]

The police had already arrested all those who worked at the British Union of Fascists headquarters, Lady Mosley discovered. As she drove out of London, alone, to return to the farm, she saw posters on the street that bore the banner M.P. ARRESTED. The evening papers carried the story of Ramsay's arrest. "They must have waited for M.," Lady Mosley wrote, "guessing that he would come up to London, which he did every day,"[13] and which Maxwell Knight surely observed him do.

Then, on Friday, May 24, British police began to round up and intern enemy aliens on British soil. Dissent and liberty had fallen casualty to the war.

NINE

The Blackout

The war is at our door.
—HENRY "CHIPS" CHANNON, *DIARIES*, MAY 23, 1940

BRITISH POLICE OFFICERS ARRESTED TYLER KENT ON CHARGES OF
larceny and imprisoned him on Cannon Row until the Home Office
could ascertain whether the British government could establish a case
to prove that he had violated the Official Secrets Act of 1911.

He vanished.

Very few people knew the circumstances surrounding his arrest
and his subsequent disappearance, and the matter of his activities—
which called forth grave suspicions on both sides of the Atlantic—
remained a closed secret to those few who did know about them.
The British authorities silently engulfed their captive American in an
isolation from which he couldn't call for help or make his situation
known. Kent now stood in a dark parallel to the many Muscovites
who had vanished into the night of the Lubyanka. The Americans in
the Department of State and in the embassy—few knowing Kent's
whereabouts—maintained a vigilant silence.

Franklin Gowen, the second secretary who had witnessed Kent's arrest and the seizure of his archive, now fielded any calls or visits made by people who knew Kent at the embassy. Gowen pretended to be Kent on the telephone so that callers continued to imagine the code clerk was working as usual in the Code Room. His own voice was unlike Kent's.

"What I do to confuse people calling for Kent is to say that I have to speak in a low tone because there are so many people around," Gowen writes in a subsequent report. "This seems to work very well with those who call up Kent. I also tap the keys of a typewriter very near my telephone. This confuses the listener on the phone, who thinks it really is Mr. Kent speaking, with a typist working near the phone."

An employee representing P. Larsson & Son, tailors on Great Pulteney Street in Soho, telephoned Kent on the afternoon of his arrest, according to Gowen, to ask him to return pattern books and to pay them a bill that amounted to ten pounds, nine shillings. Gowen also took a call that afternoon from Enid Riddell, the Right Club friend of Anna Wolkoff.

"Is that Mr. Kent?" she inquired.

Gowen replied, "Yes."

"Won't you come around for a cocktail this afternoon at about 6:30?"

Gowen, as Kent, replied that the foot traffic in the room was such that he "would have to be very short and could not speak very loud," but that he would either call her back, or simply show up for cocktails. "Will it be at the same place?" he asked.

"Yes," she replied, "right around the corner from your place, at three, Chesham Street, second floor."

Gowen relayed the contents of this brief conversation to the ambassador and then called Norman Kendal to let him know. Kendal, he reported, "was '_most happy_' to know this," and immediately arranged to have Riddell's telephone tapped. When another call came for Kent from 3 Chesham Street, Gowen cautiously didn't pretend to be Kent but told the caller instead that Kent had gone out somewhere.

Gowen remained on alert for calls coming into the embassy for Kent well into the night. He was at the ambassador's house when the embassy operator informed him that a message "had been received by phone for Kent."

Gowen returned to the embassy and waited by his phone until 10:45 p.m., when a call came in from a man who said, "Mr. Kent, will you come to three, Chesham Street? If you knock at the door I will open."

Gowen left a message at Scotland Yard requesting a car and an officer. "Ten minutes later Detective Moss arrived at the Embassy in a private car with a chauffeur," Gowen writes. They drove to within two blocks of the building and proceeded on foot to the house. Gowen rang the bell, "and a man appeared in his shirt sleeves at the door of the basement or so-called 'service' floor, which is about six to eight feet below the surface of the street. The man said, 'Who is that?' and I answered 'Mr. Kent.' He said, 'Oh yes, I'll be only a minute. Will you please wait?' We were in utter darkness. The same man opened the door, and as I stood back a few steps in the black-out he said, 'Mr. Kent.' I said, 'Didn't you know Mr. Kent was coming?' He said, 'Yes, I have something for you,' and handed me a note." Enid Riddell was not in, as Gowen had hoped she would be. He took the note forthwith to Scotland Yard, in the company of Detective Moss, where he found none of the officers who had accompanied him earlier in the day to 47 Gloucester Place.

"I was told they were all out on urgent business," Gowen reports. "The note was to the effect that the writer was most anxious to see Kent, had waited for him until 9:45, and had something important for him. It was signed 'Enid.' It also gave the address of the restaurant

La Coquille in London, with the words, 'At this address.' I arranged with Scotland Yard to take immediate action to place secret service men on the watch at the restaurant, to tap the phones at 3, Chesham Street, and to keep the house under observation. I then proceeded in the same police car to within about half a block of 3, Chesham Street, and stayed there until about 2 a.m. to keep watch on the house myself. I had planned to take the numbers of any cars that might pull up there, and to find out all I could. Nothing happened."

Inspector Pearson told Gowen the next day that he had raided the house, "but to no avail." Under questioning, however, Enid Riddell disclosed to Scotland Yard that La Coquille was the restaurant where Kent had been expected to meet her for dinner the evening before, with the Duca del Monte and other friends.

Patricia Dalgliesh telephoned Kent on Thursday, May 23. Under the impression that she was speaking to Kent, she invited him to meet her for lunch with friends at the Berkeley Hotel. "As I answered with some uncertainty as to being able to attend the lunch," wrote Gowen, "the woman remarked that it would be all right to leave word with the maître d'hôtel."

At 11 a.m. on May 24, Catherine Ridley called Kent, and invited him "to dine with her that evening 'to meet some friends,'" Gowen writes. "This information was also immediately passed on by me to Scotland Yard."

The last calls Gowen reported came from Catherine Georgesky and Mrs. Samuel Allen, respectively. Georgesky told Gowen, whom she assumed was Kent, "My brother has come home on leave—he is now in the country—I'd like you to meet him—how about this evening—phone me at Western 3K82." Mrs. Allen wanted Kent "to have a cocktail with her," as Gowen put it. These women called Kent while Gowen was dictating his report, dated May 28, eight days after Kent's disappearance. None of these callers had any inkling that Kent had vanished.[1]

Mrs. Kent greets her son in Hoboken, New Jersey, on December 4, 1945, after he had spent nearly five years in British prisons. (PHOTO COURTESY OF THE LIBRARY OF CONGRESS)

Not so Irene Danischewsky. She didn't immediately know what role (if any) the embassy had played in the raid, nor must she have connected Gowen with the embassy. On her release, she called the embassy to alert Kent's employer that the police had raided his rooms. When she left the premises at 47 Gloucester Place, the police were still conducting their investigation. In a letter she wrote at the end of the war to Kent's mother, Irene assured Mrs. Kent that she had phoned the embassy "to secure help for Tyler," and that she had not known "that the Embassy was 'in on it.'"[2]

On May 21, the day after his arrest, Irene called Kent at the embassy and spoke to Gowen, who convinced even Irene that she was speaking with her lover. Irene suggested lunch. Gowen instructed her to meet him at the embassy; Irene told him she would come, and that she'd meet him outside. When she arrived at the embassy, the policeman on watch, who had accompanied Gowen and Knight on the raid, informed Gowen that she was Kent's mistress whom he had encountered at 47 Gloucester Place. Gowen sent word with the embassy porter that Kent wanted her to wait outside "until about one o'clock."[3]

Inspector Pearson was either present in the embassy, or close at hand. "As the woman knows me," he told Gowen, "I'll walk home with her. I'll tell her that if she keeps on interfering with Kent or your Embassy I will get her in trouble with her husband."

At this point in the war, the British might be forgiven, if not excused entirely, for taking such draconian measures against unproven disloyalty to the Crown. The pluck and luck of Dunkirk hadn't come yet. Through the murk of the news blackout filtered word of the conquest of France and the dire fate that awaited the British soldiers driven in blind retreat to the French coast. Britons were preparing for the German invasion.

On May 26, Harold Nicolson advised his wife, Vita Sackville-West, to procure the means with which to end her life. "I think you really ought to have a 'bare bodkin' handy so that you can take your quietus when necessary," he wrote from London, where he served as a Member of Parliament. "I shall have one also. I am not in the least afraid of such sudden and honorable death. What I dread is being tortured and humiliated. But how can we find a bodkin which will give us our quietus quickly and which is easily portable? I shall ask my doctor friends."[4]

In *Five Days in London: May 1940*, John Lukacs quotes a survey published on May 25 that concludes, "The public mind is in a chaotic condition and ready to be plunged into the depths of an utterly bewildered, shocked, almost unbelieving dismay. The whole structure of national belief would seem to be rocking gently."[5]

This was the climate into which Tyler Kent had vanished. For ten days after his detention, those who knew about his arrest maintained a conspiracy of silence about what had become of him. His Right Club associates quickly realized that he had disappeared. Christabel Nicholson, whom Scotland Yard "detained" on May 26, when asked by MI5 agent Marjorie Mackie why she thought Tyler Kent had "gone," said that "they had been unable to get into touch with him." That was on May 21, the day after Kent's arrest.[6] Others who knew Kent had tried to reach him at the embassy, but Franklin Gowen, through his vocal trickery, had deceived them into thinking that he was at his desk—for the time being. Ten days later, British police transferred Kent across the Thames to the rat-infested Brixton Prison, where criminal suspects languished while awaiting further disposition.

On the other side of the Atlantic, the code clerk's mother, Anne Patrick Kent, wondered why she hadn't received any word from her son lately about the state of his health, which had been troubling her. She had written the embassy to inquire about him, but information in this era still traveled slowly and incompletely. Because no friends or allies at the Department of State informed her, Mrs. Kent remained innocent of any news concerning the whereabouts of her son until the end of May.[7]

In London, meanwhile, rumors began to swirl that an employee of the American embassy had been arrested. "Knowledge that a man connected with the American Embassy has been arrested by the police under a serious charge has become widespread, and it seems to me that it would now be wise that our consent be given to a simple statement being issued by the Home Office to the press," wrote Ambassador Kennedy on May 31 to Secretary of State Hull in a rushed telegram classified "Personal and Strictly Confidential." Kennedy advised Hull that Scotland Yard "states that issuance of such a statement would no longer prejudice their investigation, and the other British authorities indicate they have no objection."

A draft of the statement follows: "In consequence of action taken by the American Ambassador in co-operation with the British authorities, Tyler Kent, a clerk who has been discharged from the employment of the American government, has been under observation and has been interned by an order of the Home Secretary under the Defence Regulations."[8] Kennedy, in this dispatch, informed Hull that in its original draft the statement hadn't mentioned Kent by name. "In order, however, to allay unwarranted speculations as to the identity of the individual, it seems to me wiser to give this man's name," he wrote. "The names of other people, British subjects, who are connected with this case and have been arrested have been published. No mention, however, has been made of any connection between these individuals and Kent."[9]

Kennedy's telegram had gone out at noon that Friday; it was noon that same Friday, five hours later in Washington, when Hull replied, authorizing Kennedy to give his assent to the Home Office statement. It was an instantaneous response, as such things went then. The weekend, both men knew, would blunt the news on both sides of the Atlantic.[10]

The time had come to inform Kent's mother. The matter fell within the job responsibilities of Breckinridge Long, an assistant secretary of state, who delegated the task to J. Howland Shaw, director of Personnel Matters, who arranged for a messenger to meet with her at the Department of State minutes before Hull sent his authorization telegram to Kennedy. This official subsequently sent a memo to Long about his meeting with Mrs. Kent. "After a brief introductory conversation," he wrote, "I informed Mrs. Kent that the Department had just received cabled information that her son, Tyler Kent, who had been discharged from the American Embassy in London, has been under observation and has been interned by the British government."[11]

According to his account, Shaw's messenger gave Mrs. Kent a misleading impression. The State Department hadn't only just learned of her son's internment. The man compounded the misimpression when she asked him when Kent had been discharged from the embassy and he told her "about two days ago so far as I knew." Although he may not have known how many days truly had passed since the date of Kent's discharge, he ought to have known; he was representing the director of Personnel Matters, after all. By assigning this task to a relative underling, however, Shaw—acting at the request of Long, who took orders from Hull—couldn't stand accused of deception. He was merely limiting Mrs. Kent's access to the truth. He told her, Shaw's messenger wrote, "that the Department and the Embassy at London would make every effort to keep her informed regarding any developments, but it was a case in the hands of the British authorities and beyond the control of the United States government," which was true, and added, "In response to her question I informed her that she could scarcely be justified in drawing any inferences or implications from the information which was now available to her, and she must endeavor to be content merely with the facts as I had given them to her."[12]

It was a cold, impersonal way to treat the widow of a veteran consular official with associates in the department, who, as an official's wife, had been a valued member of the Consular Service. Shaw's messenger noted that Mrs. Kent, "a woman about fifty-seven years of age," had "recently sustained a fractured leg and was in a crippled condition when she came to the Department." He wrote that she was "of strong character and received courageously the tidings which I gave her. She was evidently, however, very much affected, but did not come immediately to a full realization of the plight of her son, although she spoke of possible execution." Shaw's man concluded his memo: "Before she left the office I warned Mrs. Kent about the publicity which is expected in this case, hinting that she might wish to avoid it personally. I am not sure, however, as to what action she will take in this respect."[13]

On State Department stationery, in the presence of Shaw's messenger, Mrs. Kent wrote a short note, addressed to the Secretary of State by title rather than name, in which she asked him to obtain further information concerning the arrest of her son, and to keep her advised of his whereabouts and his welfare. The next day, June 1, she retained the services of a lawyer, Edmund Campbell, whom she specifically asked to find out from the Department "what act or acts on the part of my son prompted our Ambassador to turn him over to the British authorities rather than send him back to the States, at this moment when England is in the mad fury of war."[14]

Officials at the State Department, acting out of fear and guilt, kept Mrs. Kent at arm's length. They treated her as if she were a threatening busybody who had no right to pry into a matter of state that happened to concern her son. No one in the department ever acknowledged her position as a State Department widow or paid deference to the loyalty that such an allegiance might have invited. From the top of the bureaucracy down, those involved in the Kent matter treated Mrs. Kent as they might have treated anyone with whom they had nothing in common other than some bureaucratic matter of a low importance. As men with wives and mothers, however, they acted with well-informed and self-protective urgency and as a team. Mrs. Kent, they perceived correctly, embodied a force with which they didn't want to contend.

On June 5, Mrs. Kent once again appealed to the Secretary of State. "My dear Mr. Secretary," she wrote, "I beg you to review carefully the following case which, since it concerns my only son, is in effect my own case. It is also, I believe, one which has been handled in a manner disloyal to the protection of our citizens in foreign countries, and especially to our citizens in the service of this department abroad."[15] She assumed, because she had not learned otherwise, that Ambassador Kennedy had turned her son over to the British authorities without any knowledge of the Department of State or the secretary, and she addressed this detail when she wrote. "Apparently this astonishing action was taken by our Ambassador in London without consulting you, for it seems the first news the State Department had of the matter came as a result of a personal cable which I had asked them to send a few days previously, asking for news of my son's health."[16]

No one had yet told Mrs. Kent why the ambassador had fired her son or why British police had detained him. "I do not know of what offense my son is charged," she wrote. "Apparently, however, the offense of which he is suspected is a political and not a personal crime. According to my information from the Department, my son had been under investigation by Scotland Yard for several weeks prior to his dismissal, and his dismissal occurred in order to facilitate his arrest by the authorities of a foreign government." Mrs. Kent understandably found this detail astounding. "Regardless of the acts of which my son is suspected of having committed," she wrote, "it is inconceivable to me that this country could so treat one of its own citizens in its own Foreign Service. He has not been convicted of any offense,—and how unfair it is under these circumstances, and on the suspicion of a political offense, to turn him over to the authorities of another country during the hysteria of war, for it seems to me that the only fair course would have been to repatriate the offending clerk at once with the recommendation that he be dismissed from the Service on safer soil than that of a nation at war seeking to try him before a military court."[17]

Mrs. Kent admitted what others who knew him could have said of Kent. "It may be that my son has been imprudently outspoken. His birth and the greater part of his upbringing abroad, while his late father held various consular posts, together with a singular ability to master foreign languages and foreign thought, have led to a youthful opinionated manner of expressing himself, —and besides he is bitter over the uselessness of the present carnage. But whatever error on his part may have brought about his present predicament, I plead for his own people not to desert him, and I appeal to you now to use all of your good offices to have my son sent home from England at once."[18]

In closing, Mrs. Kent also wrote, "It would be a great consideration if you could spare a few moments to see me personally in this matter."[19]

When they mentioned the Tyler Kent affair, men in government service often expressed parenthetically the respect in which they held Kent's family. Robin Campbell, the son of Sir Ronald Campbell, the British ambassador to France, wrote a letter to Sir Alexander Cadogan, the British foreign minister, on June 8, to tell him that William Bullitt had talked to him about Kent "the other day." "He said he had known him for a long time; that he came from a very good family, but was a complete rotter and always had been."[20] Ambassador Kennedy, when he had occasion to speak of Kent, verbally doffed his hat to Mrs. Kent. In his diary Breckinridge Long observed of Kent that "He comes from an old Virginia family, was recommended by Harry Byrd . . ."[21]

Bullitt, ambassador to France, and Kennedy, ambassador to Great Britain, square off against each other while trying to influence the hand of the Military Affairs Committee in Washington, D.C., on January 10, 1939. (PHOTO COURTESY OF THE HOWARD GOTLIEB ARCHIVAL RESEARCH CENTER AT BOSTON UNIVERSITY)

Yet the qualities that these men and others acknowledged never compelled any of them to lift a finger on behalf of Tyler Kent for the sake of his family. On the contrary, they reacted to news of his alleged misdeeds with hair-trigger rage: "The sooner you shoot him the better," Bullitt told Campbell, and, as Campbell wrote Cadogan, "he kept on repeating 'I hope you will shoot him, and shoot him soon: I mean it.'"[22] Had America already entered the war, Kennedy later told a Scripps Howard reporter, "I would have recommended that he be brought back to the United States and been shot."[23] Shooting Tyler Kent—and how and when—was one matter that Kennedy and Bullitt, who otherwise cordially despised one another, might happily have discussed.

The benefactors and connections both inside the State Department and beyond it, about which Kent evidently had boasted, now fell silent:

Moore, Carr, Byrd, and even Hull. Cordell Hull especially determined to keep Mrs. Kent at bay. Mother and son had become pariahs to their State Department friends, because to those few who still remained, they now represented a liability in the State Department civil war that continued to blister between the old guard politicos and the faction represented by Undersecretary of State Sumner Welles, who occupied the number-two State Department job that Walton Moore had coveted. Now Welles, as undersecretary, had more power than Hull, and more influence. While the secretary of state had too much political acumen to try to outmaneuver Welles, and thereby held onto his job, Walton Moore and his protégé William Bullitt fully intended to take their revenge on Welles, a cause that would require the ear of President Roosevelt. You don't attract the president's kindest considerations when you befriend either the man, or the mother of the man, caught conspiring against him.

Add to all this the awkwardness of the death of Henry Antheil, the code clerk whom Tyler Kent replaced in the London embassy at the very last minute, much to the annoyance of Joseph Kennedy. On June 14, 1940, the Helsinki embassy sent Antheil across the Gulf of Finland on a Finnish Airlines plane to retrieve documents that members of the American embassy in Tallinn had left behind when forced to flee to Finland, to escape the rapid advance of Soviet troops on the Estonian capital.[24]

It was a sixty-mile journey from which Antheil never returned. His aircraft went down into deep waters six miles off the Estonian coast, shot down by gunners on an enemy submarine. The submarine crew then gathered the classified US documents that Antheil had been sent to rescue. Like Kent, Antheil habitually helped himself to confidential documents—some falsified, others not. Robert McClintock, secretary of Legation, discovered many of them in manila envelopes in Antheil's clothes closet. As Breckinridge Long confided to his diary: "The clerk who was killed in an airplane flying from Tallinn to Helsinki as courier seems to have been somewhat indiscreet." He added, "Examinations of his effects after his death disclosed copies of some code messages in his room and a confidential letter he was not supposed to have which apparently had been opened and was addressed to Kirk in Berlin."[25]

In view of what subsequently came to light about Kent, Long found the information about Antheil disturbing, to say the least. "Both of them spoke Russian and were associates," he noted, "and both of them at least were indiscreet."[26]

Cordell Hull, who brilliantly could always remove himself from any situation that might cause political embarrassment, naturally wanted to distance himself from episodes like those involving Antheil and Kent. At the time that Mrs. Kent pleaded with him on her son's behalf, Hull was actually planning to succeed Roosevelt as president, or at least as the Democratic candidate.[27] No sitting president had ever campaigned for a third term, and Roosevelt hadn't yet signaled that he intended to introduce his name as a contender at the Chicago convention in early July. Hull had reason to believe that Roosevelt would support him as a candidate; indeed, the president had told him that he would in so many words. As secretary of state, Hull cleaved to the president's foreign policy—regardless of whether or not he liked it. In the civil war raging between interventionists and isolationists, Hull surely read the letter from Mrs. Kent with a sense of dismay, if he read it at all. She meant trouble. He doesn't appear to have responded.

Welles at this time was curiously noninterventionist. His trip through Europe, known as the Welles Peace Initiative, undertaken without Hull's approval, had inspired very little hope that Hitler could be restrained, although Mussolini and Count Ciano, the dictator's foreign minister and son-in-law, had impressed Welles with hopes of the possibility.

On June 10, France fell. Italy then declared war on France. Roosevelt fumed. At the University of Virginia Law School commencement ceremonies, where he spoke that day, the president declared that Italy had stabbed France in the back. The Welles Peace Initiative had died.[28]

It was a dark day in Europe, but that day decided the course that Roosevelt subsequently took. In July, at the nominating convention in Chicago, he permitted his name to be entered in the balloting process. Thus began his active assault on the isolationist resistance that until then he had so shrewdly baffled, even as he had cultivated a back-channel correspondence with Churchill that Kent had all but exposed.

On June 11, Ambassador Kennedy informed Secretary of State Hull that the governor of Brixton Prison, at the behest of the War Office, had issued the following oral communiqué to Kent: "As the officer from the War Office who saw you here on the 28th May 1940 informed you, you have the right to consult a solicitor, if you so desire. Since I notice that, unlike many of the 18B prisoners, you have not done so, and since also you are not a British subject, I have sent for you to remind you of your right to see a solicitor, so that there shall be no misunderstanding about the matter."[29]

In a memorandum dated the next day, G. Howland Shaw wrote that he had telephoned Mrs. Kent to inform her "on the basis of telegrams just received from the Embassy in London" that he "was in a position to state: (1) that her son will be charged and put on trial shortly; (2) that the trial will not be a military one or under military law; and (3) that her son will have counsel and that a representative of the Embassy will be present at the trial."[30]

Justice would be done even as bombs rained down from the heavens.

TEN

The Dungeon

*It must have cost him a tremendous effort to keep his courage so
bright during all those months in London when I was seeing him
very frequently; it was always he who cheered me.*
—IRENE DANISCHEWSKY TO ANNE PATRICK KENT,
JULY 1941

A WOMAN OF SOME REFINEMENT, DAUGHTER OF WHITE RUSSIAN
émigrés, carried off to exile in 1916, as she once put it, "By a nurse, an
undernurse & a nursemaid," and educated in Catholic schools, Irene
Danischewsky disliked the police raid that she witnessed on the morning of May 20 at 47 Gloucester Place. To her, the police intrusion represented a shocking explosion for which nothing in her experience had
prepared her. As she wrote at the end of the war to Kent's mother, "the
circumstances of the arrest were extremely painful & embarrassing to
me." She had no idea "who the five or six men were who literally 'broke
in' upon us, on that morning of May 20, 1940," who then separated the
lovers and "independently searched" them. She also found offensive

the manner with which the police addressed her lover, as though he were already an established criminal.[1] Which of course he was.

As Gowen reported, Maxwell Knight possessed a certain sensitivity to the nature of Irene's relationship with Kent. The MI5 officer, true to his name in the circumstances, allowed her to dress—if under police supervision—and let her go home. The full force of the experience struck her outside. "I seemed to drift into the park feeling as though a skyscraper had fallen on my head & all my limbs been torn out of their sockets," Irene later wrote to Kent. "It was such a gorgeous day and we had planned to go to Kew!"[2]

In that state she telephoned the embassy to alert Kent's colleagues of the crisis. Convinced that Kent had fallen victim to some police blunder, Irene must have assumed that the embassy had cleared up the matter when she phoned Kent and arranged to meet him outside for lunch, unaware that it was Gowen who was instructing her to wait.

As he escorted her home, Inspector Pearson brought her up-to-date with a series of sharp bulletins calculated to frighten her and undermine her self-esteem. "I was threatened," Irene later wrote in a letter to Kent's mother, "that if I persisted in demanding to see Tyler & trying to help him, I would find myself in jail! It was pointed out that under regulation 18B anyone maintaining contact with a person of proved 'enemy sympathies' could be detained." She continued: "Then a Scotland Yard official (one of those present at the arrest & who had questioned me a great deal) told me that I was 'one of at least 4 women' whom Tyler was in the habit of 'entertaining'! That kind of dirt was used many times to persuade me to make a break with Tyler or to blacken his character."[3]

Pearson's warnings ring now, as they did when Irene heard them, with an extralegal chord consistent with the tone of the police raid on Kent's rooms: a political sting for the purpose of capturing prey of far greater stature than the code clerk.

The success of the officials' creative performance, their arrest of the code clerk, and his captivity all depended on top secrecy. But Irene Danischewsky witnessed the operation—and walked away. When she appeared at the embassy at lunchtime, Inspector Pearson could reasonably suppose that she might endanger its secrecy, so he made it his job to frighten her into silence. It was an ill-considered approach to employ with a woman of Irene's intelligence, suggesting a certain obtuseness if not unseemly panic on his part.

To Pearson's credit, and to Knight's, the police examination of Irene Danischewsky's apartment took place when they knew her husband would be absent. Alexander Danischewsky hadn't yet gone off to war, was still living at home, and was, according to Irene, unaware of her relationship with Kent. Nothing that Inspector Pearson said or did that afternoon, however, would have silenced her. She immediately determined to find out Kent's location, and, when she did, she demanded to see him.

❧

Why Irene Danischewsky came to violate her marriage vows she never explained for the record. Her husband, Alexander, came from a family of eight children, five sons and three daughters of Israel and Elena Danischewsky, prosperous Russian émigrés of Jewish origin. In fleeing the Russian Revolution, his father and family had abandoned an established tar and turpentine business and fled the city of Archangel for London, where, in the Sydenham neighborhood, he launched himself as an entrepreneur.[4] Alexander and Irene had been married for six years, childlessly, at the time that Irene met Kent. In January 1940, Alexander Danischewsky was serving as an infantryman in the British Army. (He subsequently served in Asia, where he took part in the Burma Campaign as a gunner.)

Irene evidently loved her husband, worried about him during war-time, remained his wife up to the time of his death, and, in an interview in the 1970s, asserted that, apart from her affair with Kent, she had remained faithful throughout their long marriage. She eventually came clean to her husband about her relationship with Kent. Always open about her feelings, she never expressed embarrassment over any of them. Not that she was ever overly indiscreet, but, on occasions when she might have done so, she never exhibited any shame in her comportment. She never apologized either for her infidelity or for loving Kent.

Tyler and Irene met under the romantic spell of the White Russian Ball, in which the attire, music, and the very language itself dictated the illusion of attending a court ball in St. Petersburg. The imaginary circumstance nevertheless felt enchantingly real to the White Russian émigrés who came together to reclaim their lost world in the shared spirit of nostalgia. Herself the child of White Russian émigrés, Irene drifted naturally through this scene. A gallant Virginia courtier with fluency in Russian and a palpable sense of entitlement, Kent could convincingly pretend that he belonged.

Right away Irene came to his rooms to see him, and thus began their passionate affair. How much of his heart Kent gave her remains a mystery, although given his vanity and narcissism, we might doubt that he gave her much. Whatever he did give flattered Irene and inflamed in her a passion that gave her great joy and at the same time spoke for itself. The lovers shared the romantic illusion of exile that shades so easily into delusion. She came to adore him completely and accepted him for everything he said he was. As Jean Cocteau once said of his visits to Marcel Proust, "I listened with the ears of my heart."[5]

Irene wrote to Mrs. Kent that she was "politically aloof." She was neither anti-Semitic nor pro-Nazi, although she understandably may have harbored anti-Bolshevik thoughts, an attitude later set aside when

Hitler invaded the Soviet Union in June 1941. They had a good time together, Kent and Irene. He liked Russian women. He found her entertaining, even out of bed: well-read, well-spoken, and able to converse in Russian. She knew good places to visit on foot, or farther afield in the countryside, by car, especially in the soft spring of that year. Who knows? In his time with Irene, Kent may have found a relaxing diversion from his other, more pressing concerns: his archive, whether to use it, and how. For her, he may have provided a diversion in the vacuum of aimlessness created when her husband joined the army.

An adventure such as she enjoyed with Kent would not have been uncharacteristic of the other Danischewsky in-laws, which may explain why Irene showed no sense of remorse about her actions. The Danischewskys comprised a great, colorful tribe. Israel Danischewsky commanded the affection of his large family, and as her letters attest, Irene, along with her husband's sisters-in-law (none Jewish), had a strong attachment to the patriarch. In Sydenham, he ran a cheerful if eccentric household. Their Hasidic lineage, as well as their Russian heritage, happily distinguished the Danischewskys but didn't altogether define them.

As newly arrived émigrés, they had made the North Russian Association in Baron's Court the center of their social life, discovering there the Russian exile colony. Irene's brother-in-law Monja, chiefly a screenwriter, later produced *Whisky Galore,* and wrote the scripts for *The Battle of the Sexes* and *Topkapi.* He also wrote about the North Russian Association in his memoir, *White Russian—Red Face,* and the assorted émigrés, rich and poor, with whom he and his brothers put on plays and attended dances, the latter of which "were formal and old-fashioned but extremely gay and our English friends liked to be asked to them."[6]

"We were romantically minded, our family, and have remained so," Monja Danischewsky wrote. "Romance was something to be encouraged and nurtured." Alex, "a romantic with curly hair," was "the poet of the family."[7]

Given the romantic and generous, worldly and successful family into which she had married, Irene seems to have been acting in keeping with its spirit by entertaining a *folie d'amour*. Then again, this family—who had only decades earlier fled Russia for their lives, and established themselves not without difficulty on British soil—would have found any police intrusion unsettling. Irene's determination to stay by Kent's side after his arrest might have troubled the patriarch and his kin far more, however.

At first, as Gowen reported in his *aide-mémoire*, and as Irene wrote in a letter to Mrs. Kent after the war, Scotland Yard tried to frighten Irene away from taking up Kent's cause by threatening to report her liaison to her husband. British authorities even examined her status as a naturalized citizen of the UK. Meanwhile, American and British authorities plotted together to conceal Kent's whereabouts so he couldn't get word out through, or to, any interested person, including Irene, about his arrest or detainment.

Irene simply wouldn't accept his disappearance. She fought to visit him *in loco uxoris*, wearing away at Maxwell Knight until he finally decided it safer to let her see him. Her outrage and belief that Kent was an innocent victim fueled her passion. "I admire him for his many great qualities of courage & character & because I consider now & always have that the circumstances in which he found himself were extremely unjust & harsh," she wrote Mrs. Kent in 1945. "The only thing which can impress me are his own words— & the only explanation he gave me shortly after his arrest. That whatever he did, he considered it for the best interest of his own country & mine."[8]

In Brixton, Kent lived the slow-going prison life. He took news as it came, ate his prison food, and waited more or less in silence for word to come about his case, his situation, his mother. But however he waited, he waited on the convenience of others, repaying the insult of imprisonment with an attitude of indifference. When permitted, he issued only the tersest of communiqués, and only to his mother. She sent him a message on June 3, to which her son belatedly responded: "Received your note, thanks. I am quite well, don't worry."[9] The embassy transmitted this message to Mrs. Kent on June 24, via the State Department.

Twice the War Office advised him that he had the right to consult a solicitor. In fact, the public prosecutor *wanted* him to do so. By June 11, the prosecutor had prepared the basis of a case, planning to charge Kent with larceny, and the graver offense of violating the Official Secrets Act of 1911. He didn't bring charges against Kent, however, although impatient to do so, because to make a case that Kent had violated the Official Secrets Act, the prosecutor needed copies of the Churchill-Roosevelt telegrams that Kent had shown to Wolkoff. Those messages had to serve as evidence to persuade a jury to believe that Kent had transferred to Baroness Wolkoff information damaging to the British war effort.

These telegrams were the property of the US government. The public prosecutor had asked the Department of State for the opportunity to examine them, through Ambassador Kennedy. The ambassador, having consigned his code clerk to them with no apparent reluctance, now found himself the intermediary from whom British authorities needed help in the difficult matter of securing State Department cooperation. Cordell Hull and his team consented to let the public prosecutor use two Churchill telegrams, both sent to FDR while he was still First Lord of the Admiralty, which Kent had allowed Wolkoff to copy—intentionally or not. The Americans refused, however, to let the public prosecutor have either the Churchill telegram of May 16, sent while prime minister to Roosevelt, or Roosevelt's response, which Kent had shown to Wolkoff, and which Christabel Nicholson had copied by hand. Both of these provided evidence far more damaging to Kent, not to mention Christabel Nicholson, whom the British authorities had interned and intended to prosecute on charges of espionage.

"Churchill's letter was a plea and a confession of defeat," Breckinridge Long confided to his diary. "The President did not accede to his request, but the very correspondence might be hurtful. So we withdrew permission to see or use it on the theory they had enough to convict without them."[10]

Thus began a stalemate that lasted for weeks. Kent could have solved this problem by pleading guilty to the charges as any top-notch solicitor would have advised him to do, or so the British authorities believed. But Kent made no move to engage a lawyer with whom the public prosecutor could negotiate a plea bargain. Eventually it fell to Kennedy himself to secure a solicitor for Kent, when, on August 1, the public prosecutor entered charges, among others, of two counts of larceny and violating the Official Secrets Act.

Kent spent these long summer days in the cramped twilight of uncertainty. At this time he could imagine more than one outcome to his situation, and for that reason, in his state of passive stoicism, he may have felt almost buoyant. Irene had won the right to visit him conjugally in prison. How much her visits lifted his spirits we don't know. He was never anything but reticent about her, and none of his later letters to her survive to provide clues to how he felt. For almost his entire life, he kept the wartime letters that she wrote to him. Not all of them, but those from January 1, 1944, through 1945. In these fifty-plus love letters—so informative on a range of subjects, including life in wartime London—Irene provides private glimpses of a violently emotional, often angry, and sometimes affectionate man. He came to depend on her as his only contact with the outside world.

The angel in his life, Irene never lost her faith in his essential goodness and innocence. She brought him food and books, tended to his belongings, mended his clothes, and liaised between him and the world in various ways: in letters to his mother, in legal matters, in negotiating sessions with Maxwell Knight. Days turned into weeks; weeks became months; months stretched into years, during which Kent remained foremost in Irene's consideration.

His plight accelerated her passionate love for Kent. This love, which inspires the language of her letters, and gave Irene the energy to go to such extraordinary pains on his behalf, may have dismayed the prisoner even as he came to depend upon it. Kent, though, may have expected of Irene nothing less than unconditional love. His sense of wronged entitlement ran deep, after all.

In the meantime, heroism hung in the air above the English Channel and the southern coast of England. In the summer of 1940, the pilots of the Royal Air Force took to the skies in Hurricanes and Spitfires to battle warplanes dispatched by Air Minister Hermann Goering in wave after wave of bombing, intended to bring Great Britain to its knees so that Hitler's troops could invade. The Battle of Britain had begun. The monstrous titans clashed almost soundlessly and outside the visible limits of business as usual in the warmth of those summer months. Few even knew that their destiny as a people depended on the outcome.[11]

In August 1940, in the course of this epic engagement of weaponry and opposing wills, the public prosecutor formally entered his charges against Kent. Through the offices of the New York law firm Breed, Abbott, and Morgan, Ambassador Kennedy personally arranged to engage a British solicitor for Kent named Graham Maw—an evocative name, on several counts, if ever there were one.

Kent's defense took the case on or around August 4, with a trial date set for August 9. That timing might seem criminally swift, but, as it happened, the trial was postponed, possibly by agreement between the prime minister and State Department officials representing Roosevelt, who couldn't risk the public criticism to which Kent's trial—no matter how secret—might expose him. Preparations for the trial extended into the last week of October, and the trial of the Code Room spy began as the presidential election drew to a close.

ELEVEN

The Trial

Defend the children of the poor & punish the wrongdoer.
—Motto above the entrance to the Old Bailey

Thanks to British physicist Robert Watson-Watt, his countrymen could, in the course of the Battle of Britain, anticipate the approach of enemy aircraft. His radio detection and ranging technology—shortened to RADAR before losing its capitalization—gave them an advantage on which the daring young pilots of the RAF built the success of their striking force against the massive Luftwaffe assault. In the air war of 1940, German pilots inflicted terrible losses on the British, but they never knew how close they had come to victory. Instead, the British exacted a surgical toll on the German bombers, forcing Hitler to shelve Operation Sea Lion, his plan for invading Great Britain. The RAF had frustrated his scheme to knock out British forces on the Channel coast from the air and launch his invasion by water. The summer drew to an end. The weather promised to turn nasty on the armada the Nazis had assembled.

Changing his strategy, Hitler began to punish the British by mercilessly bombing London at night. He wanted to crush their indomitable spirit, even if that entailed the immense slaughter of British civilians and the decimation by fire of whole city blocks. The *blitzkrieg* came in September, a sort of unstated drift in the Nazi war aim. Hitler initially had misgivings about the use of terror, which he soon shook off. Subsequently the Nazis gave themselves up to a *Walpurgisnacht* of military murder.

"From September 7 to November 3," Winston Churchill wrote in *Their Finest Hour,* "an average of two hundred German bombers attacked London every night."[1] The Blitz took London by surprise. No one had made preparations for this kind of airborne terror. No bomb shelters existed, nor any organizing system for the protection of citizens.

"The blitz," Malcolm Muggeridge wrote, "was a kind of protracted debauch, with the shape of orderly living shattered, all restraints removed, barriers non-existent. It gave me the same feeling a debauch did, of, as it were, floating loose; of having slipped one's moorings." It "became a sort of apocalyptic *son et lumière,* a nightly spectacle widely appreciated. When it began, with sirens sounding the alert, everyone scattered—to air raid shelters if they had one, or to cellars and basements or to special little nests under tables or stairs; wherever they might hope to have some sense of security, real or illusory. A few, in places like the Dorchester, tucked up in beds arranged in the basement, resplendent in dressing gowns and negligees; many others repaired to the nearest underground station, where they bedded down on the platforms and along the draughty corridors, apparently oblivious to the roar of trains, coming and going, and the passengers passing."[2]

As he passed his dreary days and bleak nights in the confines of Brixton, awaiting his trial, the Blitz provided Kent a certain relief from life as usual. He recalled it to his mother in a letter written in 1943:

"Speaking of bombs, I was in London all during the Blitz and I shall be able to tell you some day what it feels like to have them raining down on all sides and the sky full of flares, flames and smoke. Nobody in America has as yet had that experience. Take it from me, it is quite a thrill."[3]

—◆—

On October 23, *Rex vs. Tyler Gatewood Kent* opened at the Old Bailey, a venerable institution in the center of London, nestled in a warren of backstreets between St. Paul's Cathedral and the Thames embankment. It began in an atmosphere of unhurried solemnity in contrast with the racket raised by wartime chaos outside the courtroom windows, covered with brown paper to ensure secrecy. The trial was held *in camera*. The press was barred, as were all but those directly involved in the proceedings.

American Embassy Consul John Erhardt, who had known Kent in his youth, attended. He had served in Liverpool while the Kents did the same across the Irish Sea in nearby Belfast, where William Kent served as consul. In the younger Kent's trial, Erhardt served as the US embassy witness.

Also present, as it happened, was journalist Malcolm Muggeridge, at the time in the Field Service, a Home Office unit, to which he was attached for wartime duty. Colonel Ross-Atkinson, his commanding officer, had assigned Muggeridge to observe the proceedings. "There was no really valid reason for my presence at the Old Bailey," Muggeridge later recalled, "but each day I gave Col. Ross-Atkinson a new thrilling installment of how things were going, which he greatly appreciated; especially any episodes reflecting on MI5's handling of the case—of which there was no lack."[4]

Muggeridge found the spectacle of the proceedings absorbing. "The fact that every now and again the sirens sounded, and one

The Old Bailey today in the Holborn area of London, with its famous inscription.
(PHOTO BY AUTHOR)

and all—Judge, Learned Counsel, prisoners, witnesses—repaired to underground cellars to await the All Clear, only added to the drama. Outside, such sound and fury; inside, the Judge with his wheezy dispassionateness, doodling or listening with closed eyes to interminable cross-examinations. A strange, remote, barely human figure; glasses on beaked nose, layers of wig, and folds of cloth about his withered person, fingers tapping, or scribbling down a word or two."[5] This was Justice Richard Tucker of the Central Criminal Court.

Arguing the case for the Crown was Sir William Jowitt, solicitor-general and, as such, a member of Churchill's Cabinet, whom the prime minister had appointed in May. A political historian once described Jowitt as "one of the political world's most nimble survivors."[6] He had served as a Liberal MP (1922–29), a Labour attorney general (1929–31), a National Labour candidate (1931), and, in 1939, a Labour MP.

Maurice Healy argued for the defense.[7] (Maw was Kent's solicitor, Healy a barrister. In England, only a barrister can argue before a judge. Maw put together Kent's defense team, including his barrister.) To Healy fell the task of defending Tyler Kent against two charges of larceny for having removed copies of documents from the embassy to his apartment, and five charges of having violated the Official Secrets Act of 1911 and its subsequent amendment in 1920. F. H. Hinsley and C. A. G. Simkins tell us in *British Intelligence in the Second World War* that the act was "widely drawn with a view to easing the task of the prosecution in cases involving the unauthorized acquisition, use, or retention of official information."[8]

The Official Secrets Act was and still is a catchall law, as Hinsley and Simkins explain it. "In the 1911 Act Section 1 penalised spying by providing for punishment where the information is calculated to be, or might be or is intended to be directly or indirectly useful to an enemy, and there is a wrongful intention amounting to a purpose prejudicial to the safety of the state; and Section 2 of the 1920 Act stipulated that communication or attempted communication with a foreign agent is evidence of obtaining or attempting to obtain such information."⁹ The law antithetically places on anyone in communication with an individual acting as a foreign agent the burden of proof of innocence. Churchill, as Home Secretary, had helped author the original act, proposed at a meeting that he chaired in July 1910 at the offices of the Committee of Imperial Defense in response to a wave of German spy fever.

As David Stafford writes, on a summer Friday afternoon in 1911, "when the House [of Commons] was virtually empty," Churchill steered the Official Secrets Act into passage. "The new Act eroded some long-standing principles of British law," Stafford observes in *Churchill and Secret Service*. "It not only reinforced the law against espionage, but also clamped down heavily on the unauthorised release of official information. Section 1 made it a felony for anyone, for a purpose that could be prejudicial to the safety or the interests of the state, to communicate any plan, drawing or other piece of official information that could be useful to an enemy. The hypothetical language meant there was no need to prove that actual harm has taken place. Guilt could be inferred from the circumstances of a person's behavior or character. It would be enough, for example, for a person simply to be caught in certain restricted places: the onus would be on the accused to prove innocence, not the prosecution guilt. Section 2 of the Act made both the unauthorised communication *and* receipt of any official information an offense. It was, in short, a highly illiberal and Draconian measure."¹⁰

That Tyler Kent had violated the Official Secrets Act had far graver implications than just larceny, but the larceny charge played an important role nevertheless in the Crown's case, because it supplied a plausible means of securing Kent's conviction in the event that a jury found him innocent of charges that he had endangered Britain's wartime security.

Healy, for the defense, asked Justice Tucker to dismiss the case altogether on the grounds that Kent, as a diplomat, possessed diplomatic immunity. This exact issue, on close inspection, forms an aspect of the law that at the time of *Rex vs. Kent* had been incompletely formulated—possibly because it had come up so infrequently in preceding centuries. Citing chapter and verse, Healy drew his definition of diplomatic immunity from Blackstone, a venerable sourcebook of British law, and *Hall's International Law,* to argue that only when "he commits any offense against the law of reason and nature, such as conspiring in the death of the King in whose land he is," can an ambassador be "condemned and executed for treason" or "tried for a criminal offense by the courts of the state to which he is accredited." Quoting Dicey's *Conflict of Laws,* he further argued that "The privilege of an ambassador or diplomatic agent extends to all persons associated in the performance of the duties of an embassy or legation."[11] Healy also asserted that, because the alleged acts of larceny had taken place in the embassy, they lay outside the jurisdiction of the United Kingdom, "and it would appear that no waiver of privilege could cover that point."[12]

On the matter of diplomatic immunity, Jowitt, for the Crown, conceded that Kent had possessed it—up to the moment when Kennedy waived it. Jowitt also insisted that from this moment, Kent was subject to British law. Exactly when Kennedy had waived Kent's immunity was unclear. He claimed to have waived it on May 19, before Knight broke into Kent's rooms, but no evidence ever supported this claim. Kennedy also claimed that the State Department had authorized him to waive it.

But that very morning, the opening day of Kent's trial, Kennedy conveniently had boarded an ocean liner that was steaming toward New York, a situation that prevented him from taking the stand.[13]

"It does not appear to be forthcoming, Mr. Healy," Justice Tucker intoned flatly, "and the matter must rest there."[14]

Healy insisted that after an ambassador had waived the diplomatic immunity of an agent, said waiver couldn't be enforced until the agent had ample time to leave the jurisdiction of the country in which he was serving. "An ambassador cannot rob his own subject of protection. It would be entirely contrary to the general principles of international law and the comity of nations that an ambassador should hand over one of his own subjects out of his own protection into the hands of the country in which he was arrested."

"What is your authority in regard to the question about reasonable period?" Justice Tucker inquired.

"Alas, it is the one thing that I cannot put my finger on today," Healy replied weakly.

But Healy eloquently pleaded for this extension of the privilege. "It would be a shocking thing in modern days where people take to a diplomatic career as a career and are moved from office to office and then country to country, if some person, having been persuaded to venture into a country—it might be to the Moscow legation where at one time Mr. Kent was—and through some malevolence on the part of the Ambassador, or for some reason, he suddenly found his diplomatic privilege waived. Then it would be a monstrous thing that he should be handed over to the mercy of a country into which he never would have ventured unless he had that protection. For these reasons, my Lord, I submit that there is no jurisdiction in this court to deal with this case."

Healy could cite no authority to support his assertion that the "premises of the Ambassador" were beyond the jurisdiction of the Crown. "I can only say that it is one of those matters that appears to have been assumed. One is familiar with the fact that no rates are payable in respect of an embassy"—the last sentence meaning that embassies don't pay taxes.

"But what is that based upon?" asked Justice Tucker.

"Surely it must be based upon the fact that the territory is outside the jurisdiction?"

"I do not know. It may be merely based upon the government's attitude towards foreign countries." The justice continued: "The whole doctrine of diplomatic privilege is an uncertain one. The learned writers are not in agreement as to whether the doctrine of diplomatic privilege is founded upon the fiction of ex-territoriality or whether it is not."[15]

What Justice Tucker called "ex-territoriality" historians more commonly call *extra*territoriality—a part of Chinese diplomatic tradition for a millennium. For Western powers in China, Great Britain prominent among them, extraterritoriality provided the rationale that allowed them to operate outside Chinese jurisdiction up to and including the time of Kent's trial. Justice Tucker nevertheless chose to see the issue from the angle of "an article published in the year 1895, where the learned author quotes a number of international lawyers as to the doctrine of ex-territoriality and states that the majority of the opinions are against the doctrine of ex-territoriality, and say that it does not exist at all. I do not think that the doctrine of diplomatic privilege has anything to do with ex-territoriality."

Without ruling on Healy's request to dismiss the trial, the justice adjourned the proceedings on day one in order to give Franklin Gowen, subpoenaed as a witness by the Crown, the time to hunt for Kennedy's letter of dismissal, which the ambassador had dispatched via Maxwell Knight to Kent on Cannon Row. Before he adjourned, however, Justice Tucker also heard a request entered by Healy to uncouple the Kent trial from that of Anna Wolkoff, scheduled to be heard concurrently. Because Kent didn't stand charged with conspiracy to assist Wolkoff in her use of the documents that he had shown her, Healy argued that Kent ought not to be tried jointly with her. In this matter, Tucker decided for Healy and granted Kent a separate trial, to be followed immediately by the trial of Baroness Wolkoff.

No document ever surfaced showing that Kennedy had waived Kent's immunity, or had even received permission to do so before Knight and company broke into his quarters and took him into custody. The prosecution produced the letter formally dismissing Kent from his embassy job—Knight had delivered it to Kent in his jail cell—the following day when the trial resumed.

Justice Tucker rejected Healy's plea to dismiss the case, siding with Jowitt, who had argued that Kent no longer possessed diplomatic immunity on August 1, when the charges against him were formally made. The trial proceeded.

Kent's lawyers entered a plea of not guilty on all counts. One by one, the prosecution called its witnesses: Maxwell Knight, promoted to major for his artful orchestration of the Kent-Wolkoff affair; Captain William Derek Stephens, deputy director of Naval Intelligence at the Admiralty, called as a witness to testify that the documents sent by "Naval Person" in the United States (Roosevelt) would be useful to an enemy; Guy Liddell of MI5; Franklin Gowen; Detective-Inspector Thomas Thompson of Scotland Yard; Detective-Inspector James O'Brien, also of Scotland Yard; Nicholas Smirnoff, the émigré photographer; Detective-Sergeant Harold Sutling of New Scotland Yard; and Hugh Rose Foss of the War Office Code and Cypher School.

The parade of witnesses continued on day three: Hélène de Munck and Marjorie Mackie of MI5; Thomas St. John Glasse, a staff officer in the Treaty Department of the Foreign Office, who produced the monthly lists of the Foreign Embassies and Legations and thereby verified the names of Jean Nieuwenhuys and Francesco Marigliano as second secretary of the Belgian embassy and assistant military attaché of the Italian embassy, respectively, as well as the locations of those embassies; Captain Thomas Argyll Robertson of the Department of

Military Intelligence; Malcolm Argles Frost, director of Intelligence at the BBC; and Harold Keeble, a Scotland Yard detective-inspector called briefly for testimony deemed unnecessary.

Once these witnesses had provided testimony and undergone cross-examination, Healy asked Justice Tucker to dismiss the larceny counts. Just as they couldn't prosecute someone who took papers from Paris to London, British police couldn't prosecute Kent for taking papers from the embassy to his home. He was still working the extra-territoriality angle.

"Larceny is continuous through every country it takes place [in]," the judge declared. "Case proceeds on this count (the extraterritorial question being open to question), and on the original charge that the telegrams were taken from the Ambassador, not the Embassy." He left it up to the jury to decide whether there was any intention to steal.

Then Kent was sworn in, and Healy began questioning him. He was trying to show that Kent had removed the documents from the embassy in London, as he had removed them from the embassy in Moscow, because, as Kent put it, he "gradually began to acquire evidence of American diplomats—agents—who were engaged in actively taking part in the formation of hostile coalitions in Europe, and all sorts of things of that nature, which they, of course, had no mandate to do."

"The idea that was maturing in my mind," Kent told Healy, "was that the circumstances might be brought to the attention of, say, the American Senators."

Kent singled out the following for mention: Bullitt in Paris and Biddle in Warsaw, both subjects of the White Paper issued by the German government, to prove that America had sought to encourage the Poles against the Germans before the war began, based, so the Germans claimed, on documents the conquerors had found in Warsaw.

Healy drew from Kent an assertion that he felt he had a duty to inform the American people of the policy discerned in the documents, which was to get America into the war. Indeed, of his duties, it was the higher one. Kent confessed candidly that he was anti-Semitic, and claimed that his experience of the Soviet Union had intensified his anti-Semitism, although he protested to Healy that he did not advocate violence as an anti-Semitic instrument of German policy.

In his defense, Kent professed ignorance of Anna Wolkoff's activities, but asserted that he had indeed shown documents, including Churchill's telegrams, to Captain Ramsay. He stated that when Wolkoff had asked to borrow them, he had assumed she was acting on behalf of Captain Ramsay. "I only knew Anna Wolkoff in relation to Captain Ramsay's more or less political activities, in a general way," Kent testified.

He also claimed to know very little about the Right Club—of which Captain Ramsay had made him not only a member, but a steward—except that it was somewhat political, anti-Semitic, anti-Masonic. He knew, he said, five members of the Right Club at most. His discussions with Captain Ramsay had less to do with the Right Club than with ideas they shared in common. "My conversations with Captain Ramsay were mostly on political matters," he insisted, "possibly unrelated to the activities of the club, and I did not discuss the club situation with him in any detail whatsoever." He had not attended meetings of the club. He knew nothing of the ledger when Captain Ramsay brandished it and asked him to keep it for him. "I did not know what it was at the time," Kent testified. "It was a locked ledger, with a brass lock on it."

Jowitt began his cross-examination of Kent at the end of day three and took it up again when the court reconvened on day four, Monday, October 28, after a weekend break. In his line of questioning on day four, Jowitt sought to elicit testimony from Kent that would betray pecuniary motives for appropriating embassy documents. He drew from Kent the acknowledgment that Barry Dennis, editor in chief of the International News Service, had interviewed him for a job in

New York in March 1939. Jowitt allowed the jury to infer that Kent, when he returned to Moscow, had intended to make use of documents that he had copied in his work as an INS correspondent. Kent also acknowledged that he had started to copy documents in London within the first ten days on the job. Among the documents supporting this statement were letters between the FBI and Scotland Yard that police had found in Kent's rooms. Jowitt invited Kent to explain how these related to the "higher duty" that Kent insisted provided the justification for the archive he had assembled.

Kent expressed his surprise that such a correspondence existed, "and the thought occurred to me at the time that there might be other people in America who would be interested in knowing that the American tax-payer was doing work for a foreign power, that is to say, paying for it. Then I later investigated this question in the archives of the Embassy, and I discovered that it was based on an executive agreement dating back to 1919 and was quite legitimate, and subsequent to that I lost interest in the matter."

Jowitt, however, drew Kent's attention to a letter dated November 7, also found in 47 Gloucester Place, that, as the solicitor-general put it, "deals with a certain man whose name begins with the letter F, who is regarded as a most important link in the Soviet Military Intelligence activities directed against" the British nation. "You see," Jowitt pointed out, "that they are asking for his business and private addresses to be searched, and if he could be thoroughly interrogated?" The jury could have no doubt of the value such information might impart to someone in Kent's position when Jowitt quoted the following passage from the letter: "We think it probable that a search of his premises may provide us with the names of persons who are now operating in the United Kingdom on behalf of the Soviet Government, and we are naturally anxious to get as much information as possible to assist us in our investigations here."

Though suspected of it, Anna Wolkoff hadn't yet been found guilty of espionage. To find Kent guilty of violating the Official Secrets Act, a jury needed proof only that Kent had been in contact with a person suspected of being an enemy agent, because he was the unauthorized purveyor of information that Kent himself conceded on the stand could be useful, "directly or indirectly," to an enemy.

Jowitt's cross-examination cast doubt on Kent's alleged motive—that he had a "higher duty," and eventually had intended to show relevant documents to the American people. Jowitt wondered how showing documents to Anna Wolkoff had anything to do with Kent's higher duty. Kent's defense: that he had given the copy of the Churchill telegram to Wolkoff because he thought she was going to take it to Captain Ramsay, for whom she acted as aide-de-camp. Jowitt pointed out that the telegram had nothing to do with any interest Kent shared with Captain Ramsay. He probed Kent on this matter. Kent held his ground, and convincingly so, when he told the solicitor-general that Ramsay hadn't known about the secret and possibly subversive correspondence between the First Lord of the Admiralty and the president, and was considering raising a question about it in Parliament. Jowitt quickly changed the subject. Kent's argument might show the jury too easily that Captain Ramsay was serving Kent's sense of higher duty, however indirectly.

Jowitt shifted his questioning to Wolkoff instead, regarding her anti-Semitism especially, and her pro-Nazi sympathies. Kent insisted that he hadn't known that Wolkoff was pro-Nazi, that he "had no reason to suppose that she was pro-Nazi," or anti-British.

"And you tell the jury that, having known Anna Wolkoff intimately for some time, you had not the least idea whether she was pro-German or pro-British?" Jowitt protested.

"As far as I knew, Anna Wolkoff was not particularly enthusiastic about the war in general, nor was Captain Ramsay or a great many other people in this country," Kent replied. "But that does not necessarily constitute her as being anti-British."

It was an enlightened response . . . which Jowitt backhanded down the line.

"So you selected as a person—a person who was not particularly enthusiastic about the war, to use your own phrase—you selected that person as somebody whom you would allow to browse at pleasure through your documents?"

Jowitt followed this rally with a series of half-volleys that established that Wolkoff pretty much had the run of Kent's rooms, which he had left unlocked for her convenience on at least one occasion. Moreover, the baroness had had easy access to Kent's archive, which he hadn't secured under lock and key.

Self-possessed and articulate, Kent handled himself throughout Jowitt's cross-examination with presence of mind. In the transcript, he sounds like a consular creature from birth—as he was—who preempted matters of grave diplomatic importance when the situation appeared to him to be falling into the hands of the wrong people. The archenemy who emerges from his testimony is not the president but the Foreign Service officers, who, as Kent answered Healy, were telling "half truths" to the executive branch about "the European situation as it was developing from 1933 onwards." On that basis the executive was making foreign policy. He singled out Bullitt in France and Biddle in Poland, reinforcing the Nazi White Paper, and, in cross-examination, accused Bullitt of "making false commentaries to the French government," and acting in such a way that "could involve the whole country in a catastrophe."[16]

In his autobiography, Muggeridge recalls Kent as "one of those intensely gentlemanly Americans who wear well-cut tailor-made suits, with waistcoat and watch-chain, drink wine instead of high balls, and easily become furiously indignant. They always strike me as being somehow a little mad. . . . A tour of duty in Moscow had given him a maniacally hostile attitude towards the Soviet regime, and an extra hatred of Roosevelt and his policies, besides fortifying his anti-Semitism."[17]

Toward the end of his cross-examination, Jowitt touched on two matters that could only reinforce doubts about Kent's character and stated motives. First in importance came the letter that Kent had written to Alexander Kirk, the *chargé d'affaires* in Berlin, whom Kent had known when they both had served in Moscow. As we've seen, the letter—dated February 24, 1940, and unknown to Ambassador Kennedy—asked Kirk whether he could secure a job for Kent in the Berlin embassy. Jowitt introduced it as evidence to suggest that Kent might have hoped either to sell his archive to the Nazis if he secured a transfer to Berlin, or that, once there, he might have continued the practice of appropriating documents perhaps in order to sell them.

Kent also had lied to Captain Knight about the glass negatives that the MI5 agent-runner had found in Kent's rooms. Smirnoff, the Russian émigré photographer, had made them when he'd photographed the Churchill telegrams that Wolkoff had borrowed. When Knight asked him about these negatives, Kent had told him that he'd photographed the documents himself to try out a camera he was interested in buying from one Hyman Goldstein, another clerk at the London embassy, since transferred to the Madrid embassy. He had lied, he told Jowitt from the stand, to protect Wolkoff, who he didn't realize had also fallen prey to the sting operation that Knight had conducted against him. He explained that this quick invention had come to mind because Goldstein had departed for Spain but hadn't yet reached Madrid, just then out of reach. The fabrication thus was harder to trace. Jowitt either overlooked or disregarded the obvious anti-Semitic aspect to the story.

Anna Wolkoff hadn't yet been tried and found guilty of acting as a foreign agent. She did stand accused, however, of being one, and enough evidence came to light at Kent's trial to suggest that she was, in the words of the amended Official Secrets Act, a "person who is or has been or is reasonably suspected of being or having been employed by a foreign power either directly or indirectly for the purpose of committing any act either within or without the United Kingdom prejudicial to the safety or interests of the State." By his own admission, Kent had shown Wolkoff information "directly or indirectly useful to an enemy"—in innocence or otherwise—so any jury would have found it impossible not to conclude that Kent had violated the Official Secrets Act.

In his summing up, Justice Tucker supplied the jury with a trenchant overview of the Official Secrets Act and its amendment that, in the transcript, reads like a barely veiled instruction to convict. As for the larceny charge, the justice provided a stark definition of the crime in his instructions. "If you take something, whether it is a piece of paper or a copy [of a] letter from the person to whom it belongs, it is no defence to say: 'But he would have torn it up in a day or two; it was no part of his permanent documents.' If it is stealing, it is stealing, and that is the matter for you to decide; but the seriousness or the technicality of it is for me."

On the subject of anti-Semitism, Justice Tucker proved more judicious. "This question of anti-Semitism crops up again and again in this case. Of course, in normal circumstances, if we were living in a world (I was going to say) where sanity prevailed, as in the good old days, people would be entitled to dislike Jews or not, as they wished. But one cannot shut one's eyes to the fact that anti-Semitism is one of the foundations of the creed and ideology of our enemies. That is the importance of it in this case: not peoples' likes or dislikes of Jews, but the fact that it is part of the Nazi creed and doctrine."

In his cross-examination, Jowitt had questioned Kent at some length about the anti-Semitic stickers, or "sticky-backs," that Wolkoff had left in his rooms, unbeknownst to him—or so he claimed. Justice

Tucker in his summing up added to this evidence by quoting from the letter, as he called it, that Wolkoff mailed, with the assistance of MI5, to Lord Haw-Haw. He quoted in its entirety, as well, Kent's letter to Kirk in Berlin. He reviewed the evidence *in extenso* and included in his review, as required, a summary of Kent's defense.

The jury retired for deliberation at 3:35 p.m. on Monday, October 28, 1940. It took them just twenty-five minutes to reach their verdict. They found Kent guilty on all five counts of violating the Official Secrets Act, and guilty on one count of larceny. Word reached the State Department via a news bulletin on ticker tape, within hours: "London—Tyler Kent today was found guilty by a jury at Old Bailey at a secret trial on charges of violating the British Official Secrets Act. Judge postponed sentence until after trial of his alleged confederate. Her trial opens tomorrow."

Wolkoff, too, was found guilty.

Justice Tucker sentenced Kent and Wolkoff on November 7. Kent received seven years of penal servitude, Wolkoff ten.

Muggeridge asserts that under other circumstances Kent would have appeared as a hero to many for trying to draw attention to Roosevelt's secret efforts to join the war in Europe. "When his sentence had been pronounced, Kent made an indignant protest, pointing out that he had acted throughout as a patriotic American anxious to keep his country out of a ruinous war. This was doubtless genuine enough, and if his illicit disclosure of secret papers had been leftwards instead of rightwards directed, he would have found himself, like Daniel Ellsberg, numbered among the contemporary saints, and appeared on post-Christendom's most notable stained glass window, *Time* Magazine."[18]

Mother's Plea

Nobody can misunderstand a boy like his own mother.

—NORMAN DOUGLAS

DANIEL ELLSBERG, WHO HAD WORKED IN THE DEFENSE DEPART-
MENT and the State Department during the Vietnam War, was a stra-
tegic analyst at the RAND Corporation when he photocopied the
7,000-page study of US decision-making in Vietnam commissioned
by Secretary of Defense Robert McNamara on which Ellsberg had
been working. This report entered history as the Pentagon Papers
when, in 1971, Ellsberg gave the study to the *New York Times,* the
Washington Post, and seventeen other newspapers. The US government
took Ellsberg to court on twelve charges of felony that, had he been
convicted, could have amounted to a prison sentence of 115 years. As
Malcolm Muggeridge observes, Ellsberg lived to become an American
hero of the anti–Vietnam War era. His trial, unlike Kent's, was dismissed in 1973 on grounds of governmental misconduct and figured
in the Nixon resignation.

The Tyler Kent affair, unlike the Daniel Ellsberg story, was buried alive. Although the results of Kent's trial made the news and Frank Kelley's account appeared in the *New York Herald Tribune* of November 8, 1940, with an accompanying photo of Kent, the story conveyed no sense of Kent's defense nor, perhaps understandably, any reference to the Churchill-Roosevelt correspondence prior to May 10, when Churchill became prime minister.

Word of the secret correspondence surfaced in the House of Commons in November 1941, when a Labour MP and bitter Churchill foe raised the issue. Herbert Morrison tried to put it to rest—the correspondence, its unorthodox and extralegal character, and Kent's role in trying to make it public—but it gathered force, especially in the minds of American isolationists.

Mrs. Kent put immense energy into drumming up support for her son in Washington. It was impossible for her to do so in London, where, throughout Kent's ordeal and imprisonment, she never went. She wanted to go to England and applied for a passport, which she was denied. More than anyone else she campaigned on her son's behalf: first, to secure more-lenient treatment for him from the time of his arrest, and then, as time went by and word of his arrest and the nature of his misdeeds emerged in more detail, to clear his name and obtain justice for him in American courts.

Though she utterly devoted herself to her son, Kent never rewarded her with much warmth. His reticence evidently pained her, but she never let that pain affect her maternal feelings. Distance and wartime barriers to communication undoubtedly aggravated her pain. After his arrest, Kent seems to have compounded the problem. He sent his mother two taciturn messages through the embassy to assure her that he was okay. For perhaps a year after his arrest, he didn't write her. He ascribed this fact to his tendency to be a "rotten correspondent."

Instead, he asked Irene Danischewsky to correspond with her. Irene tried to reassure Mrs. Kent when, in July 1941, she wrote that Kent couldn't quite trust himself to write to her, that "he was feeling very deeply for you & there were many difficulties in the way." She explained to Mrs. Kent that she was "mistaken in thinking that he has lost his faith in your faith in him but he is afraid that you have heard things to his disparagement & it hurts him to think that he cannot give you his defence."

Both Kent's sisters wrote to him, in 1941 and 1942, to tell their brother how much their mother was working on his behalf, and what a toll his troubles and her efforts had taken on her health, including attacks of angina pectoris. "Mother has had to sacrifice most of her friends on your account," Phoebe wrote bluntly on October 4, 1941, "but in spite of everything she still keeps faith in you and in the future."[1] Both sisters pleaded with Kent to write to their mother.

To G. Howland Shaw Mrs. Kent confided in January 1941 that "the consistently aloof attitude that her son has taken towards her since his troubles" indicated "an abnormal mental condition."[2] Mrs. Kent reiterated this notion, also put forth by Malcolm Muggeridge— that Kent might have become somewhat unhinged, and that his acts betrayed a certain emotional instability—in a five-page letter to President Roosevelt on July 24, 1942. In this appeal, she requested that her son be transferred to a Canadian internment camp—short of freeing him altogether—writing: "[W]hen he realized through your cables that before it was over the United States would have to drink the cup of woe to its dregs, I think he became a little mad."[3]

Kent may have been too distraught to write to his mother in the months following his trial, especially when his appeal, argued on his own behalf, failed. It became the darkest time of his imprisonment. In February and March 1941 in Wandsworth Prison—where Oscar Wilde famously had begun his own sentence some forty-five years earlier—Kent went on a hunger strike, feeling that he was succumbing to a nervous breakdown. It's not a stretch to imagine that he was. He faced a long imprisonment in the company of hardened criminals for committing an act, he claimed, that he innocently and blithely—if not madly—assumed to have been entirely appropriate and patriotic.[4]

Mrs. Kent never doubted this to be the case, and in her letter to the president she expresses some of the themes and beliefs that informed her son's behavior. "Our forebears came to this country before the American Revolution from Scotland and England, and my son has no other strain in his veins. We tilled the soil in the beautiful Shenandoah Valley of Virginia and became lawyers and doctors and preachers among those green hills from the colonial days until the present. The men in our family were rebels in the Revolution, soldiers in the War of 1812, died for the confederacy during the Civil War, and took part in the Spanish-American conflict." She sketched this family history to prepare her explanation of her son's subsequent career, and to show how, as a "keen observer and a very sensitive nature, he soon grew to hate the Communist methods and to have a great sympathy for the Russian people."[5]

Kent was a born student of international affairs, Mrs. Kent told the president. "During five years my son spent all of his vacations traveling in every corner of Europe. Hungering for the truth, speaking fluently several foreign languages, and being a very adaptable young man, it is extraordinary what representative persons he was able to contact in the various countries."[6]

In January 1941, in her interview at the Department of State with G. Howland Shaw, Mrs. Kent "attributed her son's downfall to the fact that he had been very lonely in Moscow, had been badly treated by commissioned officers there, and had thereupon been taken up by one of the secretaries of the German Embassy who had filled him with Nazi doctrine."[7] In her letter to the president she mentioned no such thing. Mrs. Kent, in her letter to Roosevelt, ascribes to her son a credible conviction that in 1939 Europe was headed for war. "In January 1939, he came home for a short vacation. We had many long talks. I found him grown serious and very troubled at the gathering war clouds and what he considered the American lack of understanding their significance. His reasoning was very clear and simple, i.e., side by side in the comparatively small congested area of the continent of Europe there could not exist Western culture and medieval despotism."[8]

Here in her thinking and, as she understood it, in that of her son intruded the theme of civil war—the seismic disruption to family honor and patriotism that still sent tremors through their lives as civil servants, and thus influenced how they perceived and interacted with the world.

"Poland was an unfortunate No Man's Land," Mrs. Kent wrote naively to Roosevelt. "Since mankind still knows no other way to settle its differences by force, a European Civil War was inevitable, with Russia and Germany as the principal actors. The same thing had occurred in our own Civil War when the clashing views of the Northern and Southern states had to be fought out seventy-five years ago." Mrs. Kent added, "My son also said very earnestly: 'This war must be localized by the great powers. It simply must not spread to the west; if it does there is no telling what will happen . . . Japan will attack us.'"[9] It was an easy statement to make after the Pearl Harbor and Manila attacks.

In Mrs. Kent's view, all that befell her son came about because he wanted to keep America out of yet another civil war. He was like a child trying to solve the marital problems of his parents. Victim of civil war, and dispossessed by it, he couldn't let it happen yet again, especially when the wrong side in the diplomatic equation seemed to be promoting it once again.

"Finally, in January 1940, when he sent his hopes for the bulwark of American strength in peace rather than in war crumbling under his eyes," Mrs. Kent wrote, "desperately he did the very wrong thing in showing copies of some of the cables to an esteemed friend, a Member of Parliament, and asking his advice. Knowing him as I do, my intuition tells me that my son was simply fanatically afraid of the spread of the war. He knew the stark, selfish realism of the European mind so well. Should we become involved, he believed the whole continent of Europe would turn itself into a self-sustaining fortress, from which could sally forth for years deadly sorties of submarines and planes. His burning passion was that we in the New World let the whole nasty, fighting mess of the Old World wear itself out, while from Hudson Bay to Patagonia we would guard jealously against the spread of the disease to these shores."[10]

In her zeal to seek justice and a surcease to the grim nightmare of her son's imprisonment, the stalwart and passionate Mrs. Kent eventually became convinced of the rightness of her son's cause—if she ever had any doubts—and fervently sought common cause with Roosevelt's political foes to vindicate him. In September 1944, the State Department issued his long account of the circumstances of Kent's arrest and trial, and almost simultaneously Joseph Kennedy issued his stunning denunciation of Kent—that if America had been at war when Kent's activities came to light, he would have had him sent home and shot.[11]

In April 1941, after his hunger strike, prison officials moved Kent to Camp Hill on the Isle of Wight.[12] His life had much improved, as he assured his mother in the occasional letters he now wrote her. At this minimum-security prison, he regained his health and composure. He worked on local farms during daylight hours, grew tan in the summertime, built up his strength, and tried to remain stoic as he waited out the war. In his free time, he read the many French and Russian books that Irene sent from London, along with British and American

Camp Hill Prison today, on the Isle of Wight, where Kent served
the majority of his seven-year sentence for larceny.

periodicals. As he resumed a correspondence with his mother, whom officials allowed him to write every fortnight, he tried not only to allay her worries about his health, but also to caution her about the efforts she made on his behalf, which included various legal strategies hatched by Don Harlan, a Detroit lawyer with a heartfelt if overheated commitment to Kent's cause. Harlan wanted to argue his case before the Supreme Court.

Kent, in his island repose, could see the folly of any such legal efforts. He thought the charges against him politically driven, and feared that he might have to face more charges upon his return to America after the war. He remained wary of arousing unnecessarily adverse publicity, willing though he was to confront Kennedy, who had already done just that.

He urged his mother to write to Irene, who, he wrote, "has been very kind to me during this period and comes to visit me as often as possible."[13] As for Harlan, "your Supreme Court lawyer," as Kent called him, he was skeptical. "I don't very much approve of the Supreme Court move, as from a purely legal point of view the State Department has an air-tight case. Please tell me something about the conditions on which Mr. Harlan took the case," he wrote. "Have you fallen into the hands of shysters, or are they decent people?"[14]

Kent knew that in the United States—thanks to the State Department press release and Kennedy's remarks—a groundswell of support for him had risen among isolationists, constructionists (who hold that only Congress may declare war), pacifists, and others. A. J. Muste and Scott Nearing wrote letters on his behalf to the State Department. Many of his supporters wrote to Kent. Somehow Kent had achieved his ambition if not his ultimate goal: influencing official American policy. In the eyes of his new confederates, he had become a martyr. He must have known this, even in his isolation. No longer the clerk or an anonymous man, he had burst forth into history.

Thirteen

Goodnight, Irene

With all my love and a kiss, good night, darling.
—Irene Danischewsky to Tyler Kent, August 3, 1945

Irene nurtured the sense of innocence betrayed that sustained Kent in those dark hours that he shared with England. Willingly and passionately she partook in Kent's ordeal to the extent that she could. Her shock at seeing her innocent lover so rudely apprehended brought forth in Irene an immense spirit of battle. It gave birth to a new self: passionate, devoted, aggressive, and great-hearted.

Kent wasn't her only cause; during the war she also ran shelters for bombing victims made homeless. Yet she found time over those four long years to invest in a more personal war on Kent's behalf. Her mad love for him fed her efforts to help him. The violation of his arrest and conviction fueled her passion. Her war on his behalf may even have made life in wartime Britain more bearable. In turn, the war, Kent's imprisonment, and her husband's absence gave Irene great freedom with which to lavish her feelings on Kent. In this rich climate her passion for him could expand and grow.

Whether Kent loved Irene at all is hard to say if not impossible to know. His letters to her have vanished. He was never really inclined to express himself in terms of personal feelings. "Write to me soon, darling," she wrote him, "and if you can, don't use your diplomatic training in your letters to me. I still can't understand the need for formality in your letters, but am not making a complaint, as I have liked all your letters." In another: "[A]s for you, honey—of course you are terribly Anglo-Saxon and quite incomprehensible to us lesser human species, and very impressive in your dignity & reserve."

They quarreled in writing and in person as lovers do, and shared moments of whimsy, exchanging fantasies of how, after the war, they might meet, and where. But how long, if Kent had not been taken from her, would their affair have lasted? He had other sexual dalliances, as she knew and seems to have accepted. Before the shock of his arrest they were relative strangers, though after Kent's imprisonment their conversation became very intimate. Still, Irene regretfully wrote, "Even before we parted you were quite incomprehensible to me, & I could weep now over the opportunities I lost to get to know you, and to let you know me. (On the many mornings when we used to meet.) It looked then as though there would be time enough to emerge slowly from the coating of reserve which everyone wears (even the Slavs who have been drilled into civilization). But as things happened it was a tragic waste of time (well, perhaps not waste!)—I was much too diffident with you, darling, perhaps you remember it, like an inexperienced school girl;—it was stupid?—but the theme is a difficult one to write about."

In the end, it didn't matter. It's not important whether Kent could return Irene's expressions of love in prison or whether he shared her passion. For over four years, he languished. In those years, Irene became the one person permitted to see him. Besides his mother, she

6 Palace Court today, the location of Irene Danischewsky's apartment.
(PHOTO BY AUTHOR)

alone corresponded with him. She linked him to his lawyer, to MI5, to prison authorities, and, at first, even to his own mother. She loved him.

"In my last letter to you," she wrote Kent, concerning their sexual union, "referring to the arts I think I wrote mainly about the technique of the art & perfection of execution. It would be difficult to overestimate this. But of course its main value and delight would be lost if the design were not a genuine & spontaneous one. It would also be hampered by a lack of consequence because the abandon required for the complete expression of a talent would be missing. Yes, the possibilities were all there but the design was not clear. It became clearer to me at least, just a fraction too late. That is what I have regretted so bitterly."

The sexual idyll they had shared before Kent's arrest—however much Irene may have regretted its absence—supplied her wartime rapture with the force of an erotic reality. She already had possessed him physically. Now her love for him could grow unfettered unless he rejected it—which under the circumstances Kent couldn't possibly afford. He needed her too much. Her letters to him suggest that he struggled furiously against her unconditional love.

She began her letters to Kent "Darling Tyler," or, less frequently, "My Dearest Tyler." She grew ever more affectionately expressive in signing them. "Good night, my love, I shall finish this letter tomorrow:—and a kiss" or "Well, darling, I am overcome with a wish to sleep & I must leave you in this letter—the better to dream of you, my love." "Darling," she closed one letter, "do you remember what I told you once in the vaults of the Old Bailey? I say it again. With complete conviction—and I kiss your hand. You have all my love." What had she told him? "I spoke the truth some months later," she wrote subsequently, "when I told you at the Old Bailey that I would love you all my life."

She expressed her rapture freely and at times quite playfully. "Penelope was a lady who could retire for 20 years to her latticed room at the top of a tall tower & work on her tapestry all day & unpick her stitches by night—then too, she had the faith of a reunion to sustain her. My blind pledge to you is worth another 20 of hers! But would you rather it were the identical one, darling? *Tous les baisers,* with my love, your Penelope Irene." "I love you, and until we meet, I send you *tous les baisers,* Irene," she signed a letter to him several weeks later. "I kiss you & I kiss your hand," went yet another envoi with a touch of the courtly love to which they both pretended now and again.

She knew how effusive she could be. "I have never written such 'affectionate' letters as mine are to you," she admitted, and, "I love you much too much. You must have realized that I loved you better than I said I did in 1940. Or than you could have guessed at the time. It is the same way now, but I may have to stop saying it soon." She reveled in the joy of intimacy that her letters allowed her. We can image his responses as taciturn at best.

Her openness versus his formality formed a theme in her letters in the guise of the Slav and the Anglo-Saxon. "I know from long association," she wrote in one of her last surviving letters, "that the Anglo-Saxon outward reserve is a protective shell which covers a nature more soft, sentimental & vulnerable, but less temperamental and sincere than the average Slav." In her analysis, the English were "temperamentally cold—but very warm-hearted and often succeed in being sincere—(with an effort!)—that is just generalizing—but it's a nice character amongst other nations. You are too much of an individualist to come under any category. I know that you are not cold; if you make me believe that you are really cold-hearted, I shall leave you at once." She astutely told him, though, that "you need, for your happiness, a much deeper relationship and a degree of loyalty than that which satisfies the average person. Regardless of nationality."

Once his intimate sexual companion, Irene now became his intimate friend in every other way. They even became spiritual companions of a sort as she suggests in her first letter of 1944 to him: "[T]hank you for spending New Year's Eve with me; it was very nice—I wonder if there is anything to such foolish superstitions?" She never hesitated to let him know of his unceasing presence in her thoughts. "I often wonder if you have shared at all in the very close companionship I have felt with you during all this time—or has it been an entirely one-sided experience for me alone?

"Speaking on the spiritual plane," she continued, "you have never been alone for a single night—or day either—except when I was possibly working so hard & was so tired that my mind was a blank anyway. To illustrate my point—even my habit of sleeping has changed. I always sleep now hugging a pillow case with both arms because it gave me a measure of relief to hold on to something & could act as an 'absorber' and a gag—I swear that I have known when you were particularly 'in the dumps'—nothing could persuade me otherwise! The time in Wandsworth is one example—I can't bear to dig up that misery even now—so I'll change the subject."

For his part, Kent needed her and relied on her. We can glimpse some of his rage and frustration—arisen from his forced passivity and his lack of control, to which she remained sensitive—between the lines of her letters. She rarely reminded him of her loyalty as she did in one letter written to reassure him of her affection: "I love you, you know that; & because I can't have a bad thought of you—you probably know that, too—and because I have never allowed anyone to speak badly of you even in the very early days when I could not see you. You may not know that."

She did respond forcibly, however, to his outbursts. When she had failed to challenge a decision by the governor of Kent's prison to prohibit visits, and Kent had sent her what she called a "very censorious letter," she wrote: "I do not quarrel with your right to write to me in your own particular way—or to administer a rebuke which I may deserve from you—because we have only these letters in which to express our thoughts—and because I have promised you all my loyalty & given you that right many times over." However, she continued, "Since you feel that you must punish me in your letters,—darling,—please, don't do it so ferociously. I don't know where to turn after receiving a letter such as the last."

These visits meant a great deal to them both, yet they lasted altogether too briefly—half an hour at most. For this monthly opportunity, Irene had to travel to the South Coast of England by train, board a ferry to Newport, then make her way to the prison. The round-trip consumed an entire day, and on occasion these visits grew tearful and anguished. "It was a nice visit & I enjoyed it very much, Tyler Pocahontas!—Although you were in your worst 'baiting' mood & things seemed against us & my own spirits were very low."

She understood his stress and always let him know it. "You do not have to remind me that your nerves are a little tense," she wrote. "I know what you have to contend with and I appreciate that you must give some vent to your feelings—looking back, I don't know how you have managed to remain so 'dauntless' during these wasted years. You hold all my respect and admiration, my sweetheart, but because we live in an inarticulate age, these are not easy sentiments to express. You know all this and more, darling, without my telling you—just to know that however 'formal' your style you do not really wish me to alter my own 'effusive' outpourings of the heart."

Well, perhaps he did. "I am somewhat insulted by your suggestion that I might be capable of using 'indirect pressure' or of taking vengeance on your 'helpless' self. For what? For why? And why 'helpless'? There is nothing I want, and you are not at all helpless in our assorted relationships—which is a good thing! Anyway, you are judging me on the level of the vast majority of women, & that is all wrong! It is nice to feel we have reached the stage of friendship and understanding when

I don't really mind very much your only too frequent insults. You don't 'play fair'—or else I'm used to a different set of rules!—When have I ever used those nasty little tricks during our long correspondence? On the contrary I have been 'told off' for writing too often & too much. Darling, I was very glad to receive your letter today."

Irene's unconditional love must have comforted Kent in his darkest moments, and, in the relative ease of his dull captivity, it must have distracted him if nothing else. He may have grown uneasy, however, about her rapturous tendency to idealize him, to make of him someone he knew he wasn't—even if he played a role in her imagination that he had encouraged her to entertain. She called him "Mon Prince d'Aquitaine." That title properly described Edward the Black Prince, son of King Edward III and father of King Richard II, but never king himself—a man dispossessed.

"You say in a post-script," she wrote Kent, "that you wonder if I shall ever understand your true character. Perhaps I have invented you entirely: how can I understand you better if I have not already understood you correctly by intuition alone? You must know fairly well how I think about you as my letters have not been very reticent, specially of late." Then she fashioned for him a flight of genealogical reverie that he might have found both alarming and quite pleasing. "I was so interested to hear about your progenitress, the Princess Pocahontas. You had not told me this story before, but it fits in beautifully with the character I have invented for you. Haven't I often told you that you look like a prince in fancy dress? Specially of late. In adverse circumstances it becomes more visible. I can 'invent' a character for your ancestress with equal ease. She was a completely autocratic & arrogant lady & God help anyone who crossed her will," Irene continues. "She was generous to her enemies & to the unfortunates because she despised them so much that she could not accept their feelings too."

How much of this invention do you suppose Kent himself contributed? "It made her impatient," Irene writes, "to see so many stupid people because her own standards were so high & could not be explained to them even if she had tried to do so—but she would not bother to do so. And indeed it would have been no use. It was really this that made her contract T.B. & not the climate & die in this country. Of course that is not all, but I'll tell you the rest when we go visit her tomb. In the meantime you could give me your version in your next letter."

In her next letter, Irene continued to address Kent's apprehension that she might not entirely understand him. "Of course I know that you are fickle, Tyler—Pocahontas—you think it is wiser to warn me in your letter about your nature. I wonder why? Is it because I persist in writing to you in an intimate manner? Do you think that I am a total idealist? You write in your letter: 'I think that you have to a certain extent invented me & that I shall not turn out as you expect. Don't let it go too far or else we shall not recognize each other when the "day" comes etc.'"

Beneath her questioning protestations, beneath the scent of Fugue by Roger & Gallet, with which she scented her letters to Kent, we can just make out the man in prison. Boldly, she wrote, "If I had to give an account of why I have stayed near you during this long time, I should say that at first I couldn't help myself; I was overwhelmed by an anxiety which I could not control, also by a sense of injustice—because whatever wartime measure led to your misfortune I think it is an injustice beyond repair or reason. But the chief reason for my persistence is still that 'unknown quantity.'" She assured him, "The only way in which I could be badly disillusioned would be if you were to say that I should never have tried to see you after May 1940 or written to you—that you did not want me to stay near you. Because then I really have tormented myself for a long time and plagued you into the bargain. To no purpose."

That he preserved over fifty letters that Irene wrote to him from January 1944 until his release from prison in October 1945 testifies to the value they had as rare, articulate messages of supreme love such as few men ever receive. Perhaps they gave him some sort of proof of redemption. Maybe they represented little more than a record of that time in his life when he achieved a certain notoriety. However he felt about the documents, Kent, a self-styled student of history who once had assembled a very different archive of correspondence, kept them and thereby preserved a record of life in wartime London.

Her letters teem with descriptions of the war-torn city, from when Hitler firebombed it with self-propelled V-1 and V-2 rocket bombs, known as doodlebugs, through the days leading up to the invasion of Normandy, to the final victory.

In January 1944, the air raids once again had started up. "There is a pretty noisy air raid going on at this moment—quite reminiscent of the old days," Irene wrote on January 21. "And a nasty pink glow to eastward. I am wondering if 'they' mean anything by it this time. I have just had to put on my tin hat to go upstairs to the 'ladies room'— (this is such an inconvenient & old-fashioned school building)—I shall remember this experience as a sign of these times. The shrapnel is coming down with loud clinking noises on the cement playground outside & the gunfire is so terrific that I can be sure we would not hear a bomb if it came down in the vicinity. I have just had another tour of perfection and found a nasty pink glow to westward as well as to eastward, so it looks as though the extremities of London are 'getting it' tonight."

The planning for Operation Overlord, directed by General Eisenhower, brought Americans to England in great number. "The Americans who are overrunning London and other places all look so light-hearted and bent on having a good time," Irene wrote. "I wonder if they have any conception of what they might be in for. They are terribly spoiled too; their clothing, canteens, accommodation, & entertainments are ridiculously lavish. At least they are in London. How are they going to do any fighting? You might enlighten one about your countrymen." She observed "Of course they (the Americans) will start off with at least one big advantage—they are wonderfully well-fed! And if soldiers march on their stomachs they will be great heroes in this war."

On February 4, she indicated that "We had quite a raid last night & another one in the early hours of this morning. With real bombs again this time. Some of our centres in this area have taken in 'Bombed Outs' today & I have just received the news that I must take over one of these centres tomorrow morning. Not Saunders Grove, but another one nearby which already has about 100 people & more drifting in. This sounds as if it were a bad raid, but actually it was very short & sharp & not at all up to the standard of the bad old days. It will be interesting to try my hand at the main job of work for which I have been trained & I hope that I shall remember all the rules & regulations & complicated legal junk which I am supposed to know."

It may seem as though Irene spent every waking moment writing to Kent, but she still found time to socialize. She wrote to him about Mrs. Churchill's Aid to Russia Ball at the Grosvenor: "It was a very unfamiliar spectacle and everyone looked rather sheepish about it. The food was horrible but there was lots of champagne and other drinks. Immediately on the left of our table were two long tables reserved for the Russians (Military Mission & Embassy)—I had quite a good time dancing with various Russian uniforms; on the right were some English society people & then the Americans. About halfway through the evening a famous 'Lady' on our right became very drunk & publicly beat up her husband. The Russians thought this was better than a cabaret and stood up to get a better view. An American at the other table ventured to protest about these 'goings on'— & was cursed in the most flowery language that I have ever heard—moreover the society lady then became so exasperated that she smashed a cup of hot coffee on the husband's head and the coffee dripped all down his face and white front. Then the press photographers arrived and photographed the happy family scene. What do you think of it? I have never seen such a breakdown of the conventions even in the Latimer Rd. Market."

On February 19, she wrote Kent over the course of several days, during which the Germans accelerated their bombing campaign. "I was more frightened than during the former raids; I think that my will to live must have become quite healthy again—or my wish to see you even greater. In any case the best I can do now is to pretend an indifference to the bombs, whereas before I really felt quite indifferent." She saw "that a lot of fires are still burning & that people have that uncombed and tired expression which we all wore back in 1941." But the real fireworks, as she put it, started the next night. "Our school was very badly blasted & the top floors put out of action—fortunately the ground floor which was reinforced was alright except for the windows—almost before the raid was over people started coming in, many in great distress. The other rest centre nearest to us had received a direct hit & could take no people—also two of the staff had been killed & it was burnt to the ground. It was the old kind of raid with fires burning all round—only much more concentrated & not so long."

Five nights in a row the Germans hammered Irene's part of London. "On Tuesday night, we were showered with incendiaries as well as other unpleasant things—there were dozens of them on the playground, but by some miracle none of them fell on the school. Some of the men in the centre went out and put these out with sandbags. We had lots of babies & children in the centre vomiting with fright & giving other natural demonstrations of terror & some of the grownups were just as bad."

On March 21, as she was writing Kent from her apartment across the street from Kensington Palace, an air-raid siren interrupted her.

"The 'warning' has just sounded & can no longer be treated with disrespect," Irene explained, "so I must leave this letter, my heart, & prepare to go 'downstairs' if necessary. I would just hate to take a spectacular leap off my very high balcony right into the middle of Bayswater Rd., all for the sake of an incendiary bomb."

She resumed again at 2:15 a.m. "The raid is over—it was quite a nasty one!—there are fires on three sides of us, but not so close as the one on Tuesday last. I have phoned my centre but I find that it was comparatively quiet down there. I would much rather be there in the 'blitz' than here. Most of the tenants here are perfectly 'awful' during a raid. Some of them rush straight off to the tube station as soon as the alert goes. Another couple bring down their radiogram as though it were a most valued article & heaps of suitcases. One poor old lady has heart attacks & another one becomes very quarrelsome. Fortunately for me I have the moral support of Adele (my next-door neighbor). Our reaction is to giggle a little hysterically every time something comes down. This must be just as annoying for the others as their particular reaction is to me."

She did see the lighter side of all the terror, too. "There is a great shortage of tin hats in London & ordinary civilians are quite unable to buy them, but shrapnel is very bad even during a small raid, so it has become quite a usual sight in London after the 'alert' has sounded, to see people hurrying off to shelters with pots, pans, & even enamel basins & bedroom utensils on their heads. I assure you, darling, it is quite true & no one even looks surprised at the sight."

"I have just heard the news that our offensive has begun," Irene wrote Kent in a postscript on the morning of June 5, as D-Day neared. "The anxiety & excitement is terrific. All during the night, as I was writing to you, the noise of planes was overwhelming—may the loss of life not be too terrible! I have been out of the centre for a few minutes and the whole of London seemed to be holding its breath—the wireless says it is the coast of Normandy which is being invaded. Poor France! Here we are to stand by & go on as usual."

Then Hitler launched a new aerial terror on London.

The V-1s, as the first flying bombs were known, began to arrive on June 12. "During this last week," Irene wrote Kent on June 30, "I got 'bombed' at my home address, fortunately not too badly. But the doors were blown off & the windows 'went'—today we 'got it' at the centre where I went to relieve during the afternoon (all the windows blew in!). Tonight I am relieving yet another centre & we are expecting quite a population at any moment. It is truly difficult to find time to write any private correspondence. I have had to dodge the 'boomfs' several times while writing this letter. The tiresome thing about these flying shells is that there seems to be no break with them at all—we are almost constantly in a state of alert—I don't know that the hush-hush which surrounds the whole business is very wise, either because rumours become quite fantastic & always exaggerated. But it is not necessary to exaggerate anything in this case."

On the night of July 16, Irene wrote from the Amberley Rest Centre. "The raids have eased off somewhat, but I have been assigned to a particularly gruesome 'incident' when we had about 350 people in one centre & a great number of injured & a heavy death toll; in fact, it was one of the worst incidents in the whole of London, & fortunately it is not often that one bomb can cause quite so much damage." She apologized for writing such depressing letters, adding, "It is a most depressing job to have to listen to so many tragic stories & to witness the most tragic scenes. Probably I have formed a quite distorted vision of this latest form of bombing through having constantly been in contact with its most desolate side from the very beginning."

"Last night was one of the worst raid-nights we have had," she reported just three days later. "Fly bombs came over at the rate of about one in every 3 minutes & this went on during the whole night.

Several times the centre I was in rocked on its foundations. It was horrible! However, nothing actually fell nearer than about 1/2 mile away." She wrote, "Do you know that some of these beastly things glide on you quite silently & the first thing you know is the ceiling falling down or the windows blowing in? I think that is what makes these raids so much more unpleasant than the old ones."

In another letter she wrote, "We had a batch of poor old women 'bombed out' from a local infirmary in my centre, who arrived in their night clothes and who had all left their false teeth behind in their hurry to get away. This was causing them great anxiety so I sent our handyman to see if he could salvage their teeth. He brought them back together all jumbled up in a towel and you should have seen the commotion it caused trying to sort them out again!" She added, "As usual terrible tragedies are all mixed up with utterly ridiculous situations & sometimes I don't know whether to laugh or weep!"

The new, hair-raising stage of the war forced her to confront her thoughts about it, which until now she hadn't. "I have tried to reason out why I have avoided thinking about it apart from the normal instinct to escape mental strain (& my lack of political perception!)—I think, at first, it was because the blow which fell on you & because I love you, on me, was too heavy to allow for any thought, & later because London became involved as a scene of battle & I was not able to see anything but our own 'section' of the battle. And now, as it was then, my pity is too aroused for the unfortunate & quite innocent people who are blindly taking the full brunt of these air attacks. They, too, don't reason about it at all. It is an effort to keep sane in these maddening conditions—& stupor under bombardment is one of the best mental safeguards." She concluded: "There can be no good enough reason for this war. . . . I can remember what you used to tell me back in '40, only I did not listen carefully then."

"This morning we had quite a spot of local excitement," she said one day in late August. "A flying-bomb came down in the park nearby, opposite here, & ripped all the curtains in this house & blasted the windows out again. My Scotch friend, Adele, was with me when it happened. She has only just returned from Scotland and it was her first close meeting with the 'doodlebugs'—when the dust had cleared away I found her wedged tightly under my bed. (I was still in bed) & a gramophone I've got here was still playing Noel Coward's 'Stately Homes of England'—This is a stupid but true 'bomb story.' So we both got a little drunk today to celebrate our escape and went to see a film about the American Civil War (what's the matter with the Americans? & why are they still so preoccupied with the Civil War?)—anyway, it was very restful after the strain of modern warfare." She seems unaware that the answer to her question had become the love of her life.

The British government officially called the doodlebugs "gas mains," to conceal their origins and to give Londoners a false impression of faulty infrastructure rather than wartime aggression. "Whilst writing this letter," Irene wrote on October 25, "there has been first, one of those mysterious 'bangs' which are generally referred to as the 'local gas mains'—because at first we would not recognize that such a thing as V-3 (or V-2) whatever it is, existed at all. No warning at all, just bang!—fortunately they are so infrequent that they do not cause London, as a whole, any bother; then there was a warning and a solitary flying bomb 'passed over' much too close to be comfortable. So we are not quite finished with all that yet."

On November 14: "Every time I write to you, we seem to be having a raid. Two doodlebugs have just crashed somewhere not too far away. There have been three distinct 'gas mains.' These latter are becoming more troublesome. My friend, Ludmilla, was called out with her ambulance last Friday on one of these V-2 incidents. She was so shaken by it that she has been white & sick for several days, & I have had to keep her with me to try to soothe her nerves. It really did sound very gruesome. Thank goodness there has been nothing very near this place, as yet, from this new menace. Incidentally, now that Mr. Churchill has admitted that we have been having V-2s for the past month and more, we need no longer call them 'gas mains'!"

Finally, on Christmas Eve, Irene found the words to express to Kent how and why she had come to loathe the war. "I dislike all modern politics & politicians intensely, as you can imagine. More than ever now. What I distrust most about it now is the way people are blinded and deceived by the intense & completely ruthless & stupid propaganda drummed into them from all angles. I regret that people, in the masses, have ever been taught to read or can go to the picture cheaply, or find it necessary to own a wireless. These things are being used as a drug. It has become a physical impossibility, in any country now, to form an individual and unprejudiced opinion, & I believe that we had more freedom of thought in the middle ages—when people could be burnt at the stake for saying what they thought but could not be drugged into not thinking at all."

Irene went on to say: "Because this is a war which we are fighting for our existence (propa: for the more intelligent) and for our freedom (ditto for the more credulous), it seems that any sort of deception & childish device is justified. I think it is an insult to all our generation! It may be that through our negligence we reached a point where this war could not be averted and that there is nothing for it now but to fight it out—but it disgusts me that the people who are bearing the brunt of it (& I think this applies to every country) should be constantly bamboozled by concealment of truth, distortions, & idiotic propaganda."

The rocket bombs still fell on London, and Allied forces were decimating German cities—a shattering experience far worse than anything Irene describes, to judge from the Berlin diaries of Princess

Marie Vassiltchikov, another White Russian, with whom Irene might have seen eye to eye.

"Even apart from the obvious loss of lives," Irene continued, "the price of this war is terrible! I don't suppose that you know just how awful it is. I hardly dare write of the miseries I have seen in the course of my social work even in this, my very private letter to you. I have even had to play a small part in the giant deception scheme. Herding terrified women & children during a raid and telling them they were safer there—giving them sweets to avert panic (and because sweets are rationed, they did nearly forget the raid)—I've helped evacuate children to 'safer' areas & then found out that they had been dumped into billets which were nothing short of criminal. Girls in their teens uprooted from their homes by act of law, and sent to factories to try to live on an impossible wage. The hospitals and various homes are full of them now. Soldiers' wives, by the thousands, having to ask for charity, free food, clothes & medicines, because of impossible army allowances (slightly improved now following a long outcry)—I could write a perfectly ghastly book but would not dare for fear of 'impeding the war effort.'"

Historians subsequently overlooked the war she was describing when trying to account for the Labour victory that banished Churchill from 10 Downing Street after VE Day.

"I would estimate the number of casualties on this home front as being at least equal to all casualties by enemy action on all fronts," she told Kent. "The breaking up of homes has been like nothing before in history, because not only the men have been gone for long periods, but the women have been taken away too & even the children dumped. I can't imagine what the showdown will be like! You write that individuals must make their happiness in spite of governmental activities & that we may soon have to sign on the dotted line for our 'ration' of affection—at present, honey, we can't even do that. Happiness is not like butter and there is no black market for that commodity. I don't think it can be even earned or won. It is probably just a gift from heaven—like love itself—& can only be seized or missed when the rare gift turns up."

She finished her screed at 4 a.m. on Christmas morning. "I must be mad!" she said, admitting that "these hellish five years have been worth living through because I see you sometimes & have an occasional letter from you. And because 'all the king's horses & all the king's men' have not divided us—not for all the tea in China."

Kent and Irene entertained the idea of meeting after his release, set for 1945. He had received a sentence of seven years, but he earned time off for good behavior. "I hope that we will be able to meet again just as before—or, somehow, one day," she wrote him in February 1944. "It would be lovelier than before—but a dream like that is almost too romantic to be believed. And there will always be my family affairs—and your mind will be on serious matters—and the 'powers that be' do not encourage dreams in any case. And fate itself will probably be against us because it would be too much like real happiness—for me at least!"

On May 8, 1944, she confessed, "I can't begin to make a guess at what you will do, or what I will do, or what will happen in the future. I resent the fate which literally tore us apart at such a time & at the very beginning of that lovely spring—and I know that it is very possible that we will not be able to meet again." She also refused to indulge Kent's fantasies. "You also write, rather skeptically of an island where one might regain one's independence on coconuts & fish. It sounds interesting & enticing & completely imaginary. It is not that coconuts & fish are so revolting, but the ties of domesticity are enormously powerful. A holiday on such an island would be heavenly, but even that is too misty to speculate about."

Despite her dreamy romanticism, Irene seems to have had few illusions about the chances of joining up with Kent after the war. In any case, she may not have felt an overwhelming need to do so. She loved her husband and worried about his safety in her letters to Kent. Kent's freedom seems to have mattered most to her. "When I can know that you are free it will be like coming back into the world for me too, for the first time since May 1940. I shall never forget that morning, when I seemed to drift into the park feeling as though a skyscraper had fallen on my head & all my limbs been torn out of their sockets." She returned often to those days leading up to Kent's arrest in 1940 with regret and nostalgia, as though she only wanted to repair the damage. She wrote in that same letter, "[Y]ou know I want the chance to confirm our friendship—it really was rather 'awful,' the circumstances in which we were separated—interrupted & tossed into misfortune! There are some broken bits to be mended! I would like to 'pick up' just where we left off."

In June 1945, after the war had ended in Europe, she admitted that "It was silly of me not to 'open up' and really talk to you when we were together. I loved you then a great deal more than you could guess, and I have decided that to be reticent for the sake of pride or any other foolishness at such a time is worse than stupid. If by some 'miracle' you came along now, I think I would 'lose my memory' over the past five years completely—it looks as though nothing has changed. You had a date for lunch. Where did you go? I wouldn't even ask you that question then. A lot of people are out sunning themselves but there is a dearth of chairs because many of them were burnt to keep the bonfires up on V.E. nights. The scent of the lime trees is heavenly & maddening—and I miss you—'*éperdument*'—I can't find the expression!"

She wrote, "It will be a great misery to me if I am unable to be with you for, at least, a little while when you are released. Our long and good 'companionship' in misfortunes should have made that the logical & quite natural conclusion." She knew the odds stacked against a potential reunion. "It does not look as though that will be possible, but I don't despair altogether—and later on we shall meet if you wish it. It does not matter at all where. There has never been less 'freedom' in the world than today—but if you & I both want to meet strongly enough no amount of red tape will prevent it."

By now, Kent's release from prison was all but assured; the only uncertainty was when it would happen, and under what circumstances. The war had ended. Several months earlier, however, they had fretted gloomily about the prospect of his release, even though the Allies had started to bomb Berlin. Kent asked Knight for help. To do so, he first wanted Irene to sound him out. In March, after some hesitation, she agreed, and on the 29th, she called on him. "He received me very kindly," she wrote Kent later that day, and "listened to what I had to say very sympathetically."

Knight instructed Kent, via Irene, to submit a request for an interview with him. Kent did this through the governor of his prison. Next, under pressure from Kent, Irene called Knight—the freshly minted major—to ascertain whether he'd received the letter that Kent had written him. In May, she met Knight for a cocktail at the Hyde Park Hotel. He told her that he planned to visit Kent that week or, in the event that VE celebrations prevented him, the week following.

"My dearest darling," she wrote Kent, "of course I can't advise you, and you will decide best what is in your own interest, but I do beg you not to let any outside consideration influence you against your own interest. You know quite well that you are much too proud sometimes— I am sure that Major Knight will be friendly and if he seeks for further information, which I'm sure he will, it will not be directed against you."

In a memorandum that he made of Irene's original request on behalf of Kent for an interview, Knight noted that Kent wanted to find out if it would be possible to have the deportation order, issued at the time of his arrest, revoked. This mattered to him even more than his release. Knight gathered from Irene that Kent was "not anxious to return to the [S]tates, in case he is made use of by contending political factions." Kent knew what was coming. Knight informed the Home Office, to whom he issued his memo, that "if in due course Kent does apply to have an interview with me, this should be granted," because "Both Inspector Thompson and myself formed the distinct impression that Kent is anxious to come forward with a little more information." He concluded pragmatically: "As far as we can see, no harm could be done, and it is possible that one or two of the loose ends of this case might be cleaned up."[1]

Knight visited Kent at Camp Hill on May 11, 1945. "As I had rather anticipated," Knight wrote in a subsequent report, "Kent's object in asking to see me was to ask for advice, rather than to volunteer information." Kent said that he felt the nine months of jail time he had spent waiting for his trial should count with the time he had already served, but the authorities disagreed. It was a matter, Knight told Kent, over which he had no influence. Kent also brought up the deportation order, which he understood would be activated when Kent finally left prison in the fall. Kent explained "to the best of his belief," as Knight put it, that a deportation order "only provided for the conveying of a person beyond the territorial limits of the United Kingdom," and that "it did not specify any particular country to which a man could be deported." Again, Knight had no say in the matter and told Kent to take it up with the "proper authorities."[2]

Kent also wanted to know if Knight thought it likely that "when he got back to the [S]tates certain parties" would put him on trial again. Knight had no idea, but the fact that Kent even asked the question indicated that he knew better. "I then took the opportunity of this visit to discuss one or two aspects of this case," Knight wrote. "After a somewhat long discussion regarding the Duke Del Monte, I succeeded in getting an admission out of Kent that, when he met this man with Anna Wolkoff, he did know perfectly well that he was an official from the Italian Embassy, and he also knew that the pseudonym 'Mr. Macaroni' was indeed an alias, and a rather silly one at that. He maintained that he had no idea that Anna Wolkoff was going to transmit information which she had obtained from him out of the country, via Del Monte or anyone else. I feel forced to record that I am now prepared to believe Kent. I consider that Kent's weakness is his incredible ingenuousness. He is even more naive than most Americans regarding diplomatic matters and Intelligence work. I think that, although Kent was bereft of all sense of honor with regard to his actions while employed by the United States government, the Espionage angle simply never occurred to him. I have no doubt that his experience was cleverly exploited by flattery, both by Del Monte and Wolkoff."[3]

This damning conclusion helped Kent in no way, although, as Irene, who spoke to Knight after the interview, informed him, "Knight has sent the report he promised to send—his interview was quite satisfactory from his point of view," and "He quite definitely promised to help as far as he could, within his province." His province in the matter ended abruptly at the borders of the Home Office in the Palace of Whitehall, however.

The Home Office could arrange with the US Department of State how and when Kent returned to America. That was all. By May 10, the day before Knight's interview with Kent, as a Home Office document shows, the British government had proposed to deport Kent as soon as possible following his release from prison. A Foreign Office official wrote an officer of the Home Office on July 21, 1945, a kind of written instruction on the matter. "The State Department specially desire that he should be put on a ship going direct to the United

States of America so that there can be no question of his getting out of United States jurisdiction. They also feel, as doubtless we do too, that it would be undesirable that he should be hanging about in this country between release and embarkation: they have primarily in mind that he might stow away on a vessel going elsewhere than the United States of America."[4] The Home Office agreed.

When word of this arrangement reached Kent, he wrote to an officer of the embassy named Stebbins on August 7 to ask him to convey a request for the cancellation of the deportation order. He also threatened to sue the British government if they held him in prison beyond his remaining sixty days should they fail to deport him, and he imperiously informed Stebbins that the Department of State was obligated "contractually" to provide him with first-class steamship passage.

Irene wrote to ask Kent whether he wanted money for his journey. The British government was obliged to finance Kent's passage, but it was also entitled to use any money that Kent might have available. When the time came, his mother sent the embassy £40 for traveling money, most of which prison authorities used to cover expenses that he had incurred as a temporary prisoner after his release from Camp Hill at Brixton Prison, where he was held for an additional six weeks because a strike by dockworkers on the Thames had delayed the departure of the freighter on which the British government had booked his passage.

Irene devoted herself to Kent's needs as long as he required her help. She continued to consult with his solicitor. She also arranged to repair his suitcase ("black with leather straps"), and to gather his clothing, which Mr. Maw had kept for him in storage. "In the meantime," Irene wrote Kent on July 23, "I have suspended all other interests (no great activities anyway!) until I feel that I have finished the job which I promised to do for you (Do you remember? At the Old Bailey in Nov. 1940?)—it has been a strange history! And it is quite true that we are more intimate now. It has been the one really lovely thing which has emerged. Whatever happens in the future we have a tremendous amount to talk about—and a completely unshakable friendship!"

Kent asked her to keep "a reserve of money handy," which she agreed to do, although she did decline to have his evening outfit "vetted," as she put it. "Although it is very crushed," she pointed out, "it would become so on the journey anyway, or do you need it at once to make a debut?" In a subsequent letter, she makes it clear that they both hoped that Maw could persuade authorities to arrange a swift return home by private means if possible. Indeed, Kent's solicitor investigated whether British authorities "had any objections to Kent's family chartering a family plane" to take Kent to the United States.

Meanwhile, Irene had accumulated a sizable collection of luggage, for which arrangements had to be made so that it could accompany Kent on his homeward journey. She listed these as:

- wardrobe trunk (containing clothes)
- one black suitcase
- one brown leather case "like a Gladstone bag" containing "papers and photographs!?!"
- one brown leather box case of collars and ties
- one tin box with index files containing papers

She also listed his clothes, many lovingly seen to for repairs by Irene: "1 heavy wool plaid coat, 1 navy cloth ditto, 1 grey tweed ditto, some grey tweed cloth, 1 navy striped suit, 1 black cloth ditto, 1 grey summer flannel suit, 2 grey suits (1 stripe, 1 flecked), 1 evening dress—tails & dinner jacket, 1 leather jacket, 1 hunting jacket, lots of shirts—collars—ties, cotton underclothing—white socks, 3 pyjamas—dressing gown—slippers, patent leather shoes, very few handkerchiefs & absolutely no socks! 2 felt hats—other oddments—box of studs—case with brushes & toilet things, etc." From his collection of

American Customs officials process Tyler Kent's
arrival after serving his sentence.
(PHOTO COURTESY OF THE LIBRARY OF CONGRESS)

personal snapshots, some of them erotic, she took for herself one of him that was better, she wrote, than the newspaper photo she'd carried around with her for almost six years.

"Don't worry!" she wrote to reassure him. "You showed me most of your photographs during our brief period of liberty. Sometimes I think you have forgotten that we were 'on the way' to becoming very close friends even at that very early date. And that we had exchanged quite a number of 'confidences.' Try to remember! I believe that if I had been more free we could have found a real happiness together. As it was, we have never had an 'evening' together, and that is always the best time for a woman & for the development of closer understanding. You acquired other interests of which, by the way, I was instinctively aware. But I was also instinctively aware that our friendship had much deeper roots than is usual. Therefore many things which might have broken up our friendship were, in comparison, not sufficiently important. The fact that we have somehow survived the shocks, political panic in 1940 (which you don't realize) machinations, long separation, unhappiness & time itself, is a remarkable demonstration. And so it has impressed the very few people who know the history."

Irene wrote her last surviving letter to Kent on the evening of Monday, October 8, 1945. Her stationery bore the logo of an eagle, wings outstretched, circumscribed by the Latin motto, *Per ardua ad astra* ("Through struggle to the stars," which the RAF had adopted as their motto in 1912). Kent was still in Brixton Prison, where on October 4 he received the deportation order "in the prescribed manner." He was due to leave on the 14th.

"Darling Tyler," she wrote, "I had a word with Mr. Maw; he knows nothing about the money your mother sent but suggests that it may have been sent direct to Home Office. Also he has no news of actual boat, etc." She continued, "I hope that I shall see you and that we can get things straightened out," adding, "Everything is near enough ready—but you still have not told me of any etceteras you may need while traveling." She concluded that she was "sorry that I got 'upset' during our scanty visit—the truth is that beneath a fairly smooth exterior, my nerves are at trigger point—Do you need more warm underclothing? I've put a scarf in the pocket of your big coat.—Very hastily, but most affectionately, your Irene." She added a postscript: "You can buy me some really nice black silk stockings in America— but don't send them, as I shall have no use for them until later. With a 'kiss' which I can't give you now—*tu comprends*—yours, Irene." And a second postscript, a PPS: "I'm only too glad to use my 'coupons' for you—and those stockings your mother sent more than account for anything." So ran the last words that Irene Danischewsky is known to have sent Tyler Kent.

Kent's ship, the *Silver Oak,* a Cunard White Star freighter, sailed from Tilbury, near the mouth of the Thames, for New York on November 21, 1945, five years and two weeks to the day from when Justice Tucker sentenced Kent at the Old Bailey to seven years' imprisonment. The day before, under police guard, he went by taxi to Irene's apartment at 6 Palace Court, at the northwest corner of Kensington Gardens, to check over his property and baggage. Here, outside the confines of prison, he once again saw Irene—but only briefly. They parted for good the following day when police drove him again to her apartment to collect his baggage, before proceeding to Tilbury, where he boarded the *Silver Oak* for the voyage back to America.

EPILOGUE

Absence of evidence is not necessarily evidence of absence.
— DAVID MARKSON, *VANISHING POINT*

I CAME UPON THE ABOVE APHORISM ON THE EXPRESS TRAIN BETWEEN St. Petersburg and Moscow, seeing for myself those places where Kent had lived, worked, and played in Moscow. It popped up in *Vanishing Point*, one of David Markson's brilliant and unique late works of fiction.[1] How freshly the aphorism applies to the case against Tyler Kent, I thought then, and still do. As far back as 1937 in Moscow, and later in London, Kent may have been feeding those classified letters he had copied and taken home from the Mokhovaya House Chancery on cold, dark winter evenings to a contact of Kurt Jahnke, a pro-Soviet German who, under the aegis of Rudolf Hess and the Abwehr, acquired abroad diplomatic and political information for the purposes of Nazi propaganda.

Jahnke's intelligence bureau came to the attention of British intelligence in 1945 through one of his agents, Marcus Marienhofer, code-named "Dictionary." British intelligence identified him as an outsider in Jahnke's outfit who held the modest position of unofficial informant. He, like Jahnke, had become disillusioned by Hitler perhaps because he, too, was an enthusiast of the Soviet Union. Jahnke ran agents in the UK, US, and almost certainly the USSR before and during the short-lived Nazi-Soviet alliance.[2]

The daughter of a Jahnke agent in the UK, Augusta Kell-Pfeffer, had provided a detailed description of Jahnke in 1941 for British intelligence: "He is tall, about six feet, and rather fat," her interrogator noted. "He has a roundish face, brutal and vulgar. He has peculiar eyes like a pig, she thinks bluish, and he has a habit of dropping his eyelids when thinking or pretending to think. He has bushy eyebrows, and what she called an 'important' nose. He rarely smiled but had a hard laugh. Had mouse-colored hair. He has fat hands, with well-manicured fingers and highly polished nails. He wore a ring on his little finger."

Kell-Pfeffer also observed that "He was well-dressed, but although his clothes were of the best he could not wear them well." He usually carried gloves with him. "He was a good shot, though not a sportsman," she added. "Very fond of women. Fond also of wine," she noted, but too clever to get drunk. A glutton, he dined always at the best restaurants. "He was a frightful snob, very ambitious and greedy for power. He was rolling in money. He was a great animal-lover. He was a heavy smoker, both in cigars and cigarettes. He was very reserved."[3]

Jahnke's origins remain obscure. He engaged in opium- and cigar-smuggling as a young man in San Francisco. In 1917 he earned a reputation as a man unafraid to take risks when, on behalf of the Imperial German military enterprise, he engineered the explosion of an ammunition dump in New Jersey. He ran the German espionage system in the Americas in 1918 from Mexico City, and sometime after February 1921 returned to Berlin, where, by 1927, he had become a deputy in the Prussian Diet, acting as a double agent for the Russians and Germans.

Walter Krivitsky—the top European Soviet spy who defected to the West in 1938, later assassinated in a Washington, D.C., hotel room in 1941—was familiar with Jahnke, who by the 1930s had become a very rich "self-made" man. The Nazis embraced Jahnke, and in the

1930s he put together his organization under Hess and in collaboration with a man named Pan Pfeffer (father of Augusta, above), a loyal member of Hitler's entourage, who, like Jahnke, had an office in Hess's building at 64 Wilhelmstrasse in Berlin. Jahnke, however, operated from his house at 26 Steglitz. He kept his "registry" in the basement and maintained an office on the ground floor, from which he oversaw the acquisition of information supplied by his agents in London and elsewhere.[4]

Jahnke eluded British intelligence agents until 1955, when MI6 finally ran him to ground. In their custody, he claimed that Kent had supplied him regularly with information from 1937 until 1941, when he ceased to provide him with anything useful. If Kent had indeed been Jahnke's agent, he couldn't have laid hands on anything significant on the Isle of Wight. We plausibly can suppose that in 1937 our sublimely arrogant and self-confident young American embassy clerk allowed himself to become a small-time agent for this colorfully detestable master spy.

By 1941, the British knew of Jahnke and Pfeffer both, though not Jahnke's purported connection to Tyler Kent. MI5 did know in February 1940 that most of Ambassador Kennedy's correspondence with Washington had turned up in Berlin. An MI5 informant familiar with Jahnke had brought this information to the attention of British intelligence, and on February 15, MI5—as it routinely did in such matters, it now appears—belatedly informed Herschel Johnson.

By this time, MI5 already had filed away its observation that Tyler Kent, the new code clerk, had been seen in the company of Ludwig Matthias, although they said nothing to Johnson about this—oddly, because, in his report to Captain Guy Liddell, the agent who informed Johnson of the leaks described Johnson's mystification and concern about a probable source. "Mr. Herschel Johnson said that he thought it almost impossible for anyone in the American Embassy in Berlin to have given away 'practically everything from Ambassador Kennedy's dispatches to President Roosevelt, including the former's interviews with British statesmen or officers.'" Kennedy, the MI5 man reported, "sent his reports <u>only</u> to the State Department in Washington, usually by direct cable from the American Embassy under arrangements of which we were well aware."[5] The first secretary understandably expressed his disappointment that MI5 had not brought this security leak to his attention earlier. He settled on the conjecture that the British Foreign Office was leaking the correspondence.

Jahnke did have a source in the Foreign Office and may well have received his information and documents from that informant, who left London in 1939. American diplomatic reports continued to flow into the ground floor of 26 Steglitz in Berlin through March 1940, however. These reports came from a Russian-born agent named Petroff—known also by the pseudonyms Orloff, Peters, and Petersen—who left the UK after March 1940 to become a special agent in Europe for Reinhard "Hangman" Heydrich, head of the dreaded *Sicherheitsdienst*, Hitler's secret intelligence agency. If Jahnke was telling the truth and really did use Kent as a source, Kent's contact in London was probably Petroff, who would have moved in the same Russian émigré circles. Jahnke may also have sent Matthias to England to accompany Kent on his voyage from Norway to Newcastle.

All of these suppositions linger openly in the realm of surmise because there remains to this day an absence of evidence to show the connection. Kent might well have wanted to be reassigned to Berlin in order to get closer to Jahnke. Nothing has yet surfaced in the available KGB files that mentions Kent. Yet Jahnke, double agent though he was, may not have been working for the NKVD. Tanya Iliovskaya Alexandrovna was, but Kent may not have supplied his Moscow mistress with the material that he managed to slip to Jahnke. That went through his friendly contacts in the German embassy in Moscow, the young Foreign Office apprentices who worked for the SS and of whom Martha Dodd writes. A low-level informant, Kent sold documents so that he could live as he felt he deserved to live: as a highly educated Southern gentleman in a corrupt land of gangsters and Jews.

All this would have struck William Bullitt as more than plausible. He was always convinced that Kent was a low-level spy. The former ambassador might have had something to say on the subject, but by the end of World War II his thoughts were elsewhere. He became increasingly conservative in his views on international affairs after the bitterness of his break with Roosevelt over the matter of Sumner Welles. In the postwar years, he became a member of the zealously anti-Communist China Lobby, and an outspoken critic of Roosevelt's foreign policies in the Soviet Union and China. In 1967, the year he died, Houghton Mifflin published an astonishing work that Bullitt cowrote with Sigmund Freud, *Thomas Woodrow Wilson: A Psychological Study*, in which the authors provide a penetrating analysis of another Democratic president whom Bullitt came to deplore. Did it ever cross Bullitt's mind that Wilson's birthplace, Staunton, Virginia, was also the home of Kent's family on his mother's side? Wilson also served as president of Princeton, which Kent later attended. *Grasping at straws*

On December 4, 1945, Tyler Kent debarked from the *Silver Oak* at Pier 3, Hoboken, New Jersey. A battery of reporters greeted him, along with his mother. "Of average height and with clean-cut features and wavy, chestnut-colored hair, Kent looked pale and worn." So reported the *New York Herald Tribune* on December 5. "He was met by his mother, Mrs. Ann H. P. Kent, who has fought almost constantly against his conviction in Britain. She had paced the cold, wind-swept pier from 9 a.m. until her son hurried to her at noon." The article remarks on the formality of the reunion, adding, "Kent kissed his mother and said, in a marked British accent, 'Darling, how are you?' She answered, 'It's nice to see you again.'"

Kent admitted to reporters on his arrival that he had indeed removed the confidential documents from the embassy without the legal authority to do so, but added that he considered he'd had a "moral right," and said that he was willing to testify about America's entry into the war before a Senate committee investigating the Pearl Harbor attack. "The former Embassy clerk characterized as 'pure invention' the formal accusation that he intended to pass the documents on to Nazi agents," the *Tribune* reported.[6]

"Only the rabid Isolationists in America still believe that Kent is anything but a convicted thief, and his arrival has aroused little interest, though an eager, if skeptical, audience could no doubt be found for any statements which he may wish to make,"[7] an MI5 memorandum quite shrewdly observes on the occasion of Kent's arrival in the United States. Kent sidestepped any hopes that these "rabid Isolationists" or any others may have entertained that he would go to Washington and explain himself, even though he led his supporters in Congress to believe that he might when he told reporters, "I'm very glad to be back in the United States. I think in the near future I will have something to say of interest to people of this country." Instead, Kent lay low, and on June 30, 1946, in his mid-thirties, married the forty-six-year-old heiress, Clara Hunter Hyatt, ex-wife of a State Department official, in Nuevo Laredo, Mexico.[8]

Mrs. Anne Kent died at the age of seventy in New York, in 1954.[9]

Tyler Kent didn't settle permanently into the life of a gentleman farmer after his marriage. In the 1950s, he and Clara left farming behind them to set out aboard their yacht *Sea Turtle* on a series of private cruises, eventually settling in Palatka, Florida. But even still, Kent couldn't quite let up on Joseph Kennedy, or the Kennedy family. In Palatka in 1961, he was publishing a hate sheet called *The Putnam Sun*—"Palatka's Only Independent Home-Owned Newspaper"— which he used to vilify blacks, Jews, Communists, and Kennedys, not

Kent in middle age at the Castillo de San Marcos
in St. Augustine, Florida, in the summer of 1963.
(PHOTO COURTESY OF THE HOWARD GOTLIEB ARCHIVAL
RESEARCH CENTER AT BOSTON UNIVERSITY)

Kent addressing the Sixth International Revision-
ist Conference in February 1986. (PHOTO COURTESY
OF THE HOWARD GOTLIEB ARCHIVAL RESEARCH CENTER AT
BOSTON UNIVERSITY)

to mention the Kennedy cabinet.[10] In 1963, he made an unsuccessful attempt to sue Joseph Kennedy for defamation, based on the remarks Kennedy had made in 1944 about Kent's activities when he was a code clerk.[11] The ravaging stroke suffered by Joseph Kennedy and the tragic circumstances of the JFK assassination on November 22, 1963, overtook Kent's anti-Kennedy efforts.

In later life, Kent issued lengthy, cogent explanations whenever the occasion arose in defense of his early efforts to expose the Roosevelt war effort. He presented his views at a forum held by the Sixth International Revisionist Conference and conducted correspondence with several of these, including Karl Otto Braun.

Thanks to his money, infamy, inflated self-esteem, and intelligence, Kent attained, late in life, the weird comportment of an elder statesman who expresses his right-wing, crackpot, racist views with a certain dignified gentility. In his strangely high-pitched voice, in an accent no longer British, but decidedly Southern, he gave an extensive interview to Robert Harris, a British television journalist who had found him in Texas, in the mobile home where he then lived. This was in 1982. He vehemently protested his innocence of pro-Nazi espionage to the very end. As he insisted in a letter to Pulitzer Prize–winning historian John Toland in 1978, "I stole, purloined, appropriated confidential documents and showed some of them to unauthorized persons—not to Germans as is stated and implied by smear-bund."[12]

But all of this still leaves another question unanswered: Was Irene Danischewsky an agent? By the time of Jahnke's confession, Maxwell Knight had gone on to other pursuits, including a career as a popular zoology commentator for the BBC. (Anna Walkoff had died of injuries during a car crash in Spain in an automobile driven by Enid Riddell.) It was far too late to go back and research the files for contacts between the Danischewsky tribe and Soviet double agents, though information on file suggested such a connection in the person of one Paul

The last home of Tyler Kent and his wife, Clara, in Kerrville, Texas.
(PHOTO BY AUTHOR)

Danischewsky. Knight, the lovable snake-and-lizard man, had spent more than a decade running Soviet agents to ground in London, but apparently he found no reason to suspect Irene of any subversive activity—even if she did live across the street from the Soviet embassy. Then again, he never knew that Guy Burgess was an agent for the Soviet Union when he worked as an investigator for MI5, either. Irene Danischewsky could have been an agent. It does seem a little odd that she became such good friends with Ludmilla, the Soviet embassy employee who had lived and worked most recently in Washington, D.C.

If Irene was an agent, how bold she was, and what a double game she must have played. How very rich in concealed irony are her letters if all along she was keeping such intimate watch on Kent to make sure that he never betrayed their secret association to the British police. She let him steam away on the *Silver Oak* without ever looking back, it seems. Whatever she was or was not, in her self-expression as an epistolary lover, Irene emerges as the heroine embodiment of the Russian soul: a dreamer, a natural with language, with a sense of humor, unpredictable, devoted, incautious.

Many years later, she told World War II historian John Costello that she came to believe Kent was guilty of violating the Official Secrets Act on the basis of what the police told her. She said so in 1982 over the phone. Costello had tracked Irene down—a widow in her seventies—and evidently revealed to her for the first time that public documents existed linking her to Kent. In his notes of their conversation, Costello wrote: "Mrs. D very alarmed and upset—told me 'quite alone,' husband [had] died, and publicity would mean exposure and make life not worth living—said very old and frail and events a very long time ago."[13]

Kent must have regretted losing Irene. He certainly treasured her letters to him, one way or another, for the rest of his life. He would never have kept them if he hadn't found in them such a rich affirmation of his best self, the ideal one that he entertained to the bitter end.

ACKNOWLEDGMENTS

My research on Tyler Kent and the period in which *Conspiracy of One* takes place has been extensive. I am particularly indebted to the following individuals who helped me locate material and provided judgment, advice, and historical background: Professor Daniel Aaron of Harvard University, Professor Christopher Andrew of Cambridge University, Pamela Bull, Professor Gary Clifford of the University of Connecticut, Wayne Cole, Professor Irwin Gellman, Professor Thomas Hodge of Wellesley College, Page Huydekuper, George Kennan, Caroline Moorehead, Professor and Mrs. James Patrick, Professor Janet Vaillant of Harvard University, and author Tim Weiner.

I have received ongoing support and great help from all the research assistants and staff at the Howard Gotlieb Archival Research Center at Boston University in the preparations for this book. In particular, I thank Vita Paladino, the current director, Sean Noel, Charles Niles, and Laura Russo for their kind assistance at all times. The Gotlieb Center has been like a home, and I have done much of my primary research with the help of papers in the Tyler Kent Archive there.

I have also made extensive use of documents from the papers of William Castle at the Houghton Library at Harvard University; the Joseph P. Kennedy papers at the John F. Kennedy Presidential Library in Boston; and the papers of Walton Moore, Mrs. W. P. Kent, Tyler Kent, John Costello, Ray Bearse, John Toland, and Irene Danischewsky at the Franklin Delano Roosevelt Presidential Library in Hyde Park, New York. I have also explored at great length the available files of MI5, the British Foreign Office, and the SOE, or Special Operations Executive, at the Public Record Office in Kew, a part of the British National Archive. The Weiner Museum in London kindly gave me access to the Right Club Red Book. I have used materials from the Reading Room at the Federal Bureau of Investigation, Washington, D.C., and the National Archives of the United States at College Park, Maryland. I am grateful to all who helped me in these institutions to retrieve what I sought.

In Staunton, Virginia, the staff at the *Daily News Leader* and the Augusta County Clerk's Office supplied valuable assistance in my search for genealogical material. In Kerrville, Texas, Cheryl Thompson at the Kerr County Clerk's Office also provided generous assistance. Louise Leahy at the *Kerrville Daily Times* kindly provided time and help tracking down essential Kent data. I also thank the staff at the Grimes Funeral Chapel for their help.

I pursued my investigations in Russia to see where Tyler Kent spent his time there, and I am grateful to many who helped me to do this. Lisa Vershbow graciously gave me a tour of Spaso House, and I wouldn't have been able to visit the Silver Forest, the Hall of the Nobility where Stalin's show trials took place during the 1930s, or other sites without the extraordinary hospitality and assistance provided by the Yenidogan family and Svetlana Soroka. Misha and Sarah Chemiakin provided the warmth of their hospitality and friendship, not to mention invaluable assistance, throughout this Russian sojourn and others.

In London, Sylvia Compton Miller provided a source of great ongoing practical support and friendship.

A number of friends read the manuscript of this book and otherwise provided the gift of their wisdom in the course of my writing. The late Arthur M. Schlesinger Jr. unfailingly advocated for the book, and he and Alexandra Schlesinger provided me with a treasure trove of anecdotes, some of which I have used in the book to enliven the story and give it historical nuance. Professor John Perry, Suzannah Lessard, Jeff Mason, Susan Blau, Kate Burak, and David Taylor all read the book and gave me valuable insights. In discussion, Walter Abish, David Baldwin, John Bowers, and Stephan Salisbury supplied essential background information based on their particular knowledge. Ken and Martha Wertz provided companionship and research on a fact-finding mission to Staunton, Virginia. I hope that all these friends know how much I value their help.

Joanne Wang and I have worked together as translators. Besides her work as a literary agent, she is also a treasured friend and reader. Without Joanne, who has brought the works of numerous contemporary Chinese writers to these shores, our literary life would be far less interesting and rich. As a literary agent, she is nonpareil, and thanks to her patient efforts *Conspiracy of One* has a superb publisher. I am grateful to her for putting me together with my editor, James Jayo, at Lyons Press. To my joy, he has been a steadfast enthusiast of the book.

I must also express my love and gratitude to Bliss and James Rand, to whom I have dedicated this book. Bliss has traveled far and wide with me and provided help and insight when I needed it, as she always has. James typed this book, and so he was its first reader. He subsequently accompanied me to England and Russia as a photographer for the project, and gave me valuable assistance at Kew.

ENDNOTES

ONE
BOY MISFIT

1   The author learned this in a conversation with a Kent School master, who, thanks to an introduction by Stephan Salisbury, a former Kent student, was able to provide the quote, although all matters involving students, current and former, are kept under lock and key, and he was unable to provide more information on Kent's brief stay at Kent.

2   Anne Patrick Kent, letter, Boston University (BU).

3   Ibid.

4   "Mr. Wm. P. Kent: First Virginia Consul Since Cleveland's Day," *Richmond News Leader*, August 16; "Kent-Patrick: Simple Ceremony at Trinity Episcopal Church," August 26, 1906.

5   Genealogical Records, Augusta County Clerk's Office, Staunton, Virginia.

6   Notes of John Toland, Conversation with Kent, National Archives. Kent explained that the "secret" to learning Russian was Indo-European grammar.

7   TK's State Department job application form, BU.

8   Loy W. Henderson, *A Question of Trust: The Origins of U.S.-Soviet Diplomatic Relations: The Memoirs of Loy W. Henderson*, edited, with an introduction by George W. Baer (Stanford, CA: Hoover Institution Press, Stanford University, 1986), p. 263.

9   Irwin F. Gellman, *Secret Affairs: Franklin Roosevelt, Cordell Hull, and Sumner Welles* (Baltimore: Johns Hopkins University Press, 1995), pp. 43–44.

10 Ibid, pp. 44–45.

11 Ibid, pp. 236–237.

12 Orville H. Bullitt, ed., *For the President, Personal and Secret: Correspondence between Franklin D. Roosevelt and William C. Bullitt* (Boston: Houghton Mifflin, 1972), pp. 66–69.

13 TK Archive BU.
14 TK Archive BU.
15 Arthur M. Schlesinger Jr. to author, conversation, May 2004, Jubilee Restaurant, New York.
16 Jack Alexander, "He Rose from the Rich," *The Saturday Evening Post*, March 11, 1939.
17 Ibid.
18 Margaret MacMillan, *Paris 1919: Six Months that Changed the World* (New York: Random House, 2001), pp. 78–80.
19 Henderson, chapter 31.
20 Henderson, p. 261.

Two
Bad Hat

1   Henderson, pp. 271–272.
2   Ibid.
3   Ibid, pp. 240–241.
4   Kennan, letter to author, February 26, 2001.
5   Grace Kennan Warneke e-mail to author, May 24, 2004.
6   Henderson, pp. 287–290.
7   Ibid.
8   Charles E. Bohlen, *Witness to History: 1929–1969* (New York: Norton, 1973), pp. 19–20; Henderson, pp. 278–280.
9   "Dear Pucia" letter, July 1, 1937, TK Archive BU.
10 Bohlen, p. 14.
11 Ibid, pp. 33–35.
12 Charles W. Thayer, *Bears in the Caviar* (Philadelphia and New York: J. B. Lippincott, 1950, 1951), p. 160.
13 Ibid, pp. 106–114.
14 Ibid, 156–164.
15 Ibid, pp. 116–129.
16 This story was related to author by Page Huydekuper, who worked with Kent in the US embassy in London, 1939–40.
17 William C. Bullitt, Annual Efficiency Report, May 1, 1935, TK Archive BU.
18 Bullitt, Annual Efficiency Report, 1936, TK Archive BU.
19 Amy Knight, *Who Killed Kirov: The Kremlin's Greatest Mystery* (New York: Hill & Wang, 1999), pp. 188–199.

20 Robert Conquest, *The Great Terror: A Reassessment* (New York, Oxford: Oxford University Press, 1990), p. 37.
21 Walter L. Hixson, *George Kennan: Cold War Iconoclast* (New York: Columbia University Press, 1989), p. 13.
22 Bullitt, *For the President,* p. 154.

Three
Anti-Semitism

1 Bullitt, Annual Efficiency Reports, April 17, 1937; September 30, 1938, TK Archive BU.
2 Ibid.
3 Louis C. Beck, November 13, 1940, "Conditions in the American Embassy Report," Franklin D. Roosevelt Library; Memorandum, Federal Bureau of Investigation, US Department of Justice, Washington, D.C., December 13, 1940, a document prepared for the president by J. Edgar Hoover, based on Beck's report, FDR Library.
4 Ibid.
5 Ibid.
6 Robert McClintock, Secretary of Legation, Helsinki, Finland, Memorandum, June 21, 1940, FDR Library.
7 "Dear Pucia" letter, TK Archive BU.
8 Martha Dodd, *Through Embassy Eyes* (New York: Harcourt, Brace, 1939), p. 256.
9 G. Howland Shaw, "Kent, Mrs. William P.," memo, January 22, 1941, TK Archive BU.
10 Henderson, Telegram to Secretary of State, #116, Paraphrase Copy, June 13, 1937, FDR Library.
11 Ibid.
12 George F. Kennan, *Memoirs: 1925–1950* (Boston, Toronto: Atlantic Monthly Press, Little, Brown, 1967), p. 83.
13 Gellman, p. 21.
14 William Castle, Diaries, Vol. 28, December 11, 1936, Houghton Library, Harvard University.
15 Schlesinger to author, May 2004.
16 Bohlen, p. 45.
17 Gellman, pp. 128–135.
18 Ibid, p. 37.
19 Ibid, p. 98.

20   Jean-Paul Sartre, *Anti-Semite and Jew* (New York: Schocken Books, 1948), p. 26.

21   Ibid, p. 27.

22   Ibid, p. 28.

23   Ibid, p. 32.

24   Ibid, pp. 32–33.

25   TK Archive BU.

26   Henderson, p. 523.

27   Department of State, February 2, 1939, TK Archive BU.

28   James L. McCamy, *The Administration of American Foreign Affairs* (New York: Alfred A. Knopf, 1950), p. 201.

29   George Messersmith, State Department Report dated February 15, 1939, TK Archive, BU.

30   *Rex v. Tyler Gatewood Kent,* Central Criminal Court Transcript, October/November 1940, p. 124, TK Archive BU.

31   Selig Adler, *The Uncertain Giant: 1921–1941,* American Foreign Policy between the Wars (New York: Macmillan, 1965), pp. 197–214.

32   Telegram #535, September 13, 1939, "Kent, Tyler G.," File 123, FDR Library.

33   Robert McClintock, Memorandum, June 21, 1940, File #123, FDR Library.

34   Joseph P. Kennedy, Telegram to Secretary of State, September 17, 1939, Antheil Files, FDR Library.

35   Charles Thayer, Telegram to Secretary of State, March 10, 1941, "Subject: Books Belonging to Tyler G. Kent," TK Archive BU.

36   *Rex v. Tyler Gatewood Kent,* pp. 108, 109.

37   Steinhardt to Secretary of State, September 30, 1940, TK Archive BU.

38   Agent's Report, Ludwig Ernest Matthias, October 8, 1939, PRO Ref: PF 51267.

39   Anthony Masters, *The Man Who Was M: The Life of Maxwell Knight* (Oxford: Basil Blackwell Ltd., 1984), p. 85.

Four
Code Clerk

1   Tyler Kent, "Memorandum: Facts Relating to the Tyler Kent Case," PRO, FO 371 151684.

2   Page Huydekuper to author.

3   Sabline, "Extract from a letter from Sabline re: the Wolkoffs, Kent, Ridley and Rayevsky," P.F. 51767, PRO 1617140.

4   Monja Danischewsky, *White Russian—Red Face* (London: Victor Gollancz Ltd., 1966).

5   Irene Danischewsky, letter to Anne P. Kent.

6   Sartre, p. 46.

7   "First General Interrogation of Kent after His Arrest Held in Ambassador Kennedy's Office, May 20, 1940," FDR Library.

8   Will Brownell and Richard N. Billings, *So Close to Greatness: A Biography of William C. Bullitt* (New York: Macmillan, 1987), p. 297.

9   Arthur M. Schlesinger Jr., *A Life in the 20th Century: Innocent Beginnings, 1917–1950* (Boston, New York: Houghton Mifflin, 2000), p. 241.

10 Joseph P. Kennedy, Diaries, March 20, 1940, Personal Papers Box 92, John F. Kennedy Library.

11 Ibid, March 18, March 20, 1940, p. 2.

12 Ibid, October 5, 1939.

13 TK Archive BU.

14 Ibid.

15 Ibid.

16 David Stafford, *Churchill and Secret Service* (Woodstock, NY: Overlook Press, 1998), pp. 40–41.

17 Ibid, pp. 154–155.

18 Masters, pp. 126–127.

19 Author not sure where he found this, but it matches up beautifully with other descriptions of Knight, and so will retain it.

20 Joan Miller, *One Girl's War* (Dingle, County Kerry, Ireland: Brandon, 1986), p. 125.

21 F. H. Hinsley and C. A. G. Simkins, *British Intelligence in the Second World War: Volume Four, Security and Counter-Intelligence* (UK: HMSO, 1990), pp. 39–40.

22 Stafford, pp. 175–180.

23 Ibid, p. 146.

24 Ibid, p. 148.

25 The Institute of Contemporary History and Weiner Library in London is in possession of this document, which the librarian kindly permitted the author to examine in July 2002.

26 Miller, p. 22.

27 Ibid.

28 "Summary of the Reports Submitted by M/Y between 23rd September 1939 and 1st week in June 1940," PRO KV2 677.

29 Ibid.

30 Ibid.

31 Masters, p. 80.

32 "Summary of the Reports Submitted by M/Y."

33 Miller, p. 26.

34 *Rex v. Tyler Gatewood Kent*, p. 136.

35 "Dear Young Lady," letter from A. Celine to Anna Wolkoff, the 22nd, PRO KV2/841.

36 Miller, pp. 26–35.

FIVE

SECRET SHARER

1 Transcript, Red Book, PRO Document H0045/2569, Weiner Library.

2 Gellman, pp. 174–175.

3 James Chace, Acheson: *The Secretary of State Who Created the American World* (New York: Simon & Schuster, 1998), p. 73. I owe this insight into the political views of Peabody to James Chace, who, in his biography of Acheson, writes about a conversation over lunch between the two men at the Elysée Park Hotel in Paris in the summer of 1938, based on *Acheson Country* by David Acheson. Dean Acheson, like President Roosevelt and most Groton graduates who had known the Rector, entertained for Peabody the utmost respect for this man who embodied the very values by which they fashioned their lives and careers. Chace writes, "When the Peabodys had departed, Dean said: 'There goes a really great man, but do you know, there's a sad anomaly here. Chamberlain doesn't understand what he's up against, but he would be a great success as a student at Groton. Churchill does understand it. He would be kicked out of Groton in a week.'"

4 Gellman, p. 175.

5 Launched in 1931, the *Rex*, according to Robert Hughes in *Rome: A Cultural, Visual and Personal History* (New York: Alfred A. Knopf, 2011), was "the world's fastest transatlantic passenger steamer, a marvel of Fascist, Futurist travel" (p. 409).

6   Gellman, p. 176.
7   Arthur M. Schlesinger Jr. to author, May 2004.
8   Gellman, p. 176.
9   Joseph P. Kennedy, Diary, March 10, 1940, p. 2, Box 92, JPK Personal Papers, JFK Library.
10 Ibid, March 1940 (exact date crossed out).
11 Beatrice Bishop Berle and Travis Beal Jacobs, eds., *Navigating the Rapids, 1918–1971: From the Papers of Adolf A. Berle* (New York: Harcourt Brace Jovanovich, 1973), p. 829. Berle recounts the incident, which occurred after Roosevelt had reluctantly let Welles go, and Roosevelt had just returned to Washington. "Presently President Roosevelt came back and I went over to see him," Berle writes. "He said Bullitt had just been there. That on Bullitt's entry he had appointed himself St. Peter. Two men came up: Sumner Welles, and after chiding him for getting drunk, Roosevelt let him in. The second was Bullitt. After paying due tribute to what Bullitt had done, St. Peter accused him of having destroyed a fellow human being and dispatched him to hell. The President said to me a bit naïvely: 'I don't think Bill will ever forgive me.' But so far as I know they never met again." Elsewhere (p. 297) Berle writes, "Roosevelt confided his resentment to Henry Wallace over lunch at Warm Springs, Georgia, in August 1944. 'He said Bill Bullitt was perfectly terrible,' Wallace recalled. 'I asked him why. He said because of that awful story he spread all over town about Sumner Welles. He said Bill ought to go to hell for that.'"
12 Gellman, p. 192.
13 *Rex v. Tyler Gatewood Kent*, pp. 67–71.

Six
The Onslaught

1   Joseph P. Lash, *Roosevelt and Churchill 1939–1941: The Partnership that Saved the World* (New York: W. W. Norton, 1985), p. 95.
2   Ibid.
3   John Colville, *Fringes of Power: 10 Downing Street Diaries 1939–1955* (New York, London: W. W. Norton, 1985), pp. 110–111.
4   Colville, p. 111
5   Miller, p. 34.
6   Ibid.
7   *Rex v. Tyler Gatewood Kent*, p. 154.
8   Ibid, pp. 76–77; Miller, p. 38.
9   Miller, p. 38.

10   *Rex v. Tyler Gatewood Kent,* p. 79.

11   PRO H0045/2569613.

12   Maxwell Knight, "Report on Right Club," PRO PF 51267.

13   Ibid.

14   Ibid.

15   Advisory Committee Report in the Case of Captain Ramsay, July 18, 1940, p. 8, PRO H0045/2569613.

16   PRO KV21070.

17   Ibid.

18   Under Secretary of State, the Home Office, Letter, PRO H0045/2569613.

19   Ibid.

20   Letter, marked "Personal," May 24, 1940, PRO H0045/2569613.

21   Knight, "Report on Right Club."

22   Lash, p. 100, spoken by Admiral of the Fleet Lord Keyes.

23   Lash, p. 104.

24   Winston S. Churchill, *Their Finest Hour: The Second World War* (Boston: Houghton Mifflin, 1953), p. 10.

25   TK Archive BU.

26   Metropolitan Police Report submitted by Thompson and Foster, PRO PF51267.

27   Maxwell Knight, "Tyler Kent," a report for Brigadier Harker on his visit to Kent at Camp Hill Prison on May 11, 1945, PRO KV2/545.

28   *Rex v. Tyler Gatewood Kent,* p. 45.

29   Kent, sworn testimony to Captain Maxwell Knight, May 29, 1940, FDR F790009–1411 (see endnote 158).

30   *Rex v. Tyler Gatewood Kent,* pp. 87–88.

31   Gladstone Report, June 12, 1940, PRO KV2/841.

32   Ibid; June 4, 1940, PRO PF 51267.

33   Anonymous Memo (from No. 7 Elementary Flying School, Desford, to Group Captain F. G. Stammers, June 5, 1940), PRO PF51267.

34   Gladstone Report.

35   MI5 Report, May 25, 1940, PRO PF51267.

36   B.5b Report, "Report on Tyler Kent," June 13, 1940, PRO KV2/841.

37   Report initialed B. A., May 25, 1940, PRO PF51267.

38   Ibid.

39   Kent, sworn testimony to Captain Maxwell Knight, May 29, 1940, FDR F79 0009-1411.

SEVEN
THE RAID

1   Maxwell Knight, copy of B.5b Report, "Report on Tyler Kent," May 9, 1940, PRO PF51267.

2   Amanda Smith, ed., *Hostage to Fortune: The Letters of Joseph P. Kennedy* (New York: Viking, 2001), p. 430.

3   Kennedy to Secretary of State, May 20, 1940, TK Archive BU.

4   B.5b Report, "Report on Tyler Kent," Stafford, p. 179.

5   Colville, p. 136.

6   Ibid.

7   Schoenfeld, "Memo Addendum," FDR Library.

8   Ibid.

9   Executive Order 8181, September 1939.

10   Smith, 431.

11   *Rex v. Tyler Gatewood Kent,* p. 72.

12   Franklin C. Gowen, "Re: Tyler Kent, Memorandum Submitted by Franklin C. Gowen, Second Secretary, London, American Embassy, May 28, 1940," FDR Library.

13   *Rex v. Tyler Gatewood Kent,* p. 141.

14   Maxwell Knight Statement, June 25, 1940.

15   *Rex v. Tyler Gatewood Kent,* pp. 46–47.

16   Gowen, "Re: Tyler Kent."

17   Smith, pp. 430–431.

18   JPK Diary, August 15, 1940.

19   David E. Koskoff, *Joseph P. Kennedy: A Life and Times* (Englewood Cliffs, NJ: Prentice-Hall, 1974), p. 236.

20   Norman Kendal to F. A. Newsam, letter marked Secret and Personal, May 20, 1940, PRO PF51267.

21   Telegram, Kennedy to Secretary of State, May 24, 1940, TK Archive BU.

22   Gowen, "Re: Tyler Kent, Memorandum."

23   See endnote 193.

24   The entire preceding account is drawn from a transcript titled "First General Interrogation of Kent after His Arrest," a session held in Ambassador Kennedy's Office, dated May 20, 1940, FDR Library.

25   Ibid.

26   Telegram, Kennedy to Secretary of State, May 20, 1940, TK Archive BU.

EIGHT
USUAL SUSPECTS

1   Colville, p. 138.
2   Ibid.
3   Richard Thurlow, *Fascism in Britain: From Oswald Mosley's Blackshirts to the National Front* (London, New York: I. B. Tauris, 1998), p. 163.
4   Ibid, pp. 162–164.
5   Stafford, pp. 176–182.
6   Thurlow, p. 163.
7   Ibid, pp. 166–167; Stafford, p. 179.
8   Cabinet Minutes.
9   Hinsley and Simkins, pp. 50, 51
10   Stafford, pp. 176–182.
11   Pearson, "Metropolitan Police Report," May 30, 1940, PRO H0045/2569613.
12   Diana Mitford Mosley, *A Life of Contrasts* (New York: Times Books, 1977), p. 169.
13   Ibid.

NINE
THE BLACKOUT

1   The preceding material is quoted from the Gowen Report, May 28, 1940.
2   Irene Danischewsky, letter to Anne Patrick Kent.
3   Gowen Report.
4   Nigel Nicolson, ed., *Harold Nicolson: The War Years 1939–1945: Volume II of Diaries and Letters* (New York: Atheneum, 1967), p. 90.
5   John Lukacs, *Five Days in London: May 1940* (New Haven and London: Yale Nota Bene, Yale University Press, 2001).
6   Thompson/Foster Report, "Subject: Mrs. Christabel Nicholson," 4/12/40, PRO PF51 267.
7   JKH to Long Memorandum, May 31, 1940, TK Archive BU.
8   Kennedy to Secretary of State, telegram marked "Personal and Strictly Confidential for the Secretary," May 31, 1940, TK Archive BU.
9   Ibid.
10   Hull to Kennedy, "Rush," May 31, 1940, TK Archive BU.
11   JKH Memo, May 31, 1940.
12   Ibid.
13   Ibid.

14 Anne Patrick Kent (APK) to Edmund Campbell, letter, June 1, 1940, TK Archive BU.
15 APK to Hull, letter, June 5, 1940, TK Archive BU.
16 Ibid.
17 Ibid.
18 Ibid.
19 Ibid.
20 Sir Ronald Campbell to Sir Alexander Cadogan, letter, "A. C.," American Department, MI5 copy, June 8, 1940, PRO PF51267.
21 Breckinridge Long, edited by Fred L. Israel, *The War Diary of Breckinridge Long: Selections from the Years 1939–1944* (Lincoln: University of Nebraska Press, 1966), p. 111.
22 Campbell to Cadogan letter.
23 Masters, p. 104.
24 Long, p. 111.
25 Ibid.
26 Ibid.
27 Gellman, pp. 214–215.
28 Lash, p. 152.
29 Kennedy to Secretary of State, telegram, June 11, 1940, TK Archive BU.
30 G. Howland Shaw, "Memorandum Regarding a Telephone Conversation with Mrs. William P. Kent," June 12, 1940, TK Archive BU.

TEN
THE DUNGEON

1 Ibid.
2 Ibid.
3 Ibid.
4 Monja Danischewsky, pp. 35, 36, 56, 57.
5 Rosamund Bernier, in a talk given at the Metropolitan Museum of Art in New York, attended by the author.
6 Monja Danischewsky, p. XX.
7 Ibid.
8 Irene Danischewsky to APK, FDR Library.
9 TK to APK, letter, FDR Library.
10 Long, p. 114.
11 Churchill, p. 343.

Eleven
The Trial

1   Ibid.
2   Malcolm Muggeridge, *Chronicles of Wasted Time: Chronicle 2: The Infernal Grove* (New York: William Morrow & Company, 1974), pp. 104–110.
3   TK to APK, letter, November 28, 1943, FDR Library.
4   Muggeridge, p. 107.
5   Ibid, p. 108.
6   Paul Addison, *The Road to 1945: British Politics and The Second World War* (London: Jonathan Cape, 1975), p. 106.
7   Kent told Toland in Mexico that Healey "was a great authority on port wine. And his nose gave him away," National Archives.
8   Hinsley and Simkins, p. 21.
9   Ibid.
10 Stafford, p. 34.
11 *Rex v. Tyler Gatewood Kent*, pp. 2–17.
12 Ibid.
13 Joseph E. Persico, *Roosevelt's Secret War: FDR and World War II Espionage* (New York: Random House Trade Paperbacks, 2002), p. 69.
14 *Rex v. Tyler Gatewood Kent*, p. 39.
15 *Rex v. Tyler Gatewood Kent*, p. XX.
16 *Rex v. Tyler Gatewood Kent.* The foregoing account of the Kent trial proceedings, including excerpts, are drawn from the transcript.
17 Muggeridge, p. 108.
18 Ibid, p. 109.

Twelve
Mother's Plea

1   Phoebe Kent, "Dear Tyler" letter, October 4, 1941, TK Archive BU.
2   G. Howland Shaw, Memo: Kent, Mrs. William P., January 22, 1941, TK Archive BU.
3   APK to FDR, letter, "To the President of the United States," July 24, 1942, TK Archive BU.

4   Wandsworth was "frightfully gloomy," Kent told Toland in Mexico. The windows were painted black, and the light was provided by blue bulbs. "It looked like something out of the Middle Ages," National Archives.

5   Ibid.

6   Ibid.

7   Shaw, Memo: Kent, Mrs. William P.

8   APK to FDR letter.

9   Ibid.

10   Ibid.

11   "Ex-Envoy Refutes Kent 'Railroading,'" Henry J. Taylor, *Washington Daily News*, September 5, 1944, TK Archive BU.

12   Kent recalled in his conversation with Toland in Mexico that Camp Hill was like "an ex-boys' reformatory. It was not a very tough place. And other than being deprived of a library, I cannot say I was badly treated." At Camp Hill, in addition to farming for the locals, Kent sacked potatoes, loaded cabbages, and worked as a tinsmith. Kent to John Toland, Kent, Tyler, Dec. File, National Archives.

13   TK to APK, August 22, 1943, FDR Library.

14   TK to APK, December 8, 1944, FDR Library.

THIRTEEN
GOODNIGHT, IRENE

1   Maxwell Knight, Memo, re: The Case of Tyler Kent, London, March 28, 1945, PRO KV2/545.

2   Maxwell Knight, Memo, re: The Case of Tyler Kent, London, May 16, 1945, PRO KV2/545.

3   Ibid.

4   Harry Hohler, for F. M. Broadmead, to L. W. Clayton, Esq., O.B.E., July 21, 1945, PRO FO371/44628.

EPILOGUE

1   David Markson, *Vanishing Point: A Novel* (Washington, DC: Shoemaker & Hoard, 2004), p. 161. Author urges reader to buy this book as soon as possible.

2   M. N. Forrest, "Report on Three Interviews with Marcus Marienhofer," May 4, 1945, PRO KV2/965.

3   "Dear Mr. Vesey," letter, September 17, 1941, PRO KV2/965.

4   I was alerted to information on Jahnke and his possible relationship to Kent by Christopher Andrew, who directed me to files in the PRO (KV2/ 543-545) I had not seen, an assistance for which I am extremely grateful; for more on Jahnke, see Walter Schellenberg, *The Labyrinth: Memoirs of Walter Schellenberg, Hitler's Chief of Counterintelligence,* introduction by Alan Bullock, translated by Louis Hagen (Cambridge, MA: Da Capo Press, 2000).

5   Memo, February 14, 1940, PRO [TK].

6   "Kent Returns, Defends Taking Secret Papers," *New York Herald Tribune,* December 5, 1945.

7   Tyler Kent, Memorandum, KV 2/545, PRO.

8   "Tyler Kent Weds in Mexico; Ex-Clerk in U.S. Embassy," *Washington Star,* TK Archive BU.

9   Item, TK Archive BU.

10 "Code Pilferer Kent Runs Hate Sheet," by Morton Mintz, staff reporter, *The Washington Post and Times Herald,* July 23, 1961, TK Archive BU.

11 Memorandum, Department of State Legal Adviser, June 10, 1963, TK Archive BU.

12 "Dear Mr. Toland," letter, February 19, 1978, FDR Library.

13 John Costello, Notes on Phone Conversation with Mrs. Irene Danischewsky, June 18, 1982, FDR Library.

Bibliography

Addison, Paul. *The Road to 1945: British Politics and the Second World War.* London: Jonathan Cape, 1975.

Adler, Selig. *The Uncertain Giant, 1921–1941: American Foreign Policy between the Wars.* New York: Macmillan, 1965.

Baer, George W., ed. *A Question of Trust: The Origins of U.S.-Soviet Diplomatic Relations: The Memoirs of Loy W. Henderson.* Stanford, CA: Hoover Institution Press, Stanford University, 1986.

Batvinis, Raymond J. *The Origins of FBI Counterintelligence.* Lawrence: University Press of Kansas, 2007.

Bearse, Ray, and Anthony Read. *Conspirator: The Untold Story of Churchill, Roosevelt, and Tyler Kent.* London: Macmillan, 1991.

Berle, Beatrice Bishop, and Travis Beal Jacobs, eds. *Navigating the Rapids, 1918–1971: From the Papers of Adolf A. Berle.* New York: Harcourt Brace Jovanovich, Inc., 1973.

Bohlen, Charles E. *Witness to History: 1929–1969.* New York: Norton, 1973.

Brownell, Will, and Richard N. Billings. *So Close to Greatness: A Biography of William C. Bullitt.* New York: Macmillan, 1987.

Bullitt, Orville H., ed. *For the President, Personal and Secret: Correspondence between Franklin D. Roosevelt and William C. Bullitt.* Boston: Houghton Mifflin, 1972.

Chace, James. *Acheson: The Secretary of State Who Created the American World.* New York: Simon & Schuster, 1998.

Churchill, Winston S. *Their Finest Hour: The Second World War.* Boston: Houghton Mifflin, 1953.

Clough, Bryan. *State Secrets: The Kent-Wolkoff Affair.* Hove, East Sussex: Hideaway Publications Ltd., 2005.

Colville, John. *Fringes of Power: Downing Street Diaries, 1939–1955, Volume 1.* New York, London: W. W. Norton, 1985.

Conquest, Robert. *The Great Terror: A Reassessment.* New York, Oxford: Oxford University Press, 1990.

Costello, John. *Ten Days to Destiny.* New York: William Morrow, 1991.

Crane, Katharine Elizabeth. *Mr. Carr of State: Forty-Seven Years in the Department of State.* New York: St. Martin's Press, 1960.

Danischewsky, Monja. *White Russian—Red Face.* London: Victor Gollancz Ltd., 1966.

Dodd, Martha. *Through Embassy Eyes.* New York: Harcourt, Brace, 1939.

Gellman, Irwin F. *Secret Affairs: Franklin Roosevelt, Cordell Hull, and Sumner Welles.* Baltimore: Johns Hopkins University Press, 1995.

Henderson, Loy W. *A Question of Trust: The Origins of U.S.-Soviet Diplomatic Relations: The Memoirs of Loy W. Henderson,* edited, with an introduction by George W. Baer. Stanford, CA: Hoover Institution Press, Stanford University, 1986.

Hinsley, F. H., and C. A. G. Simkins. *British Intelligence in the Second World War: Volume Four, Security and Counter-Intelligence.* UK: HMSO, 1990.

Hixson, Walter L. *George Kennan: Cold War Iconoclast.* New York: Columbia University Press, 1989.

James, Robert Rhodes, ed. *Chips: The Diaries of Sir Henry Channon.* Harmondsworth, Middlesex, England: Penguin, 1970.

Jeffreys-Jones, Rhodri, and Andrew Lownie, eds. *North American Spies: New Revisionist Essays.* Lawrence: University Press of Kansas, 1991.

Jowitt, The Earl. *Some Were Spies.* London: Hodder & Stoughton, 1954.

Keegan, John. *The Second World War.* New York: Penguin Books, 1990.

Kennan, George F. *Memoirs: 1925–1950.* Boston, Toronto: Atlantic Monthly Press, Little Brown, 1967.

Kimball, Warren F., ed. *Churchill & Roosevelt: The Complete Correspondence.* Princeton, NJ: Princeton University Press, 1984.

Knight, Amy. *Who Killed Kirov: The Kremlin's Greatest Mystery.* New York: Hill & Wang, a Division of Farrar, Straus and Giroux, 1999.

Koskoff, David E. *Joseph P. Kennedy: A Life and Times.* Englewood Cliffs, NJ: Prentice-Hall, 1974.

Lash, Joseph P. *Roosevelt and Churchill 1939–1941: The Partnership that Saved the World.* New York: W. W. Norton, 1985.

Long, Breckinridge, edited by Fred L. Israel. *The War Diary of Breckinridge Long: Selections from the Years 1939–1944.* Lincoln: University of Nebraska Press, 1966.

Lukacs, John. *Five Days in London: May 1940.* New Haven and London: Yale Nota Bene, Yale University Press, 2001.

Maclean, Fitzroy. *Eastern Approaches.* London: Jonathan Cape, 1950.

MacMillan, Margaret. *Paris 1919: Six Months that Changed the World.* New York: Random House, 2001.

Mandelstam, Nadezhda. *Hope Against Hope: A Memoir.* Translated from the Russian by Max Hayward. New York: Atheneum, 1970.

Masters, Anthony. *The Man Who Was M: The Life of Maxwell Knight.* Oxford: Basil Blackwell Ltd., 1984.

McCamy, James L. *The Administration of American Foreign Affairs.* New York: Alfred A. Knopf, 1950.

Miller, Joan. *One Girl's War.* Dingle, County Kerry Ireland: Brandon, 1986.

Mosley, Diana Mitford. *A Life of Contrasts.* New York: Times Books, 1977.

Muggeridge, Malcolm. *Chronicles of Wasted Time: Chronicle 2: The Infernal Grove.* New York: William Morrow, 1974.

Nicolson, Nigel, ed. *Harold Nicolson, The War Years 1939–1945: Volume II of Diaries and Letters.* New York: Atheneum, 1967.

Persico, Joseph E. *Roosevelt's Secret War: FDR and World War II Espionage.* New York: Random House Trade Paperbacks, 2002.

Sartre, Jean-Paul. *Anti-Semite and Jew.* Translated from the French by George J. Becker. New York: Schocken Books, 1948.

Schellenberg, Walter. *The Labyrinth: Memoirs of Walter Schellenberg, Hitler's Chief of Counterintelligence.* Translated by Louis Hagen. Cambridge, MA: Da Capo Press, 2000.

Schlesinger, Arthur M., Jr. *A Life in the Twentieth Century: Innocent Beginnings, 1917–1950.* Boston and New York: Houghton Mifflin, 2000.

Skidelsky, Robert. *Oswald Mosley.* New York: Holt, Rinehart & Winston, 1975.

Smith, Amanda, ed. *Hostage to Fortune: The Letters of Joseph P. Kennedy.* New York: Viking, 2001.

Stafford, David. *Churchill and Secret Service.* Woodstock, NY: Overlook Press, 1998.

Thayer, Charles W. *Bears in the Caviar.* Philadelphia and New York: J. B. Lippincott, 1950, 1951.

Thurlow, Richard. *Fascism in Britain: From Oswald Mosley's Blackshirts to the National Front.* London, New York: I. B. Tauris, 1998.

Ward, Geoffrey C. *A First-Class Temperament: The Emergence of Franklin Roosevelt.* New York: Harper & Row, 1989.

Weiner, Tim. *Enemies: A History of the FBI.* New York: Random House, 2012.

West, Rebecca. *The New Meaning of Treason.* New York: The Viking Press, 1964.

Whalen, Richard. *The Founding Father: The Story of Joseph P. Kennedy.* New York: New American Library, 1964.

Index

release concerns, 207–9, 210–11, 213–14

Russia, possessions left behind in, 54–55

solicitor, rights to, 150, 157, 158, 159–60

trial cross examination, 172–75, 176

trial testimony, 171–72

trip back to U.S. on *Silver Oak*, 214, 219–20

Kent, William (father), 1–2, 3–5, 35

Kirk, Alexander, 36, 50, 64, 124, 126, 176

Kirov, Sergei, 32

Knight, Maxwell

career, 70–71

Danischewsky, Irene, and, 207–8, 225

Fifth Column concerns, 78

Kent, Tyler, interrogation of, 119–25

Kent, Tyler, raid on apartment, 105, 109–14, 152, 153

Kent, Tyler, release concerns, 207–9

Kent, Tyler, report on, 92–93, 96

Miller, Joan, and, 69–70, 92

personality and character, 68–69

sexual identity, 69–70

La Coquille restaurant, 137–38

Liddell, Guy, 70, 87, 170, 217

Lindbergh, Charles, 47

Litvinov, Maxim, 9, 23, 26, 29, 33

London life, 59–64, 101–3, 196–205

Long, Breckenridge, 143, 147, 148–49, 158

Ludmilla (Soviet embassy employee), 202–3, 225

Lukacs, John, 141

Mackie, Marjorie, 73–76, 92–93, 141, 170

Marienhofer, Marcus, 215

Marigliano, Francesco, 80, 88, 89, 100–101, 208–9

Markson, David, 215

Matthias, Ludwig, 55–56, 106, 111, 122, 217, 218

Maw, Graham, 159, 165, 210, 211, 213

McCamy, James L., 51

Messersmith, George, 50–52

Miller, Joan

diplomatic pouch scheme, 89

Knight, Maxwell, and, 69–70, 92

Right Club, 76, 77, 78

Wolkoff, Anna, and, 89, 90–91

Molotov-Ribbentrop Pact, 38, 53, 64–65

Moore, Walton "Judge," 10, 19–20, 45–46, 50, 81, 148

Morton, Desmond, 71

Moscow embassy, 7, 10–12, 36–39

Moscow life, 20–25

Mosley, Diana, 133–34

Mosley, Oswald, 72, 73, 74–75, 130, 131–32, 133–34

Moss, Detective, 137

Muggeridge, Malcolm, 162, 163–64, 175–76, 178, 179, 181

M/Y (code name for Marjorie Mackie/Amor), 73–76, 92–93, 141, 170

Neutrality Zone, 66–67

Newsam, F. A., 118

Nicholson, Christabel, 91, 99, 141, 158

Nicolson, Harold, 141

Nieuwenhuys, Jean, 75–76, 170